D0138658

BLAKE'S ILLUSTRATIONS
TO THE
POEMS OF GRAY

O D E

ON THE DEATH OF A

FAVOURITE CAT.

Drowned in a Tub of Gold Fishes.

D 3

BLAKE'S ILLUSTRATIONS TO THE POEMS OF GRAY

BY IRENE TAYLER

PRINCETON, NEW JERSEY

PRINCETON UNIVERSITY PRESS

1971

Copyright © 1971 by Princeton University Press

All Rights Reserved

L.C.C.: 73-90963   I.S.B.N.: 0-691-06182-3

Princeton University Press expresses its gratitude to Mr. Paul Mellon
for permission to include the color frontispiece and the black and white illustrations in this book.

We are grateful to Mr. Arnold Fawcus of the Trianon Press of Paris
for making available to us his facsimile of the "Cat 1" plate for reproduction as a frontispiece.
A gift from Mr. J. Lionberger Davis made possible the use of full color for this reproduction.
The Trianon Press hand-colored facsimile edition of Blake's designs for Gray's poems,
produced for Mr. Mellon who owns the original work,
will make it possible for admirers of Blake to appreciate the delicate tints and shadings
that are barely suggested by the black-and-white reproductions included here,
and of which the frontispiece furnishes only an example.
The facsimile will be published for the William Blake Trust in 1971 in a limited edition
of 400 copies and will be distributed by Bernard Quaritch Ltd., London.

Printed in the United States of America by Princeton University Press, Princeton, New Jersey

This book has been composed in Linotype Baskerville

Illustrations by the Meriden Gravure Company, Meriden, Connecticut

NC
242
'B55T38
C.2

434181

For My Family

434181

CONTENTS

ACKNOWLEDGMENTS

YEARS AGO, when I first began the reading that produced this book, the late Yvor Winters (who had small tolerance for Blake's prophetic obscurities) advised me with good-humored skepticism: "Try to write something intelligible." I regret that I can never know if, in his eyes, I have succeeded.

As with any scholarly undertaking, many debts must go unacknowledged. But I want to make specific mention of a few of mine that cannot find a proper place in footnotes. I am very grateful to Paul Mellon for allowing me to study, and the Press to reproduce, his unique copy of Blake's 116 illustrations of Gray's poems; also to Willis Van Devanter, Arnold Fawcus, and the officers of the Morgan Library for helping to arrange for me to see the designs. The Huntington Library has been consistently generous with its rich Blake materials, as were the British Museum Print and Manuscript Rooms and the Bodleian Library while I was in England in 1968-1969. The year in England, made possible by a study grant from the American Council of Learned Societies, deepened my awareness of the complex sense in which Blake was very much of his time as an artist and illustrator.

Jean Hagstrum gave the manuscript a most careful reading and offered detailed, helpful commentary. Others for whose liberal assistance I am grateful include G. E. Bentley, Jr., Martin Butlin, Bliss Carnochan, James L. Clifford, Mary E. Cumberpatch, S. Foster Damon, Northrop Frye, John E. Grant, David Halliburton, Elsa Foster Miller, Lucio Ruotolo, Carl Woodring, and Mary K. Woodworth. Linda C. Peterson has proved not only an excellent editor but a knowledgeable student of Blake; she and Harriet Anderson made the rites of publication almost a pleasure.

David Erdman, whose unselfish learning and energy have been at the service of so many Blakeans, has long offered me generous encouragement as well as practical help. And many times again he has done so in my work on this book.

Finally, I am grateful to Willy, David, Letta, Bear, and Jesse Tayler for their affectionate encouragement of a working mother, and my husband, Ted, for the loving support he has given his working wife.

BLAKE'S ILLUSTRATIONS

TO THE

POEMS OF GRAY

He has treated his Poet most Poetically.

—ANN FLAXMAN

INTRODUCTION

WILLIAM BLAKE, as T. S. Eliot noted with dismay, received no formal education in literature. Rather, he served an apprenticeship in engraving and in the pictorial arts. Yet he read avidly all his life, and being a man of keen intelligence and strong opinions he responded powerfully to what he read, often finding himself moved to answer one art with another. On these occasions he left posterity such splendid interpretive illustrations as those to Young's *Night Thoughts*, to most of Milton's major poetry, and to the Book of Job. His final series of illustrations—those to Dante's *Divine Comedy*—was interrupted by his death in 1827.

Nearly a century later Edmund Gosse announced dramatically: "Years have passed since any discovery has been made on the field of English letters so sensational as that which Professor Grierson has the privilege of revealing in a magnificent folio."[1] The treasure revealed was a unified set of 116 brilliant illustrations made by William Blake for the poems of Thomas Gray, important designs which were privately owned and therefore little known in Blake's own time and which had dropped completely from sight since the early nineteenth century.

No one knows exactly when or why Blake undertook the project of illustrating Gray's poetry, though there are a few facts that may be used as a framework for fuller speculation. The designs must have been begun sometime after 1794, since the paper is watermarked with that date; and sometime before 1805 Blake must have presented them to Mrs. Flaxman, wife of the sculptor John Flaxman, since the volume contains his dedicatory poem to Mrs. Flaxman and is mentioned by her in a letter of September 1805.[2] The designs passed into Flaxman's estate at his death in 1826 and were sold at Christie's in 1828.

[1] *More Books on the Table* (London, 1923), p. 343, as reprinted from *The Times* (London), August 16, 1923.

[2] G. E. Bentley, Jr., very kindly quoted for me the contents of this letter before it was published in his *Blake Records* (Oxford, 1969), p. 166. (At the time *Blake Records* was published Mr. Bentley did not know of Miss M. K. Woodworth's success in dating the Gray designs 1797-1798 [see below, p. 10], and so speculated that the designs were "a recent commission, presented on Nancy's birthday, July 6th, 1805" [July 6 was in fact John Flaxman's birthday; Nancy's was October 2].)

We now know that Christie's sold the volume for eight guineas to a man named Clarke, probably the eminent bookseller William Clarke of New Bond Street, who either was buying for the collector William Beckford at the time or else sold the designs to him shortly afterward. The volume then apparently went with the rest of Beckford's library to his daughter, who married her cousin the tenth duke of Hamilton. But when this splendid library, rich in Blake materials, came up for sale at Sotheby's in 1882, it contained no illustrations to Gray, nor were they heard of for almost another forty years.

Then on November 4, 1919, a letter from Professor Herbert Grierson to the London *Times* announced that the designs had been found, uncatalogued and unrecorded, in the library of Hamilton Palace as the palace was being dismantled. Grierson's letter, though restrained, nevertheless communicates the importance of the find: "I have seen no collection which illustrates so fully the range of Blake's power."[3] On November 5 a second letter appeared, unsigned, offering additional information about the history of the volume, and it is from this letter that we learn of Clarke's and Beckford's part in its history.[4]

The Bentley-Nurmi bibliography records no further mention of the discovery until 1922, when the Oxford University Press published a full-sized monochrome reproduction of the 116 designs, with 6 designs also reproduced in color, and a gentlemanly 14-page introduction by Professor Grierson that up to the present was the most thorough published study of Blake's splendid series. Then in 1923 there appeared two reviews of the reproduction, one by Edmund Gosse (quoted above), which, though it shows a lively appreciation of the designs, is clearly the work of a student of Gray rather than of Blake; and one by Guy Eglington in *International Studio*,[5] including six reproductions of the designs and two pages of knowledgeable and sensitive criticism.

The two reviews of Grierson's "sensational" revelation were not the prelude to the numerous fuller and richer studies that one might expect. On the contrary, when B. Ifor Evans in 1940 devoted a chapter of his *Tradition and Romanticism* to "Thomas Gray and William Blake," discussing and contrasting these two widely different "pre-romantic" figures, he was apparently completely unaware that one had in fact given the meticulous attention of 116 interpretive illustrations to the work of the other. J. Bronowski (1947) was emphatically un-

[3] *The Times* (London), November 4, 1919, p. 15.
[4] *The Times* (London), November 5, 1919, p. 15.
[5] "Blake Illustrates Gray," *International Studio*, LXXIX (1924), 39-47.

4

aware of them.[6] In 1949 Ruth Lowery published a brief argument for dating the illustrations earlier than 1800, the year tentatively suggested by Grierson, but she was apparently not even aware that her own suggested date placed the designs before the 1790 text of Gray which Blake used as the center of each page, though this date is clearly evident on the title page of both reproduction and original.[7]

Other scholars have similarly ignored the designs or considered them only in passing: S. Foster Damon in his great *Philosophy and Symbols* (1924) seems to have mentioned them only twice, and Geoffrey Keynes, who in his *Blake Studies* (1949) also mentions them twice, assigns in each instance a different number of designs to the series, both of them wrong. David Erdman, in *Prophet Against Empire* (1954), refers to them several times for corroboration of other points, but it is not to his purpose to treat them directly. Anthony Blunt, in *The Art of William Blake* (1959), mentions them once in a note, by way of comparison to the illustrations Blake did for Young's *Night Thoughts*. And Jean Hagstrum, in *William Blake, Poet and Painter*, mentions them several times, but offers only one extended comment—still less than a page long.[8] In Northrop Frye's wide-ranging *Fearful Symmetry* I find no mention at all; Frye notes that "Blake's masters in poetry were Gray, Collins . . . ," and so on, but mentions no designs; and his remark that Blake's five daughters of Zelopehad may have had their source in the "five Valkyries in Gray's 'Fatal Sisters' "[9] suggests that he may not have seen Blake's illustrations to the poem, for Blake represents them consistently as three. (There are twelve in Gray.)

The pattern is clear. Even the greatest of the Blake scholars, and even those most concerned with his visual art, are generally either unaware of the Gray illustrations or not greatly concerned with them. Lately some fine work has been done more or less tangentially, such as Paul Miner's note on the use of Gray's "Fatal Sisters" in Blake's own developing symbolism,[10] or John E. Grant's discussion of the illustrations to Gray's "Ode on the Spring" as partial evidence for an interpretation of Blake's "The Fly."[11] Most recently Kathleen Raine, in

[6] *William Blake, 1757-1827: A Man Without a Mask* (London, 1947); see p. 109.
[7] "Blake and the Flaxmans," *The Age of Johnson*, ed. F. W. Hilles (New Haven and London, 1949), pp. 281-289.
[8] (Chicago and London, 1964), p. 131.   [9] (Princeton, 1947), pp. 167, 440.
[10] "William Blake: Two Notes on Sources," *Bulletin of the New York Public Library*, LXII (1958), 203-207.
[11] "Interpreting Blake's 'The Fly,' " *BNYPL*, LXVII (1963), 593-615.

Blake and Tradition, has reproduced and commented interestingly on several of the designs, although she inexplicably dates the project "early 1790's."[12] But the present study is the first to consider the entire series. It offers in fact the first mention that most of the individual designs have received, and the first detailed discussion of any of them.

How is it possible that such an important series, rediscovered so dramatically, should have had to wait almost 170 years for even a beginning of the attention they deserve? Partly it has been a matter of their availability: long lost to sight, even when they were rediscovered they were generally available to students of Blake only in the 1922 reproduction, and only 650 copies were made of that. Moreover, for all its virtues this edition does not show the designs to advantage, mainly because the pale reproductions on yellowing paper offer little clue to the fresh beauty and brilliant coloring of the original. Anything short of a full-color facsimile such as that now being prepared by the Trianon Press is bound to be misleading.

But partly, too, this lack of attention has been a matter of the history of scholarly and critical interest in Blake. Only very recently have students of his poetry come fully to remember that what we have been used to thinking of as "poems" were presented by Blake himself as part of a more complex art for which we have no proper name, since it is uniquely Blake's art: English words in something like the form of poetry (Blake increasingly called it "prophecy" or "vision"), printed from hand-drawn plates as part of a larger nonverbal design, thus combining words and pictures into a new and unique whole. Had he had access to a medium that could have appealed to ear as well as eye, he would probably have used it, for we are told by contemporaries that he sang his "songs" to his own beautiful melodies, and musical instruments in use are throughout his work symbolic of the fully lived creative life.[13]

Further, students of Blake's art, even of the pictorial art of his illuminated books, tend to forget that by far the greatest bulk of Blake's artistic output was as interpretive illustrator. The powerful Job series, published in 1825, is probably now the most famous, and justly so, but in his own day Blake was known chiefly for his illustrations to Young's *Night Thoughts* (1797) and Blair's *The Grave* (1808), except by the small following of young men that he gathered in his last days, a group calling itself "the Ancients." These young artists particu-

---

[12] (Princeton, 1968). For dating and two reproductions, see I, 90.
[13] E.g., quite explicitly in *Milton,* plate 16, and in the first and last Job designs.

6

larly admired Blake's woodcuts—the only woodcuts he ever executed—illustrating an imitation of Virgil's First Eclogue by the eighteenth-century poet Ambrose Phillips. Besides these works, Blake illustrated numerous scenes from Shakespeare, most of the major poetry of Milton, Bunyan's *Pilgrim's Progress*, Dante's *Divine Comedy*, and countless passages from both the Old and New Testaments. Professor Hagstrum calculates that Blake must have engraved "some 1,200 illustrations for the work of other writers,"[14] and although this figure includes illustrations that Blake engraved after the designs of other artists, it omits the many others that he designed but did not engrave, such as the 28 watercolors to Bunyan, the Virgil woodcuts, the designs for Blair's *The Grave*, all but 43 of the 537 illustrations to Young, most of those to Milton, and all but 7 of the 102 to Dante, and of course the 116 to Gray that we are considering here. In contrast to these many hundreds of designs illustrating the works of others, the 375 pages of stereotype engraving that make up the canon of what might be called "self-illustrated" verse[15] seem a very small part of Blake's total output as illustrator, and remind one again that though he was a poet, he was more often a pictorial artist. And though he was an artist depicting his own poetic visions, he was far more often an illustrator depicting (and modifying and expanding) the visions of others.

It need hardly be said that for Blake illustration was no servile art, never merely a matter of following the dictates of another mind and never a purely commercial enterprise. Rather it was vigorous critical interpretation: an encounter—in Eternity, he might have said—of one visionary experience with another, the dramatic confrontation of two images of the truth. Even after the failure of the Young illustrations as a commercial venture, Blake was nonetheless willing to return with optimistic vigor to the same kind of task with the Blair illustrations—another financial failure, at least for him, since the lucrative part of the job, the engraving, was taken from him and given to the more fashionable engraver Schiavonetti. And while Blake undertook some of the illustrations as paid jobs (for example, the designs for the imitation of Virgil) he executed them with no less passion and vitality.

In his widely stimulating essay on "The Eidetic and the Borrowed Image: An Interpretation of Blake's Theory and Practice of Art," Joseph Burke observes: "Blake's judgments of artists are extraordinarily consistent. They are

---

[14] *Poet and Painter*, p. 119.
[15] Again I draw the number from *Poet and Painter*, p. 119.

based exclusively on perceptual approach and on style, never on the artist's religious or political ideas, or his personal conduct, except in the case of the living."[16] Burke demonstrates that although Blake does not use the terms, his judgments are always based on the opposition between the linear and the painterly styles, with consistent approval of the former and denunciation of the latter. "If there is an Old Master by whom we would expect him to be attracted on ideological or personal grounds," continues Burke, "it is surely Rembrandt. But Rembrandt's greatness as a religious painter is for Blake completely obscured by his natural vision."

The situation with verbal art is more complicated, however, since there are no clear-cut stylistic grounds on which to divide the prophet from the impostor. In his old age Blake remarked that "One Power alone makes a Poet: Imagination, The Divine Vision."[17] But the presence or absence of this divine vision had to be deduced at least in part from the poet's religious or political ideas: "I see in Wordsworth the Natural Man rising up against the Spiritual Man Continually, & then he is No Poet" (782). Yet Chaucer's naturalism never offended him. In *The Marriage of Heaven and Hell* Blake had judged Milton "a true Poet" at least partly on stylistic grounds, but Dante, of whose visionary mode one might expect Blake to approve, is denounced for his ideology: "Every thing in Dante's Comedia shews That for Tyrannical Purposes he has made This World the Foundation of All, & the Goddess Nature Mistress" (785). He was too much "an Emperor's, a Caesar's Man" (413). But the most powerful source of Blake's antagonism is neither Dante's devotion to this world nor his loyalty to its leaders. Significantly, the failure of ideology—as well as Milton's failure of style—is at bottom a failure of humanity. On his design diagraming Dante's circles of hell Blake affirms revealingly: "Whatever Book is for Vengeance for Sin & whatever Book is Against the Forgiveness of Sins is not of the Father, but of Satan the Accuser & Father of Hell" (785). And it is for forgiveness and redemption that the poet redescends to earth in *Milton*: not to redo the passages written in fetters, but to loose the fetters. Milton was "curb'd by the general malady & infection from the silly Greek & Latin slaves of the Sword," which put him on the side of those "who would, if they could, for ever depress Mental

---

[16] *In Honour of Daryl Lindsay* (Melbourne, 1964), pp. 100-127. Passages quoted appear on p. 118.

[17] *The Complete Writings of William Blake*, ed. Geoffrey Keynes (London and New York, 1957), p. 782. (Hereafter page numbers in the text will refer to this edition.)

& prolong Corporeal War" (480). His prosody was not so much the result as the corollary of such a position. The "Monotonous Cadence" of English blank verse, "derived from the modern bondage of Rhyming," is a kind of verbal analogue of the spiritual condition of the poet who writes it and the society that reads it. "Poetry Fetter'd Fetters the Human Race" (621).

The complex interweaving of vision and error in even the greatest poets, and the importance of exposing the error in order to help redeem at once the poet and his readers, makes of literary criticism an activity on a par with poetry, painting, or music: all are activities of the creative human intellect reaching for salvation. But what, precisely, does the critic criticize? And how? If, as Burke cogently argues, "style was for Blake an essential and absolute test of spiritual truth" in visual art, it was not so in poetry;[18] there prosody and political principles become entangled with what might be called questions of spiritual humaneness, raising issues that with one or two exceptions Blake chose to meet not with doctrinal comment but with the full confrontation of interpretive "illustration." The 116 designs to Gray's poems offer clear and widely varied examples of Blake's techniques of literary criticism, of art interpreting art, commending or correcting it.

Everywhere Blake seems to have found his task the same: to locate and expose the visionary promise in others and in himself. As he observed when speaking of the brilliance of Chaucer's characterizations: "Visions of these eternal principles or characters of human life appear to poets, in all ages" (571). Or when distinguishing between allegory or fable and what he called "vision": "The Hebrew Bible & the Gospel of Jesus are not Allegory, but Eternal Vision or Imagination of All that Exists. Note here that Fable or Allegory is seldom without some Vision. Pilgrim's Progress is full of it, the Greek Poets the same" (604). Nor did he suppose that his own "visions" were uncontaminated truth: "The Greeks represent Chronos or Time as a very Aged Man; this is Fable, but the Real Vision of Time is in Eternal Youth. I have, however, somewhat accomodated my Figure of Time to the common opinion, as I myself am also infected with it & my Visions also infected, & I see Time Aged, alas, too much so" (614). Indeed, "Every thing possible to be believ'd is an image of truth," Blake affirmed in *The Marriage of Heaven and Hell* (151). That it be believed passionately and personally, not simply accepted from the belief of others, was the premise from which Blake started. And that it was an image only, constantly in need of development and revision, seems to have been Blake's experience with his own vision

---

[18] The problem of its application to visual art will be taken up below, in the Conclusion.

9

as it exfoliates in his poems and prophecies. Again, such revision of vision was in part what he conceived himself to be carrying out for Milton in his own poem by that name, and in an important sense it is what he did every time he "illustrated" the vision of another man.

But why, one wonders, did he turn to the vision of Gray, a poet whom modern readers tend to find rather dim of eye? And—a related question—when, exactly, did he do so? Grierson speculates that the designs to Gray were done in 1800 as a gift to the Flaxmans,[19] thanking them for the introduction to William Hayley that resulted in the Blakes' moving with great joy and expectation to a country cottage in Felpham, where Blake would work under the patronage and with the companionship of Mr. Hayley himself. Certainly Mrs. Flaxman did receive the designs at Blake's desire, as the poem of dedication indicates; and Mrs. Flaxman's letter of 1805 proves that she had received them before that date. Moreover, in view of Blake's delight over the prospect of his stay in Felpham, and his gratitude to Flaxman for making it possible, 1800 seems the most logical time and occasion for a gift. However, a newly discovered draft from Mrs. Flaxman's letter notebook indicates that the designs were in fact undertaken not as a gift, but as paid employment. After a sentence or two describing Blake to her correspondent, a friend in Italy, Mrs. Flaxman concludes: "Flaxman has employ'd him to illuminate the works of Grey [sic] for my Library." The draft is undated, but Professor Mary K. Woodworth, who discovered it, dates it late 1797.[20]

There is other evidence that the designs must have been done about this time. The *terminus a quo* is provided by the paper used, which carries the watermark 1794; and we do know when and how Blake came by that paper. In 1795 Blake and the publisher and bookseller Richard Edwards of 142 Bond Street reached an agreement by which Blake was to make designs to encircle the letterpress of each page of Edward Young's *Night Thoughts*, an immense poem divided into nine sections or Nights.[21] According to Blake's friend the artist Henry Fuseli,

---

[19] *William Blake's Designs for Gray's Poems* (London, 1922), p. 16.

[20] British Museum Add. ms. 39,790, fol. 4. The text of the letter and Professor Woodworth's proof of date have now been published in *Notes and Queries*, ccxv [= new series, xvii] (August 1970), 312-313.

[21] Information about the Young project is available in *The Farington Diary*, ed. James Grieg, 8 vols. (London, 1922-1928); in Geoffrey Keynes, "Blake's illustrations to 'Young's Night Thoughts,'" *Blake Studies* (London, 1949), p. 60; and in *Vala or The Four Zoas*, ed. G. E. Bentley, Jr. (Oxford, 1963), pp. 155-217.

whom Farington quotes as an authority in this matter, Edwards had supplied Blake with about 900 sheets of drawing paper for use in the project; Blake actually used less than 300 sheets for his drawings, since he employed both sides and made a total of 537 designs (of which Edwards eventually had him engrave only 43). Then he used a further unascertained number for trial proofs of the engravings; 24 of these survive as sheets on which he wrote parts of his unfinished *Vala*. A few other sheets were used to make copies of other of his prophetic works. Almost certainly it was some remaining sheets of this same 1794 J Whatman paper that Blake used for his illustrations to Gray.

His work on Young's *Night Thoughts* proved richly stimulating to Blake; from the suggestion offered by Young's "Nights" grew—at whatever distance— his original conception of *Vala . . . a Dream of Nine Nights*, as his original title page dated 1797 describes the poem. And the format of the Young designs is the same as that he employed for the designs to Gray; both encircle printed letter-press insertions—a technique he never used before or again.

text; and as Edwards presented them to the public, namely as engraved designs to Edwards, namely as watercolor drawings surrounding each page of printed

The Young illustrations exist in two different forms: as Blake presented them surrounding only some of the pages of text. There was a total of 56 separate leaves or 112 pages in the published edition (comprising the first four nights of the poem, the rest to follow in three more such parts), but only 43 designs. In other words, less than half the pages were decorated. Blake doubtless considered the series done for Edwards as in some ways a really different project from the one we see in published form. And the method of the Gray series is that of the earlier and longer form of the Young illustrations, for while Blake excised the front matter and the notes from J. Murray's 1790 edition of Gray's poems, he kept the title page and all the poems intact and in their original order, supplying a design for every single page, even blank ones.[22]

---

[22] Possibly Edwards had the pages of text laid in for Blake by one of his own workmen, as several leaves of text published with the *Night Thoughts* but not pertinent to it were cut and pasted by someone who evidently did not realize that the poem being illustrated had already ended; these sheets remain, undecorated, boxed in the British Museum with the last of the *Night Thoughts* series.

One is left to wonder whether Edwards might not also have had the Gray text cut and prepared for Blake, intending perhaps a whole series of poetic illustrations, but reneging when the first published section of the *Night Thoughts* proved financially unsuccessful. Flaxman might then have relieved Blake by offering to buy the Gray designs himself when

Edwards apparently first employed Blake in 1795, and gave him the paper at this time;[23] most of the engravings are dated June 24, 1796, which means that the drawings for at least this first part must have been finished sometime before that. G. E. Bentley, Jr., assumes that "Almost certainly by this time Blake had also completed his 537 drawings for the engravings,"[24] but I know of no certain evidence that this was the case.

According to Keynes,[25] the latest date on the engraved plates is March 22, 1797; the actual publication took place shortly afterwards, and the commercial failure of the edition must have been evident almost at once. According to J. Bronowski, it was "No doubt . . . killed by the money crisis of 1797."[26] Or perhaps it would have died anyway. But even supposing that the failure was emphatically evident at once, it would not be out of character for Blake, if he had not yet finished the originally projected drawings, to continue right on with them, either in view of an agreement with Edwards or in the hope of better luck with better days.

Blake consistently repeated visual motifs that pleased or interested him, so that a reader constantly finds similar postures or figures even in works far apart in time. The floating God-figure with arms outstretched is an obvious example. A less obvious but very frequent instance is the figure seen naked, from the back, leaping upward with one leg drawn up and back slightly arched. It appears, for example, on the plate illustrating the Argument of *The Visions of the Daughters of Albion*; on *Europe*, plate 11;[27] on the title page of Blake's illustrations to Young; as the little horn-winding fly in Blake's fifth illustration to Gray's "Ode on the Spring"; and in *Jerusalem*, plate 32 (Stirling copy). Thus one may not

---

they were done. But all this must remain mere speculation until some further evidence appears. It is also possible, for example, that Catherine Blake did the cutting and pasting jobs for both the Young and the Gray designs.

[23] Keynes, in *Blake Studies*, p. 61, says that the 1794 watermark "indicates that the pages were probably made up early in 1795, when the paper manufactured during the previous year was still being sold." But it was in fact still being sold several years after; D. V. Erdman notes in *Prophet Against Empire* (Princeton, 1954), p. 268 (rev. edn., 1969, p. 292) that "a statement by the present head of Whatman's" asserts that "their firm issued no dated paper before 1800 *except the 1794 J Whatman*." Thus 1795 is not—at least on the basis of the paper—a necessary *terminus ad quem*.

[24] *Vala*, ed. Bentley, p. 155.   [25] *Blake Studies*, p. 61.

[26] *William Blake*, p. 89.

[27] So numbered in the Henry E. Huntington Library copy; the accompanying text is numbered plate 9 in the Keynes edition (240), since the two earlier plates bearing pictures but no text are omitted from the count.

safely argue closeness in time simply from closeness of pictorial imagery. Moreover, given the great number of Young illustrations it is hardly surprising that Blake found himself repeating the successes of his own fecundity, both by revising earlier designs for the Young series and by later reworking motifs that originated with the Young.[28] The series in this way binds strands of both past and future. But even granted all this it is still remarkable that the strongest alliance of the Young designs is unquestionably with designs done for the Gray series. Some parallels are so close as to be almost literal repetitions, others merely suggestions or associations, though telling ones. But the majority by far—and especially of those that bear the closest relationships—are from the later nights, particularly Night Nine. The burden of proof would seem to be on anyone arguing that the two series were not executed close together in time.

We have, then, two separate reasons (aside from the undated draft of Mrs. Flaxman's letter) for thinking that the Gray designs were done before 1800 rather than afterwards. The first is their affinity with the *Night Thoughts* series, on which Blake may conceivably have worked as late as 1799, but surely no later. The generally accepted date is 1797, the year of Edwards' publication. Second, our knowledge of Blake's undertakings during his three-year Felpham stay and shortly afterwards is the most complete of any period in his life, thanks to the many letters written to friends and family at that time. But nowhere is any mention made of the Gray designs or of any project that sounds like them, whereas mention is made of virtually everything else Blake did between 1800 and 1805, and we know from Mrs. Flaxman's dated letter that these designs were finished and in her possession at least by September 1805.

If they were done before 1800, then how long before? As observed earlier, the 1794 watermark sets the earliest certain limit, but Edwards apparently did not give Blake the paper until 1795, and 1796 seems a safe *terminus a quo* for the Gray designs in view of the unlikelihood that Blake would begin using Edwards' paper before he was well enough along on the Young project to be sure of suffi-

---

[28] There are among the *Night Thoughts* designs several borrowings from *The Gates of Paradise* (1793): no. 13 (of the 537 designs in the British Museum) closely echoes "At length for hatching ripe"; the drawing on the back of the general title page is reminiscent of "The traveller hasteneth in the Evening" (as are several other of the *Night Thoughts* designs); no. 28 shows a figure with the exact posture and expression of "Water." Others echo designs from *America, Songs of Innocence and of Experience, The Marriage of Heaven and Hell,* and *The Book of Urizen,* as well as individual paintings such as the 1795 "Death of Abel."

cient extra paper for such an undertaking as the illustrations to Gray. Blake was poor, and too conscientious to borrow against expensive materials that he might not be able to replace. And even if the designs were originally commissioned by Edwards (see note 22, above), it seems reasonable to assume that Blake would have finished at least the first section—the one that was engraved and published—before undertaking quite another set of designs. The date may then be safely if not certainly limited to the time between 1796 and the early months of 1800.

Although we know that Flaxman "employ'd" Blake "to Illuminate the works of Grey" for his wife's library, we do not know whether the choice of subject was Blake's, or Edwards', or the Flaxmans'. Possibly Blake spoke of a desire to illustrate Gray as he had illustrated Young, and Edwards or Flaxman then offered to buy such a series. Certainly Blake had long been interested in Gray's poetry. He was probably exposed to it during his apprenticeship to James Basire (if not before), since the frontispiece of Mason's great edition—a profile portrait of Gray based on the posthumous drawing by Benjamin Wilson—was engraved by Basire in 1775, when Blake had already been an apprentice in the shop for three years. Indeed, Blake might even have been responsible for part of the work, as Basire often signed with his own name the work of his apprentices.

By 1785 Blake had read Gray carefully enough to be moved to illustrate "The Bard," for a watercolor bearing that title was exhibited at the Royal Academy in 1785.[29] That he appreciated the poetry itself and not just its grand subject is evident from his remarks about the poem some years later: "Weaving the winding sheet of Edward's race by means of sounds of spiritual music and its accompanying expressions of articulate speech, is a bold, and daring, and most masterly conception. . . . Poetry consists in these conceptions" (576). And by 1793, when he was making early notebook drafts of what were soon to become poems in the *Songs of Experience*, his drafts for "The Fly" show familiarity with the language of Gray's "Ode on the Spring": the "gaily-gilded trim" and "painted plumage" of Gray's flies, cruelly "Brush'd by the hand of rough Mischance,"[30] become in the first verse (later discarded) of Blake's draft "gilded, painted pride," "Brush'd" by "my guilty hand" (182).

It is also quite conceivable that Blake could have been influenced by friends.

[29] This is not the tempera painting by the same title displayed in Blake's 1809 exhibition, although the two are frequently confused.

[30] Unless otherwise noted, quotations from Gray are taken from the 1790 Murray edition used by Blake.

Keynes suggests that it was probably Blake's colorful friend Fuseli who influenced Edwards in his choice of Blake for the *Night Thoughts* project.[31] The preface written for the first (and only) published installment of the work is attributed by Blake's biographer Gilchrist and many other scholars to Fuseli, although Keynes thinks Edwards himself the more likely author, suggesting however that Fuseli may have written the "Explanations of the engravings."[32] Certainly Fuseli was interested in the project and encouraged it, and he did write the preface to Blake's 1808 illustrations to Blair's *The Grave*.

It seems possible, therefore, that Fuseli encouraged Blake to consider illustrating other poets as well; and Fuseli emphatically preferred Gray's poetry to Young's, whose *Night Thoughts* he had dismissed in 1775 as "Pyramids of dough."[33] According to Frederick Antal, "Fuseli seems to have particularly liked Gray's poems; those of Thomson and Young, whose *Night Thoughts* had much influenced him at an earlier date, were now too tame for him."[34] And Fuseli's biographer quotes him as having remarked indignantly: "How! do you think I condemn myself so much as not to admire Gray? Although he has written but little, that little is well done."[35] Fuseli himself did an illustration to Gray's "The Descent of Odin" as early as 1771, and later a set of three illustrations for the 1800 edition of Gray's poems—one each for "The Bard," "The Fatal Sisters," and "The Descent of Odin." The introduction to this edition offers some critical comments on the poems, the most striking being the following: "The *Fatal Sisters*, amid a variety of terrific beauties, furnish a striking instance of the unequal power of images addressed to the ear, and to the eye. The 'human entrails,' and the 'gasping warriors' heads,' that supply the weaving phantoms with texture and weights, are suffered to spread and dangle, without creating much indignation or abhorrence: had they been imitated by painting, we should equally loath the fancy that bred, and the work that exposed them to our eye." The writer of this introduction adds in a note shortly after this: "For several of the foregoing observations, the editor is indebted to the friendship and learning of H. Fuseli, Esq. Professor of Painting to the Royal Academy."[36] Fuseli's own illustration to this poem is a lively one, displaying the violence and abandon of the women at

---

[31] *Blake Studies*, p. 29. [32] *Blake Studies*, p. 63.

[33] Eudo C. Mason, *The Mind of Henry Fuseli* (London, 1951), p. 32.

[34] *Fuseli Studies* (London, 1956), p. 18. The "now" refers to the 1760's.

[35] John Knowles, quoted in Mason, *The Mind of Henry Fuseli*, p. 343.

[36] *The Poems of Gray. A New Edition* (London, 1800), pp. xxi-xxii.

their work, as they are observed by a horrified mortal who clings to the side of the cave-opening that frames Fuseli's picture. But we are decorously, and significantly, spared details of their gory undertaking, whereas in Blake's picture we are not. Conceivably Fuseli's views arose from contention with Blake over the proper way of representing this scene to the eye.

If Fuseli did influence Blake toward illustrating Gray, it was probably in 1797 or 1798 rather than 1799 or 1800, for sometime near the later date Blake seems to have begun distrusting Fuseli's motives toward him, or at least to find that he offered little actual help. The whole period was one of great difficulty for Blake. As G. E. Bentley, Jr., observes: "Between the failure of the *Night Thoughts* and the summer of 1800 Blake was only engaged to engrave designs for six or seven books, and his growing poverty was an obvious reason for accepting Hayley's generous offer of patronage in the latter year."[37] Blake wrote his friend Cumberland on August 26, 1799: "For as to Engraving, in which art I cannot reproach myself with any neglect, yet I am laid by in a corner as if I did not Exist, & Since my Young's Night Thoughts have been publish'd, Even Johnson & Fuseli have discarded my Graver" (795). From there Blake's spirits declined to such an extent that it seems hard to believe he could have done the Gray designs—at least the more graceful and comic ones—at this time. On July 2, 1800, he wrote again to Cumberland: "Excuse, I intreat you, my not returning Thanks at the proper moment for your kind present. No perswasion could make my stupid head believe that it was proper for me to trouble you with a letter of meer compliment & Expression of thanks. I begin to Emerge from a Deep pit of Melancholy, Melancholy without any real reason for it, a Disease which God keep you from & all good men" (798). And later in the same letter he supports a proffered opinion by saying: "at least I hear so from the few friends I have dared to visit in my stupid Melancholy. Excuse this communication of sentiments which I felt necessary to my repose at this time. I feel very strongly that I neglect my Duty to my Friends, but It is not want of Gratitude or Friendship but perhaps an Excess of both" (798). In other words it is lack of confidence in his own value, and in the value friends might be expected to place on his "meer compliment"; it is that "Excess" of gratitude that is the product of insufficient self-esteem.

Blake had been recommended by Cumberland to the Rev. Dr. John Trusler, who asked Blake to submit a sample illustration, apparently so that he might

---

[37] *Vala*, ed. Bentley, p. 160.

consider having Blake do a series of illustrations for a work he had then in progress. By Blake's account to Cumberland: "I have made him a Drawing in my best manner; he had sent it back with a Letter full of Criticisms, in which he says It accords not with his Intentions, which are to Reject all Fancy from his Work" (794). Three days earlier he had written Dr. Trusler to defend his "Visions of Eternity." At the close of that letter he writes with pride of the orders he has received for his designs: "Engraving is the profession I was apprenticed to, & should never have attempted to live by anything else, If orders had not come in for my Designs & Paintings, which I have the pleasure to tell you are Increasing Every Day. Thus If I am a Painter it is not to be attributed to Seeking after" (794). Blake's tone smacks a little of bravado, but it may be bravado born partly of the knowledge that the recently finished designs to Gray had been commissioned and paid for by one of the foremost sculptors of the day. Nevertheless, one can see why the period of melancholy ending in early 1800 must have been a dark time for Blake: the illustrations to Young had been a financial failure; he had found his graver "discarded" even by good friends; he was too poor to engrave *Vala*, although he felt near enough finished with it at the time to begin making a fair copy;[38] England was relentlessly pursuing a war of which he bitterly disapproved, and everywhere he looked in the outside world he saw error and blindness. In his annotations to Watson he had observed: "To defend the Bible in this year 1798 would cost a man his life. The Beast & the Whore rule without control" (383). And, as suggested above, he had begun to think of his friend Fuseli as perhaps less than a friend after all.

In that same letter to Cumberland (July 2, 1800) Blake speaks of "Poor Fuseli, sore from the lash of Envious tongues," and implies that there may as well have been some lashing in return: "he is not naturally good natured, but he is artificially very ill natured" (798). We see the affair in retrospect in a letter from Blake to his friend and patron William Butts, written in 1802 from Felpham: "I find on all hands great objections to my doing any thing but the meer drudgery of business, & intimations that if I do not confine myself to this, I shall not live; this has always pursu'd me. . . . This from Johnson & Fuseli brought me down here, & this from Mr. H[ayley] will bring me back again" (812). The complaint is repeated in a poem sent to Butts in a letter dated November 22, 1802, although the poem was written (according to the letter) more than a year before that. In the poem Blake is addressed by a vision:

[38] See *Vala*, ed. Bentley, p. 160.

And Los the terrible thus hath sworn,
Because thou backward dost return,
Poverty, Envy, old age & fear
Shall bring thy Wife upon a bier;
And Butts shall give what Fuseli gave,
A dark black Rock & a gloomy Cave. (817)

The topical meaning of "turning back" is uncertain in this context, but the allusion to Fuseli is not: the cave is an encloser and limiter (as in *The Marriage of Heaven and Hell*) and the rocks in their resistance to the creative fire are likewise constricting, impervious to the poetic imagination. But one does not have to marshal Blakean allusions to understand that Blake felt Fuseli had tried to confine and restrict him, to darken his vision, to make him be governed by the decorum that had guided Fuseli in illustrating "The Fatal Sisters."

Fuseli's side of the matter we can gather from an even earlier source, for Joseph Farington records in his diary that on June 24, 1796, Fuseli had called on him and discussed Blake: "Fuseli has known him several years and thinks he has a good deal of invention, but that 'fancy is the end and not a means in his designs.' He does not employ it to give a novelty and decoration to regular conceptions, but the whole of his aim is to produce singular shapes and odd combinations."[39] Blake would have agreed to this distinction, though not to the value judgment apparently implied. (This judgment may be Farington's rather than Fuseli's, as Farington himself clearly did not admire what he had seen of Blake's work, although he names several others who do.) But Fuseli was a successful artist and something more of a practical man than Blake, and doubtless Fuseli regarded as the counsel of good sense what Blake considered a malevolent effort to inhibit his genius.

Moreover, in 1799 and 1800 Fuseli was himself much occupied with a project that was to bring him great disappointment. During the 1790's he had been at work on a "Milton Gallery" (on the analogy of Boydell's Shakespeare Gallery), which Johnson originally planned to publish in conjunction with an edition of Milton being edited for him by William Cowper, to be illustrated by Fuseli. With Cowper's illness and the intervention of Boydell, Johnson gave up the scheme. But Fuseli went ahead and opened his gallery in May 1799. It was an unhappy failure then, and was so again in 1800 when the Royal Academy re-

[39] *The Farington Diary*, I, 151.

opened it with a banquet and the added attraction of seven new pictures. By August 1800 Fuseli had given up all hope of success for the venture.[40] It was doubtless partly this experience that prompted Fuseli's pessimism as recorded several years later by Farington: "Fuseli has little hope of *Poetical* painting finding incouragement in England. The People are not prepared for it. Portrait with them is everything—their taste and feeling all go to realities.—The Ideal does not operate on their minds."[41] It was partly a shared exasperation with such un-Ideal views that kept the breach between Blake and Fuseli (if there ever was a real breach on Fuseli's side) from being permanent; the two men remained friends until Fuseli's death only two years before Blake's.

One would guess, then, that if Fuseli did suggest the Gray project to Blake, it would have been before 1799 rather than after, both because Fuseli himself was suffering disappointment in the area of "poetical painting" in 1799 and because shortly after this time he was giving kinds of advice that Blake was unwilling to accept. Moreover, in 1797 and 1798 Fuseli was feeling highly optimistic about his own Milton illustrations and may have urged Blake to undertake a more compact and durable poet than Young, their mutual admiration for Gray helping them determine on him as the choice.

Let us, then, review the evidence. For reasons just discussed it seems likely that the designs were done before the summer of 1800. Although it is hard to tell just when the period of "stupid Melancholy" began, it would seem to have been after August 1799, for the letter describing the melancholy pleads unwillingness to write thanks as a symptom of it, whereas on August 26, 1799, Blake had in fact written Cumberland specifically to thank him for his "kind recommendation to Dr. Trusler, which, tho' it has fail'd of success, is not the less to be remember'd by me with Gratitude" (794).

We still have the period from about 1796 or 1797 to at least August 1799 to account for, and there are no certainties to guide us. We have only the close affinity of the Gray and Young designs and our knowledge that if Fuseli did encourage Blake in the project he would have been somewhat more likely to do so before 1799. Fuseli's own illustrations for the 1800 edition of Gray would seem to have followed Blake's in time, if we credit the possibility that Fuseli's views as paraphrased in the introduction did indeed arise from discussions with

---

[40] For details see Gert Schiff, *Johann Heinrich Füsslis Milton Galerie* (Zurich and Stuttgart, 1963).

[41] *The Farington Diary*, III, 91.

Blake or from a view of his "indecorous" designs. Indeed, the fact that Fuseli and not Blake was given the job by the publisher may further have embittered Blake during his period of melancholy, and may have put a further edge on his temporary mistrust of Fuseli.

On the basis of all this conjectural evidence I will suggest that the most probable time for Blake's execution of the designs to Gray was somewhere between 1797, after he had finished engraving the forty-three *Night Thoughts* plates, and early 1799, before his period of great melancholy and the subsequent departure for Felpham. Professor Woodworth's date of 1797-1798 therefore seems thoroughly convincing to me. I will further suggest that the project was undertaken as one of considerable personal interest to Blake, though possibly with the encouragement of Fuseli, Edwards, or Flaxman. And of course we now know that at some time before the series was finished it had been sold to Flaxman for his wife's library.

The manuscript itself is a work of vigorous and powerful beauty, giving in its finished state evidence of both exquisite care and that bold "Original Invention" that Blake insisted must be "Drawn with a firm & decided hand at once" (595). Bound in with Blake's designs and attesting to the high value the Flaxmans placed on the volume is an extra sheet to which is attached a smaller sheet of wove paper bearing a pencil sketch of Blake, signed by John Flaxman.

Of some interest is the enormous care and delicacy exercised in assembling the pages of this work. The title page is that of the 1790 edition of Gray published by J. Murray, No. 32 Fleet Street: here, as in each case, whoever made up the pages has cut away the margins of this edition to make a sheet about 3¾ inches wide by 5½ inches high, which he has then pasted carefully by the thinnest possible margins against a very slightly smaller rectangular opening cut into the folio drawing paper. The printed sheets are applied against the verso of each drawing sheet, somewhat high and to the right of center of the verso (and so of course the insertion appears high and to the left of each recto), indicating that from the beginning the project was envisioned as a bound or bindable "book" in its own right.

On the title page Blake has surrounded the "text-box" (as I will call the insertions) with five meticulously drawn concentric bordering lines in red ink. A single red line encircles each inserted text-box throughout the work, forming a colorful link between the printed paper and the watercolor design surrounding it.

The 1790 edition offered a blank verso for the title page of each poem, excepting a few on which was printed an "advertisement" or other commentary about the poem itself; fortunately each time a verso was so used, there happened to be a blank verso to the page before, the page bearing the final lines of the preceding poem. So in one way or another Blake was always able to supply himself with a blank text-box at the outset of each new poem, either on the verso of its printed title or on the page facing its title. These blank text-boxes Blake appropriated for his own use, listing on them the titles of his illustrations for the poem that followed; in black ink he would first write the title of the poem illustrated, then a list of numbers, one for each design, followed by his own title for that design written in longhand. On the upper outside corner of each page of design he penned the corresponding number. Two more blank sheets were left after this process was completed—the verso following the last lines of "The Fatal Sisters" (Sisters 10) and the verso following the last lines of the "Elegy Written in a Country Churchyard" (Elegy 12). The former Blake left blank; the latter he employed for his poem dedicating the book to Mrs. Flaxman.

Blake's titles are sometimes descriptive, as "12. A Muse," sometimes quotations from the poem itself, as "7. 'Shaggy forms oer Ice built mountains roam.'" Often they synopsize two or more lines or phrases from Gray in a combination of paraphrase and quotation. Blake has also marked with an "x" the line in the text to which his illustration pertains, occasionally marking a different line from that quoted in his title, in which case both are pertinent. The designs to each poem are numbered consecutively, and I have adapted from this a form of brief reference to the designs: thus "Eton 2" refers to the second design for Gray's "Ode on a Distant Prospect of Eton College." This design Blake numbers "2" in the upper corner of the design itself and also lists as number 2 in his titles to the designs for that poem.

Each design is presented as a separate picture, formally independent of whatever may appear on the facing page. Twice the facing designs seem particularly closely allied, both times in "The Triumphs of Owen": in the first pair (Owen 2 and 3), we are shown two stages of a banquet—the meal itself and the entertainment afterward. In the second pair (Owen 3 and 4) we see two sides engaged in battle—Owen advancing terribly on his enemy, and the enemy thrown back in dismay. But each of these four exists as a design in its own right; it is simply that in this one poem Blake has twice used the spread of double pages to widen our perspective on the events.

I can find no certain way of telling in what order Blake executed the designs, though the continuity of tone within the designs to each poem, and the movement of tone throughout the entire set of 116 designs, argues for a generally straightforward plan of work. Blake's method seems to have been first to sketch out his ideas very faintly on the drawing sheet, using light strokes of the pencil; some of these sketches still remain visible, especially on the few occasions when Blake changed his first plans but did not erase them. Following the pencil sketches came more careful and detailed sketching in ink with a pen, or sometimes with a thin brush. On the highly finished designs it is hard or impossible to retrace these steps, but in those left unfinished or left in their "sketchy" state (chiefly designs to Gray's three translations), the process may be clearly followed.

After the pen or thin brush came the watercolors, and finally retouching with pen and sometimes highlights of color. The highly worked designs—in terms of both use of pen and details of color—tend to be nearer the beginning. The cat ode offers some of the best examples. But even here we see none of the miniaturist effects—the gradations, or the use of color for outlining, say, lips or folds of clothing—that are visible in Blake's later watercolors. Here the effects are generally simpler, and where the colors are bold, it is in the saturation of a few colors washed on, rather than in worked-up touches or the complex juxtaposition of many colors or shades of color. Compare the highly wrought details of the Stirling *Jerusalem*'s title page to one of the brightest of these designs—Poesy 4, for example—to see how different are the effects, and how vigorous, rough, and bold the Gray. I believe that Blake's technique shifted, in this regard, during his stay at Felpham, and perhaps because of his work at miniature painting there.

In her letter explaining that Flaxman had employed Blake to illuminate the works of Gray for her library, Nancy Flaxman concluded of Blake's designs: "He has treated his Poet most Poetically." If there may be said to be a single theme uniting the entire series of 116 designs, it is the theme of the poet and the various potentialities of his role. The opening design, surrounding Murray's printed title page, depicts the crucial event of inspiration. As Gray wrote in the Pindaric tradition, Blake entitles the picture "The Pindaric Genius receiving his Lyre," and employs the conventional motif of a youth astride a soaring swan (Apollo's bird)

22

accepting with his outstretched hand a lyre apparently descending from above. Gray would certainly have known of Pindar's special devotion to Apollo—the lyre, of course, was Apollo's own instrument—and Blake's design seems also to allude, through the swan, to Apollo's role as patron of poets. That this god of poetry and prophecy should have been envisioned by the ancients as a figure of youth, light, and beauty must have seemed to Blake a clear instance of the way myth can retain elements of visionary insight.

Blake's choice of this figure for his opening design tells us a great deal about his overall view of Gray, and reminds us of the position Gray held among eighteenth-century poets. In his "The Progress of Poesy. A Pindaric Ode," Gray alludes deprecatingly to his own poetic inheritance:

> Oh! Lyre divine, what daring spirit
> Wakes thee now? tho' he inherit
> Nor the pride, nor ample pinion,
> That the Theban Eagle bear. . . .

But in associating himself with the Theban Pindar and the "great ode" (and nine of the thirteen poems in the Murray edition are odes more or less Pindaric), Gray was putting himself in a tradition consciously liberal for its time. Pindar was the supreme classical example of the wit sublime that might nobly err, of the original genius who might successfully ignore the rules. Gray was sufficient scholar to know that in fact the works of Pindar were far from lawless, and Gray's papers show that his own odes were meticulously planned; but still his contemporaries found his more daring poems dark and difficult. Samuel Monk, quoting Nathan Drake as one who "offers a convenient summary of the more popular nature of the discussion" of the sublime,[42] notes that "The Bard," "so wildly awful, so gloomily terrific," is according to Drake greater than anything by Pindar. Both the comparison and the appreciation are revealing.

So it is Gray as Pindaric genius that Blake chooses to introduce on his title page, reflecting Gray's own view of himself in "The Progress of Poesy" as well as Gray's pervasive concern with the question of the poet's role, his power and responsibilities. Gray is of course exploring the question implicitly as he exercises himself on the fringes of allowable poetic experimentation, and explicitly in one or another aspect of most of the poems represented. In "Ode on the Spring" he nominates the poet to represent mankind. In "A Long Story" he

[42] *The Sublime* (Ann Arbor, Mich., 1960). Quoted passage occurs on p. 137.

treats the poet and his audience with a knowing irony that Blake enjoys and—rather surprisingly—reflects in the designs. In "The Progress of Poesy" Gray places himself in what he considers the great English tradition; Blake demurs in part. In "The Bard" poetry is given a prophetic power that Blake rejoiced in. The illustrations to "The Triumphs of Owen" draw firmly to our attention the fact that the poem is the recital of a bard. Gray's "Ode to Music" employs poetry as extended ceremonial bow—a degradation Blake deplores. And finally, in the "Elegy Written in a Country Churchyard" Blake and Gray confront one another most elaborately over the poet's vision of death.

The order of Blake's designs follows that of the 1790 text, but there is one piece of evidence suggesting that Blake had in mind a broad division of the poems into three groups or movements, groupings not indicated in the arrangement of the edition he used. The first group comprises Gray's early poems, those written in the 1740's and including "A Long Story," written in 1750 though first published with Bentley's illustrations in 1753. The second group comprises the Pindaric odes, the translations, and two other later poems, all written in the 1750's and 1760's. The final "group" is the single famous "Elegy Written in a Country Churchyard"—a poem separated from the others not by date, but rather by popular success. This grouping into three provides a convenient basis for dividing the poems among Chapters II, III, and IV, below.

The hint that Blake had such a tripartite division in mind is to be found in the layout of three designs, all depicting the poet at work: one of these designs "introduces" each of the three groups just defined and tells something of Blake's attitude toward the poems in each group by what it implies about the spiritual condition of the poet who wrote them. The first of these introductory designs presents a youthful poet seated at work—his hair curled loose from his head in a kind of eager abandon, his eyes regarding fervently the page on which he writes. The second and third show the poet in the same seated position, though he is more sedate and enclosed in the second, then almost grotesquely hunched over in the third. The surroundings, while similar in the linear movement of the designs, grow increasingly specific and detailed, and so place Gray increasingly in the mundane rather than the eternal world. We will look more closely at each of these designs as we come to the groups they introduce.

My method in the present study has been to combine catalogue with commentary, taking the designs more or less in order and discussing them poem by poem. It seemed desirable to allow the direction of my own argument to be guided by

Blake's, for the illustrator's method was at least in part progressive and his purpose largely educative. Of some of his fellow artists Blake wrote, with the immodesty of visionary conviction,

I found them blind: I taught them how to see (543).

His art proposes to do as much for anyone who will look.

I

THE EXPANDING

LANGUAGE

THERE are no rules, fortunately or unfortunately, for reading metaphors: one simply acquires, if one is lucky, a kind of tact in handling them, a tact developed from a sense of what is fitting or ludicrous in general, and from a sense of the particular context at hand. Homer's "rosy-fingered dawn" is liable to invite most readers to visualize a real sunrise, with the first rays of light reaching out rather like rosy fingers from behind the horizon. But there is nothing in the phrase itself to prevent one from visualizing dawn as a young woman or man complete, the youth of the day suggesting the youth of the person, the pink hands suggesting perhaps pampered delicacy. It would require a context of rather heavy burlesque to suggest a comic or unpleasant redness, however, partly because of the attractive connotations of "rosy," but even more because this kind of personification now has associations of eighteenth-century decorum, associations that tend to confine the reader's response and make it relatively predictable.

It was in 1800 that Wordsworth found this kind of decorum, this kind of "poetic diction," outworn, arguing that while such figures might originally have been prompted by passion, they were by then little more than mechanical bombast. "The reader will find that personifications of abstract ideas rarely occur in these volumes," he wrote in his famous Preface to the second edition of *Lyrical Ballads*, adding, "There will also be found in these volumes little of what is usually called poetic diction." Wordsworth maintained that the public, having grown used to "gaudiness and inane phraseology" in their poetry, demanded "outrageous stimulation" of a familiar but ever shriller kind that finally blunts the mind and reduces it to a state of almost "savage torpor." What should be substituted, he urged, was a calmer voice speaking a language stripped of "foreign splendour"—a language fundamentally no different from "the language of prose when prose is well written." Wordsworth continues: "To illustrate the subject

26

in a general manner, I will here adduce a short composition of Gray, who was at the head of those who, by their reasonings, have attempted to widen the space of separation betwixt Prose and Metrical composition, and was more than any other man curiously elaborate in the structure of his own poetic diction." He then quotes Gray's sonnet on the death of his close friend Richard West, reserving for approval five of the fourteen lines and affirming that the language of those five "does in no way differ from that of Prose." Interestingly, these lines do offer some natural personifications—"in my breast imperfect joys expire"— and what would sound to a modern ear very much like "poetic diction," but the personifications are unobtrusive, so that one need not picture joys alive to accept their "expiring."

The point is that for Wordsworth the cumulative effect of the poem, and of this kind of poetry in general, was to numb response rather than arouse it, apparently because the metaphors felt dead to him. "Smiling mornings" meant not more but less to him than simply "mornings," as did the far more long-winded "reddening Phoebus lifts his golden fire." The approved lines, demanding less of the response he could not give, irritated him less.

Yet a glance at Blake's illustrations to the poems of Gray shows that the metaphors and personifications which seemed dead to Wordsworth were often to Blake the whole life of the poetry, indeed evidence of its author's genius. We have noted that Blake was not educated in literature, and it may have been partly his very lack of sophistication that made him leap the bounds of tact that restrained as sensitive a reader as Wordsworth in order to find in "poetic diction" the vitality that first gave it currency. Anyone who believes that Gray's name describes his poetry will think again when he encounters the brilliance and energy of Blake's vision of it, for the pages burn with a vitality that Blake had found in the language of the poems. Gray says in his "Ode on the Spring" that the Hours "wake the purple year": Blake depicts a strong man springing from sleep, his face glowing with rapturous anticipation, his coloring pinked to a kind of purple that strangely enough manages to look vigorously healthful. Gray speaks in his "Ode on a Distant Prospect of Eton College" of "black Misfortune's baleful train . . . the vultures of the mind": from out of the distance behind the text box swarms a crowd of gargoylelike vulturous monsters such as nightmare could hardly conceive, dark against a flame-streaked sky. In "The Progress of Poesy," where Gray speaks of Helicon's springs and the "laughing flowers" that "drink life and fragrance" there, Blake draws a gracefully elaborate scene in rich pastels, filling the page with flowers from which tiny human figures joyously curve and bend, filling pitchers and goblets to drink the charmed liquid. And so on.

Is it irrelevant to Gray's poetry that a man with a vivid visual imagination has been able to find in its metaphors a life that can be reasserted pictorially? Certainly it was not irrelevant to eighteenth-century poetic theory,[1] and while Gray doubtless did not expect quite the kind of visualization Blake supplied for his images, they were intended to be visualized. In the Eton ode Gray appeals to the river—"Say, Father Thames"—to tell him about the current generation of students: "Who foremost now delight to cleave,/ With pliant arms, thy glassy wave?" Blake predictably shows a giant father reclining in the landscape, his arm draped over a huge urn, from which flows the river; beneath him small figures swim, "cleaving" the water with their widespread arms. The huge old man wears a crown of oak leaves and acorns, and the lines of his beard, flowing hair, and long body merge with those of the water streaming out of the urn. It is a typically Blakean rendition of the lines, almost perversely so, and yet in this case Blake is not even original: the figure is a conventional visual personification, although Blake's source in this case was probably a design Richard Bentley made for an edition of Gray's poems in 1753.[2]

This luxurious edition, done at the behest of Bentley's and Gray's mutual friend Horace Walpole, was so flattering to Gray that he permitted his occasional poem "A Long Story" to be published there for the first time because Bentley was to illustrate it. This was certainly the chief illustrated edition of Gray's poems in his own time, or at any time before Blake's undertaking. And one may suppose that Bentley's designs generally reflected the spirit in which Gray hoped his poems would be visualized. Bentley made for each poem a headpiece and tailpiece, a decorated initial letter, and one full-page illustration drawing elements from throughout the poem into a single, elaborately framed unit. The full-page illustration to the Eton ode offers a number of details that Blake borrowed: his drawings of the college closely resemble Bentley's, though Bentley's are far more detailed. A boy similar to Blake's boy rolls a hoop in Bentley's picture. At either side of the picture, forming part of its frame, stand figures identified by the "Explanation of the

---

[1] See Bertrand H. Bronson, "Personification Reconsidered," *ELH*, XIV (1947), 163-177; Jean H. Hagstrum, *The Sister Arts* (Chicago, 1958); and Patricia Meyer Spacks, *The Poetry of Vision: Five Eighteenth-Century Poets* (Cambridge, Mass., 1967), for pertinent discussions of eighteenth-century poetic use of visual imagery.

[2] *Designs by Mr. Richard Bentley, for Six Poems by Mr. Thomas Gray* (London, 1753).

Prints" as "terms representing Jealousy and Madness": Blake has borrowed the torch held by Madness for his representation of the queen of Death in Eton 8; her snaky hair he has modified somewhat and given to one of the monsters suffering under Death's reign, again in Eton 8.

But the clearest and most complete borrowing in the illustration to the Eton ode is of Bentley's chief figure, "the god of the Thames," as the "Explanation of the Prints" identifies him.[3] In the center of Bentley's design reclines a large man in a pose closely resembling that of Blake's figure; he leans languidly against a large urn from which flows the water of the river, his head is crowned with leaves (rushes rather than Blake's oak leaves, as nearly as one can tell), and at his feet a young man somewhat like Blake's chief swimmer "cleaves" the waves, his arm outstretched and his bottom up. A second swimmer regards the first, from a point in the water analogous to that occupied by Blake's second swimmer.

There are some interesting departures on Blake's part, in addition to the important similarities. Bentley depicts the "passions, misfortunes, and diseases coming down upon" the boys at their sports, and shows this personified crowd as naked but ordinary men and women in a kind of orgy of misery and punishment. They are massed in a cloud that hangs over the rest of the pictures: one holds a serpent wreathed around her wrist and hand; a male figure, blindfolded, clutches a dagger in each hand, raising one as if to plunge it into the back of the figure holding the serpent. A third holds a tasseled whip; another holds arrows; another weeps, face in hands. Driving them all from behind is a skeleton, presumably the death to which, Gray says, all this "black Misfortune" leads. But Blake has avoided the human specificity of Bentley's version, substituting the vultures and monsters that swarm out of the distance to surround the playing children. Blake's monsters have some unexpected human characteristics: one vulture reaches forward with almost delicate human hands to lift away a young boy; another creature, diabolical with scales and pointed ears and a pair of snakes that ring his forehead, cavorts clownlike and points leeringly up toward the vultures, his hand wreathed with a snake similar to that in the hand of Bentley's figure. Another monster, reminiscent of Blake's famous "Ghost of the Flea,"

[3] For evidence on the one hand of the conventional use of the river god figure, and on the other of the similarity of Blake's view to Bentley's, compare both to a similar figure by Alexander Runciman (1736-1785) in his "Marriage of Peleus and Thetis." Runciman's preparatory drawing, showing the figure clearly enough, is reproduced in David Irwin, *English Neoclassical Art* (London, 1966). (Blake, incidently, employs the idiom again in his figure of "lucid Avon," Poesy 9.)

embraces with transparent hands a fleeing boy. And Blake, too, has a weeping figure, emerging at the side from what appears to be a cave and grasping—again with transparent hands—a young girl who plays, oblivious, with her doll. This weeping figure offers an interesting analogy with the figure of the sighing cave of Bard 5; both are colored a striking gray-green and have similar faces and expressions—faces recalling the Greek tragic mask, which Blake used as a symbol of oppression elsewhere in his art.[4]

Interestingly, the effect of Bentley's kind of personification is to distance the figures of passion and misfortune, to make them external agents personified according to a sort of literary gentlemen's agreement. They are the traditional allegorical figures of emblem literature, Gothic themes in a mannerist rendering. It seems relevant to recall that Bentley designed much of the decoration for Walpole's Strawberry Hill.

But Blake, although he often draws on emblem literature for both technique and design, is really trying to do something entirely different. It was not only Gray's expression "vultures of the mind" that caught his interest, but also the idea behind that choice of language. The vulture preys on carrion; vultures "of" the mind are thus both vultures that the mind creates and also vultures that prey on dead minds. In Blake's belief, the two points conflate: it is the dead mind that creates the vultures that prey on it, and that in turn fears these vultures. This is why Blake draws them partially transparent, or "invisible."

It is not that the creations of imagination are to Blake's mind less real than opaque, tangible things—quite the reverse. In the *Descriptive Catalogue* written to defend and explain his exhibition of 1809, he takes exception to those who have found fault with his representation of the "Spirits of the murdered bards" in his painting "The Bard, from Gray": "The connoisseurs and artists who have made objections to Mr. B.'s mode of representing spirits with real bodies, would do well to consider that the Venus, the Minerva, the Jupiter, the Apollo, which they admire in Greek statues are all of them representations of spiritual existences, of Gods immortal, to the mortal perishing organ of sight; and yet they are embodied and organized in solid marble. Mr. B. requires the same latitude, and all is well" (576). The point is that such beings are the objects of a vision superior to corporeal or "mortal" vision. "The Prophets describe what they saw in Vision as real and existing men, whom they saw with their imaginative and

---

[4] Hagstrum, *Poet and Painter*, p. 27, observes this symbolism in Blake, noting that Blake shares it with Fuseli.

immortal organs; the Apostles the same; the clearer the organ the more distinct the object" (576). The "vultures of the mind" to which Gray refers are, however, not the products of that superior vision which sees more distinctly; rather, as suggested above, they are the product of dead minds, of minds weighed down by fear, uncertainty, and the folly of supposing that such vultures are external and inevitable rather than internal and self-created. To borrow a phrase from Blake's "London": these are "mind-forg'd manacles."

The man with that real and superior vision is the one who can find the true vision, where it exists, and expose errors: in this instance, it is he who can ferret out the truth of Gray's figure of speech from the error of his abstract general statements. Gray is right to say that these "vultures" are "vultures of the mind," but wrong to suppose that with maturity man necessarily falls passive prey to them. Blake's vision of Gray's vision—his illustration of Gray—must then reveal the vultures as invisible because unreal after all, the figments of dead minds rather than the "spiritual existences" visible to the fearless and creative imagination. It is in instances such as this that we can see Blake trying to do something very different from what Bentley was doing, and see that it was not quite the sort of visualization Gray expected his images to evoke. It is not, however, opposed to the kind of visualization Gray expected—rather, it builds on it, trying to force it into use as a more fully active tool of language, just as the illustrations build on Bentley's designs but seek to go beyond them.

I do not believe that Blake arrived immediately at such a method of illustration, but rather that he was developing a related kind of illustration for his own illuminated printing, that is, in the designs to his own poetry and indeed in the poetry itself. As Blake was reading and annotating his copy of Swedenborg's *Wisdom of Angels Concerning Divine Love and Divine Wisdom* in about 1788, his attention was caught by Swedenborg's distinction between the "spiritual ideas" with which angels "see" in their thought and communicate in their speech, and the "natural ideas" of men. Swedenborg offers an example: "That there is such a Difference between the Thoughts of Angels and Men, was made known to me by this Experience. They were told to think of something spiritually, and afterwards to tell me what they thought of; when this was done and they would have told me, they could not." Lest one interpret this to mean that Swedenborg could not understand the angels at all, Blake remarks in his margin: "They could not tell him in natural ideas; how absurd must men be to understand him as if he said the angels could not express themselves at all to him" (94). Blake be-

31

lieved that men, too, were capable of having "spiritual ideas" and indeed of communicating them, though the ability is "unusual in our time, but common in ancient" (94).

When men who possess and understand "spiritual ideas" communicate with one another about (and with) them, they converse "in the spirit," which Blake equates with "conversing with spirits": "all who converse in the Spirit, converse with Spirits." To this Blake added and afterwards erased: "& they converse with the spirit of God."[5] Blake finally adds, in compliment to a book he was then reading: "For these reasons I say that this Book is written by consultation with Good Spirits, because it is Good" (88). It is not far from this to Blake's assertion at the beginning of his long final prophecy, *Jerusalem*: "We who dwell on Earth can do nothing of ourselves; every thing is conducted by Spirits, no less than Digestion or Sleep" (621), by which he does not mean that man is passive and at the mercy of something outside himself, but rather that these "spirits" are the real man, that force in him which moves and grows and thinks. We say, for example, that someone "has a lot of spirit," and understand a connection between functions of spirit and bodily process when we say "his low spirits made him lose his appetite." Blake has expanded and literalized the metaphor. Were he to picture it, he would doubtless give it human form.

In a well-known passage from *The Marriage of Heaven and Hell*, Blake recounts having asked the prophets Isaiah and Ezekiel "how they dared so roundly to assert that God spoke to them; and whether they did not think at the time that they would be misunderstood, & so be the cause of imposition." To this Blake has Isaiah answer: "I saw no God, nor heard any, in a finite organical perception; but my senses discover'd the infinite in every thing, and as I was then perswaded, & remain confirm'd, that the voice of honest indignation is the voice of God, I cared not for consequences, but wrote." A reader who then asks Blake "How dare you so roundly assert that Isaiah spoke to you?" has his question already answered. Blake then forestalls the reader's next question as well; speaking again to Isaiah:

Then I asked: "does a firm perswasion that a thing is so, make it so?"

He replied: "All poets believe that it does, & in ages of imagination this firm perswasion removed mountains; but many are not capable of a firm perswasion of any thing." (153)

[5] These eight additional deleted words are supplied in *The Poetry and Prose of William Blake*, ed. David V. Erdman (New York, 1965), p. 590.

We are left to hear Blake's own "firm perswasions," his discovery of "the infinite in everything." These persuasions are, however (to return to the earlier passage in Swedenborg), spiritual ideas. How, then, is one to communicate them in "natural ideas," which are the province of ordinary speech?

The answer is, of course, to expand ordinary speech. At one point in *Jerusalem*, as he has just inundated the reader with names of the characters and places of his mythology, Blake adds parenthetically:

> (I call them by their English names: English, the rough basement.
> Los built the stubborn structure of the Language, acting against
> Albion's melancholy, who must else have been a Dumb despair.) (668)

Albion's melancholy is England's melancholy, that is, the sickness from which the English—or by extension any people—suffer in their fearful unwillingness to overthrow their materialism and rationalism and hear "the voice of God." The language whose "stubborn structure" has English as its "rough basement" is the language Blake strove all his life to perfect, a language that could adequately communicate "spiritual ideas" or "vision." It would be a language of "visionary forms," both verbal and visual.

When Blake illustrated Gray he was at something of a midpoint in his development: he had completed all of his short prophecies, written most of his lyrics, and made the fine series of large color prints now in the Tate Gallery. He was at work on *Vala* and was just finishing or had just finished the huge *Night Thoughts* project. Ahead of him were his two long prophecies, *Milton* and *Jerusalem*, as well as the great series of illustrations to Milton, Bunyan, the Book of Job, and Dante. He seems to have abandoned for a time the idea of reaching a large public through his illuminated books, but with the encouragement of the early hopes for the *Night Thoughts* series there seemed a good chance of reaching this same public through illustration.

And in fact it has proved historically true that as a poet, or artist in words, Blake has always been known and appreciated most for his early lyrics; whereas as a pictorial artist, designer, and illustrator, he has always been best known and appreciated for his late illustrations, especially those to Job. His early pictorial and late verbal art have been the more neglected. This developing language, then, drew increasingly on the pictorial aspects of "vision," and in some respects, at least, did so with increasing success.

I spoke earlier, in relation to the Eton ode, of Blake's trying to build on the kind of visualization Gray expected his readers to supply for his figures of speech, trying to use it to go beyond the theory of illustration that it implies. Blake was, in this way, really trying to expand Gray's language itself; by exposing the real vision half-dormant in the language of Gray's poems Blake would be, like Los, building from the rough basement of Gray's English a "stubborn structure" powerful enough to communicate that vision.

"ODE ON A DISTANT PROSPECT OF ETON COLLEGE"

The poem opens with Gray addressing his old school, "Where once my careless childhood stray'd/ A stranger yet to pain!" He then asks "Father Thames" what "sprightly race" is there now, and uses this as a transition into the long rumination about the boys and their future that makes up most of the rest of the poem. Some play happily with hoops and balls; others study; still others break away from childish play, but with discomfiting results:

> Some bold adventurers disdain
> The limits of their little reign,
> And unknown regions dare descry:
> Still as they run they look behind,
> They hear a voice in every wind,
> And snatch a fearful joy.

Yet the vicissitudes that all these children experience are only the mild ups and downs of young lives. Such are their disappointments:

> Gay hope is theirs by fancy fed,
> Less pleasing when possest;

and such their recoveries:

> The tear forgot as soon as shed,
> The sunshine of the breast. . . .

But it will not always be so:

> Alas! regardless of their doom,
> The little victims play!

34

Turning again to Father Thames, Gray shares with him the painful foreknowledge of misery:

> Yet see, how all around 'em wait
> The ministers of human fate,
> And black Misfortune's baleful train!
> Ah, show them where in ambush stand,
> To seize their prey, the murderous band!
> Ah, tell them they are men!
>
> These shall the fury passions tear,
> The vultures of the mind. . . .

And there follows a list of these vultures and passions, among them anger, fear, shame, pining love, jealousy, ambition, infamy, and madness. Beyond, in "the Vale of Years," are "The painful family of Death/ More hideous than their queen": these are the ills of old age, seen as a band of malicious creatures acting on the passive aged:

> This racks the joints, this fires the veins,
> That every labouring sinew strains,
> Those in the deeper vitals rage:
> Lo, Poverty, to fill the band,
> That numbs the soul with icy hand,
> And slow-consuming Age.

The process is inevitable, so there is nothing to be gained by the children's knowing about it, by their being told that "they are men," and what this means. The poem concludes:

> Yet, ah! why should they know their fate!
> Since sorrow never comes too late,
> And happiness too swiftly flies.
> Thought would destroy their paradise.
> No more—where ignorance is bliss,
> 'Tis folly to be wise.

Gray's language has been criticized as stilted, and certainly it often seems so: children at play "chase the rolling circle's speed" (hoops) or "urge the flying ball." Yet most of the stilted effect of the language comes, I suspect, from the role of the speaker. The pleasures of childhood are seen by old age looking back;

boys who swim and catch birds do not see themselves as cleaving "with pliant arms" the "glassy wave" or "enthralling" the "captive linnet." And one must be well past childhood to see reading children as ones who "Their murm'ring labours ply/ 'Gainst graver hours, that bring constraint/ To sweeten liberty." Yet it is not unusual to read of childhood from a stance well outside it; Gray seems just a little farther outside than most.

But the striking thing for a modern reader is that maturity, too, is seen from well outside the experience of it, as if the poet had joined Father Thames in his position as timeless watcher. And further, all the experiences of old age are themselves "outside" the experiencer. Life is seen as the journey of ignorant innocence into the "ambush" of a "murderous band," whose members are the experiences of the psyche externalized by personification. They are in turn "ministers," a "baleful train," the "murderous band," a "grisly troop," the "painful family of Death" headed by their "queen."

As visualizers of Gray's lines we see these figures as Bentley depicts them— separate human shapes grouped apart from their victims, themselves similar to the victims in human appearance, and acting out among themselves the drama of the victims' futures. Here again, to Blake's mind, such a "vision" of the matter is not so much wrong as incomplete.

Let us look at Blake's series of designs. The title page shows a rather lankly elegant young man leaning against a wall of "Windsor terrace" (as Blake's title identifies the spot), an open book held in a hand that has dropped down by his side; he gazes across at the "distant prospect of Eton College," which appears as a small group of stylized towers looking rather like a picket fence. The lines of the drawing are almost all straight, or only gently curved; the effect is peaceful, indeed almost lifeless, and the sense of soft motionlessness is reinforced by a pastel coloring of the whole scene.

This languid peacefulness prevails in the next four designs as well: in design 2 a boy flies a kite, his body beautifully curved in a running posture that nevertheless conveys little sense of motion, but is rather like a sustained ballet position. Almost the only color on the page is the soft purplish-blue of his clothing and the faint blue of some streaks at the top of the page, indicating distant sky. Design 3 offers a somewhat closer view of the "spires" and "antique towers" of Eton, largely obscured by a gently shapeless foreground of bushy trees, among which wander two robed students and the floating "shade" of the founder of the college, Henry VI, who is absorbed in a book he holds before him. The boys, equally absorbed in their books and in one another, do not see him. The next design is that depicting Father Thames, already described; but again the tone is predominantly peaceful. Father Thames is himself rather sadly contemplative; two boys with the group of swimmers but not participating sit on the bank, bent over in attitudes of weariness or depression; and a sailboat drifts quietly in the distance.

The last of this peaceful sequence is design 5, which illustrates the range of activities of this "idle progeny." A boy in a tree hands down a nest of baby linnets to a graceful girl below; another boy walks by, looking down and "murm'ring" from the book he holds open before him; a third runs gracefully after a large hoop, his posture closely recalling that of the kite-flier in design 2. In the distance two more figures may be seen, one leaning against a tree and the other apparently also reading from a book. The cumulative effect of these young people, for whom reading is one of a group of rather infantile—certainly childishly "innocent"—occupations, is to suggest that life is bland, and best encountered with placid indifference.

One is, then, unprepared for what the turning of the page reveals: the violent flock of monstrous creatures preparing to engulf the unwitting children. (Two children are running, but it is hard to tell whether in play or in fear of their descending fate.) Gray has in his poem prepared us for this moment, first in the opening lines, where he described himself at Eton as a "stranger yet to pain," a hint that pain will come; but more obviously in the lines about the "bold adventurers" who "look behind" as they run, snatching only "a fearful joy." But Blake has offered none of this kind of direct preparation at all: his hints, where they have occurred, have been not of pain but of incapacity, to be inferred from the self-absorption of the children and their limp elegance. This amounts less to "preparation" in the ordinary sense than to a display of the children's lack of it. Yet the sight of the monsters, when it comes, is one of the most violent in the entire series of designs to Gray. And it is only the first of three discomfiting designs.

The facing page is much lighter in coloring and the motion is less violent, but the action illustrated is again an ugly one: it shows one of the "fury passions" at work.

> Ambition this shall tempt to rise,
> Then whirl the wretch from high,
> To bitter scorn a sacrifice,
> And grinning Infamy.

37

"This" youth is shown in three stages of his sad development, first as he scrambles eagerly up the left toward Ambition, a regal lady who beckons from the top of a rock or hill. Her expression is hard to decipher in the reproduction, but in the original design it may be seen to be viciously inviting. Below her, down the right of the page, falls headlong the same boy, already tempted and literally fallen. At the bottom, in his third stage, the boy lies outstretched—presumably dead—in a posture very similar to that of the figure beneath the poison tree in the *Songs of Experience*. The personified figures of Scorn and Infamy point at him, Scorn wearing an expression of outrage, Infamy grinning with a kind of delight in destruction. Infamy is interestingly seen as a subhuman figure with gargoylelike face and pointed ears; as noted, one hand points at the fallen boy in a gesture parallel to that of Scorn, while the other hand points back at the path taken by the boy as he first struggled up the rock toward Ambition, emphasizing and completing the circular motion implicit in the design. We see in stages the fate of one victim racked on the wheel of Fortune, and the stages are further defined by the coloring of the boy: as he climbs his outfit is bright pink; as he falls, his outfit is pale pink, his face bluish; outstretched he is blue entirely. It is a wry added comment of Blake's that the temptation held out in Ambition's beckoning hand is a laurel leaf.

The last of these three grim designs shows death taking over from old age:

> Lo, in the Vale of Years beneath,
> A grisly troop are seen,
> The painful family of Death,
> More hideous than their queen. . . .

At the top of the page, to the right, spread the crowned head and side-streaming hair of an aged God; the lines from his eyes, eyebrows, and beard all sweep out to the sides to join other feathery lines indicating wings. It is Blake's familiar Urizen figure with minor variations. Below and to the left, wearing a crown identical to that of the god (and to that of Ambition on the page before), sits the "queen," a hideous amazon all enwrapped with thick, ropy, serpentlike coils and grasping what appear to be blue-red fasces. Flames burst out from beneath her feet. Pouring down across the page in a diagonal line from upper left to lower right are the subjects of the poem—the youths, now aged and dying. Above, left, they are seen as bent old men and women, heads down, oppressed by age and helpless resignation. They sink down behind the text box, to emerge below

38

transformed into the torturing and tortured monsters they fear. Thus the spirit of the page shifts from the quiet and hopeless pallor of the "vale of Years" above, presided over by Urizen, to the tangled activity of decay into subhumanity below, presided over by the queen of the "family of Death." The point is clear: the man who grows old in helpless fear of himself and fear for his future, who submits himself to the blinding restrictions of a Urizenic existence, will finally become what he fears and succumb to the god he has created. It is the theme of the "vultures of the mind" again, here developed through time.

Facing this page is the ninth of the ten illustrations to this poem, done in response to the poem's closing lines:

> No more—where ignorance is bliss,
> 'Tis folly to be wise.

A youth, strongly reminiscent in appearance and posture of the kite-flier and hoop-roller before him, rushes off to the right, his hat raised back over his head, poised to catch or strike at a tiny bird just visible in the air beyond him. In the fork of a bare tree above him crouches a fat, foolishly complacent little creature who flings pestilence from two vials onto the head of the fleeing youth beneath. The design works almost like a pun. Pestilence flung onto a sporting boy epitomizes the argument of Gray's poem: yet in Blake's design it is not "human fate" or some similar figure that flings the pestilence, but rather a vision of that very ignorance which Gray maintains is the only (though temporary) escape from the pestilence. Gray's cure is Blake's cause. In his *Poetical Sketches* Blake had maintained that "Ignorance is Folly's leasing [deceitful] nurse" (14), and here the same point is made in pictorial reply to Gray.

The final illustration for this poem is a masterpiece of tone: it depicts with flawless ease the casual elegance of three young men, two of whom stand watching the third, their arms entwined, as he bends gracefully over a top he is preparing to spin. The world of "fury passions" and "vultures of the mind" is inconceivable in this context; our only reminder of what we have just seen is in the skimpy lines that arch high over the three figures, depicting the thin and barren branches of a leafless tree. For the force of contrast one should compare this design to plate 9 of *America*, where the same tree arches over a scene of genuine innocence—the tree burgeoning with birds and lovely, delicate leaves.

Blake's designs illustrate Gray's language with great fidelity and precision, but achieve at the same time a forceful and important critical commentary on the poem. Gray writes of innocent children, whose very innocence makes them helpless in the face of the awful but inevitable horrors of the experience of maturity. The few "bold adventurers" who do look beyond their present condition do not so much prepare themselves for understanding it as run from it. A few lines later even this fleeting awareness is overlooked in lines that emphasize once more the impotence of the children and the inevitability of their fate: "Alas! regardless of their doom,/ The little victims play!" To tell them what lies in store for them is to "tell them they are men!" and the poem concludes that since "all are men,/ Condemned alike to groan," there is no use thinking about it. "Thought would destroy their paradise," for the only bliss is in ignorance.

Blake believed, however, that "Innocence dwells with Wisdom, but never with Ignorance" (380), and that "Neither Youth nor Childhood is Folly or Incapacity. Some Children are Fools & so are some Old Men" (794). But the foolishly ignorant need not remain so. One of the points most vigorously made in *The Marriage of Heaven and Hell* was that men create their own "eternal lots": the angel who shows Blake the eternal lot he thinks Blake may expect—a horrible vision of spiders and "animals sprung from corruption," as Blake is such a bad man—is himself frightened away by the sight, which indeed disappears as soon as he departs and ceases to create it by believing in it. Blake then finds himself sitting on a pleasant bank in the moonlight, listening to a song about how "The man who never alters his opinion is like standing water, & breeds reptiles of the mind." Blake returns to the angel to inform him: "All that we saw was owing to your metaphysics" (156). The foolish angel is Blake's version of Gray's Eton boy grown up. As it happens, the ability to change one's mind is not at issue in Gray's poem, but then it is not really the central issue in Blake's either; rather, the inability to change one's mind is one of many lamentable results of having a stultified spirit, of allowing oneself to be herded like the old men and women of Eton 8 toward a death that is horrible because one is afraid of it. "Hell" is what a man does to himself, self-stultification of mind and body: "Mark that I do not believe there is such a thing litterally, but hell is the being shut up in the possession of corporeal desires which shortly weary the man, *for* ALL LIFE IS HOLY" (74). And, as Blake affirmed in his first version of "The Fly":

> Thought is life
> And strength & breath;
> But the want
> Of Thought is death. (183)

40

Gray's conclusion that "Thought would destroy their paradise" is thus not only wrong, but indeed shows up the source of all the hell depicted in the poem and in Blake's dark vision of the "eternal lots" these young men and women are preparing for themselves by their choice of ignorance and "fearful" joy over self-knowledge and the release of spirit and body that comes with it. Their minds breed vultures just as the angel's bred reptiles. And the fact that Blake pictures girls as well as boys at Eton, and later women as well as men shuffling toward death, emphasizes his desire to generalize from Gray's poem:

> . . . in your own Bosom you bear your Heaven
> And Earth & all you behold; tho' it appears Without, it is Within (709)

Clearly the problem is not uniquely a problem for Eton boys, nor even for the listless wealthy. Any human being who hopes for life must find it in the released powers of his own mind: "Where is the Existence Out of Mind or Thought? Where is it but in the Mind of a Fool?" (617).

Thus it is that from the first the Eton boys are drawn as rather younger than they ought to be, removed from experience by a kind of mindless elegance that suggests a peace born of decadence and makes them seem even more motionless than they are. The cues are all in Gray, who describes the boys as "idle progeny" accustomed to "The thoughtless day, the easy night." But to Gray they are "little victims," whereas to Blake they are little fools, accepting the balm of ignorance—their real pestilence—administered by the plump, mindlessly complacent little imp of the next to last illustration. They are as barren as the tree that arches over them at last.

This sequence, then, exemplifies Blake's technique of illustration. There is no design of the ten that does not derive from Gray's own language: some of the most striking and apparently private of Blake's details were indeed anticipated by an illustrator of Gray's own time, and one whom Gray avowedly admired. In what sense might Blake then be said to be expanding Gray's language and building a "stubborn structure" from its "rough" English "basement"? Are we merely offered a sort of code, which only those knowledgeable in Blake's symbolism and attitudes can hope to translate?[6]

---

[6] Occasionally Blake does employ what amounts to "code," as for example the wreath of oak leaves on Father Thames's brow. Blake regularly used the oak as a symbol, but the force of its meaning shifted for him. Most often it connotes suffering, sacrifice, and oppression, as it apparently does here.

I think that any attentive reader of Gray's poem in this version, that is, surrounded by these designs, will sense something stifling in the atmosphere of the children's play. The first response of those I have seen glancing at the designs is that the illustrations to this poem (excepting the violent designs, which impress most viewers) are "beautiful" but finally rather "dull." Yet in the terms "beautiful" and "dull" there is surely some contradiction, and in this case I believe it is one that can be explained.

Readers of Gray's poem remark on its "stiltedness,"[7] and we have spoken of the distance of the speaker from the persons and experiences he describes. But this distance is part of the decorum of the poem, and is related to that decorum rejected so vigorously by Wordsworth, who wished, by using "the language really spoken by men," to remind us that it is always men's feeling that gives importance to actions and situations; that it is human response that makes meaning. Thus when language grows mechanical, response becomes mechanical as well, and the human center of poetry is lost. The "stiltedness" to which we object and the "inane phraseology" to which Wordsworth objected are not exactly the same thing, but they are related. Both objections are—generally speaking—to the "distance" from his subject we feel in Gray. But we would surely be wrong to suppose that Gray's distance implies a lack of passionate concern, or that he does not "feel" what he says; it would probably be psychologically more accurate to say that he feels it so strongly that he must distance it in his poem. If he was "A stranger yet to pain" during his time at Eton (which I doubt), clearly he was no longer a stranger at the time of writing this poem.[8]

[7] Chester F. Chapin, in *Personification in Eighteenth-Century English Poetry* (New York, 1955), p. 70, observes that although "one or two" of Gray's allegorical tableaux still come alive for the modern reader, "much of Gray's allegorizing is thoroughly conventional. He shares the mid-century fondness for picturesque allegorical groupings." Elsewhere (p. 73) he suggests that where Gray's allegory seems "superficial" it is because the "pleasing pictures" "decorate rather than animate the verse in which they appear." It is of course always the animation that Blake seizes upon, and he finds it far more frequently than do either Bentley or we.

[8] Mrs. Spack's *The Poetry of Vision*, pp. 100-101, holds a similar view of Gray's "distancing." Discussing his "allegorical presentation of phenomena" in the Eton ode, she observes that "the remoteness of personifications from actual experience, the 'distancing' involved in the use of this device, emphasizes the horror of maturity in reality: it is too dreadful to be discussed more directly; the poet must find metaphors to make his perceptions tolerable." Bronson, "Personification Reconsidered," p. 174, remarks on the necessary decorum of generalizing one's private feelings by means of personified abstraction: "To gen-

But biographical facts and psychological speculations are not at issue. The point is that the tradition of decorum dictates what Gray's habit of mind leads him to prefer—the effect captured pictorially by Bentley, who shows us the poem as one elaborately framed picture: across the top is a swag of drapery with the head of "Folly" at its center; at the sides, terminal pillars culminate in figures of "Jealousy" and "Madness"; below, a leafy decoration bears a floating banner inscribed "Ah tell them they are men." Within, as already noted, the boys play in the manner described by Gray, while above them on a cloud their fate is enacted by allegorical figures. Thus Bentley's visualization frames the action (and so distances it) in a pictorial tradition whose verbal analogue is Gray's decorous poetic tradition.

However, where Wordsworth found in the "personifications of abstract ideas" a reduction of human feeling to mechanical formulae, Blake recognized in it a relationship to his own views about the "eternal principles or characters of human life," those forms grasped by the "vision" that is seldom lacking in "Fable or Allegory."[9] In a rather difficult passage Blake tries to explain what he means by "eternal principles": "the Oak dies as well as the Lettuce, but Its Eternal Image & Individuality never dies, but renews by its seed; just so the Imaginative Image returns by the seed of Contemplative Thought" (605). Thus, viewed imaginatively, Chaucer's characters are the same as those of Greek story: "The Franklin is one who keeps open table, who is the genius of eating and drinking, the Bacchus; as the Doctor of Physic is the Esculapius, the Host is the Silenus, the Squire is the Apollo, the Miller is the Hercules, &c. Chaucer's characters are a description of the eternal Principles that exist in all ages. The Franklin is voluptuousness itself, most nobly pourtrayed" (571). "'Voluptuousness" is of course an abstract idea, and so are "Ambition," "Scorn," "Infamy," and indeed

---

eralize was, in fact, to be civilized, and in poetry, no matter how intensely one might feel, it was not decent to autobiographize. Hence the crucial importance and intense satisfaction found in personified abstraction."

[9] (See p. 9, above.) Although he is discussing neither Bentley nor Blake, Chapin, *Personification*, p. 132, neatly defines the difference between their views of the "reality" of Gray's personifications: "Personifications become 'real' to the eighteenth-century mind when they are felt as dramatizations of the values, affections, or qualities which relate to the activities of man in the empirical world—not when they are projected as figures from a world of vision." That Blake's mind is—though visionary—in many ways very much "eighteenth-century" does not lessen the value of Chapin's distinction. For Bentley, Gray's allegorizing always returns us to the empirical world; for Blake it opens to the visionary.

"the vultures of the mind." But these are not—in Blake's view of the matter—abstracted from varied individual experience, from accidental external configurations or events. Rather they are "abstract ideas" in the sense that they exist in their "eternal reality" in the mind, and it is the visionary mind that sees the "eternal reality" in the everyday experience. One might call the notion Platonism internalized: "All Forms are Perfect in the Poet's Mind, but these are not Abstracted nor Compounded from Nature, but are from Imagination" (459). Perfection lies within the mind, not beyond it; and seeing "reality" within the appearance is a matter of how, not what, one sees.[10] "Nature becomes to its Victim nothing but Blots & Blurs" (595) only if he fails to bring his mind to bear on nature and see, in the visionary sense, its real forms. And thus it is that the true artist, copying not "Nature" but rather "imagination," can draw "with a firm & decided hand at once, like Fuseli & Michael Angelo, Shakespeare & Milton" (595). Such "drawing" is done, as Blake's examples show, in poem and picture both.

Sometimes an artist can draw accurately from his truly visionary imagination without realizing what he is about: Milton, who was "a true Poet and of the Devil's party without knowing it" (150), is Blake's most famous example. But as I have already suggested, to some extent every artist's vision is "infected," as Blake saw his own vision of Chronos infected. Gray's vision was infected in the Eton ode by a kind of fatalism that denies the power of the mind and leaves man the helpless victim of his own fears, but there remained alive in his language some of the vision that made him—in Blake's judgment—a true poet. Gray recognized that the youths he described were "idle progeny" who snatched "fearful joy," but he forgot why this was true. And he realized that their tormenters came from within—"vultures of the mind"—but forgot that "of" meant created by the mind as well as expressed through sicknesses of mind, sicknesses such as "Disdainful Anger," "Jealousy," and "Despair."

So Blake picks up Gray's cues offered in the terms "idle," "thoughtless," and "easy," and suffocates us with pastel delicacy: drawing on the same personifica-

[10] Bronson, "Personification Reconsidered," p. 174, observes of the eighteenth-century poets that "they first translated personal experience into decorous generalization; and then, without surrendering the general, reparticularized it by means of personification." The reasons for Blake's repudiation of much of the art admired in his time are suggested in the verb "to translate" and in the notion of "decorous generalization," implying as they do that the world of what Blake considered "eternal reality" was really no more than a set of polite locutions.

tions and visualizations as did Richard Bentley, he tries to avoid the distancing effect by inducing in the viewer the feeling he believes appropriate to the event. Recall that viewers often find the designs (excepting the violent ones) "beautiful" but "dull," an apparent contradiction, since what one finds really beautiful one can hardly find dull. Yet the point is that both responses are in their way called for by the designs and are necessary to Blake's purpose. "Idleness," "thoughtlessness," and "ease" are not unattractive, or their desirability would not have seduced a man as wise as Gray. But they are deadeningly insufficient, as Gray is the first to point out and Blake makes keenly vivid in design 6, where the pastel children are about to be engulfed by the dark monsters flocking from the flame-streaked sky. It is the deadening insufficiency that makes itself felt in the apparent "dullness" of the designs: Blake is communicating his sense of the stifled mind, and we feel stifled by it.

The causal relationship between this kind of beauty and this kind of insufficiency is what Gray failed to see, and what Blake's vision supplies. The point is made in design 8, where the pale aged sink to become the monstrous dead and dying; it is subtly hinted at in the increasing paleness of the ambition-racked boy, and finally reiterated in the visions of Folly as the real pestilence-flinger in design 9 and of the barren false innocence in design 10.[11]

Gray's metaphors and personifications were written to be visualized; Blake complied—and then used this very visualizing capacity in Gray's language to go beyond it, to make connections and arouse feelings only dimly present in some of Gray's figures of speech. Partly because of Blake's own beliefs about the existence in the mind of the eternal forms of things, he responded immediately and easily to Gray's habits of personification; indeed, he undoubtedly found in them one of the proofs of Gray's genuine poetic vision. And therefore, while he shared with Wordsworth a passionate concern for "Albion's melancholy"—the illness of a mechanized humanity—he did not identify the illness by quite the same symptoms, nor did he recommend the same cure.

---

[11] It is interesting that Blake's use of the bare tree to imply barrenness is also prefigured in Bentley, for his frontispiece to the 1753 edition offers a humorous compliment to Gray and deprecation of himself by showing the "poet" seated with his lyre beneath a richly foliated tree, while seated near him the "artist," a comic ape, works at his easel beneath a bare-branched tree. It seems unlikely that Bentley was Blake's source for the symbolism, as Blake had been using it for years and it was a well-established symbolic idiom. But the affinity does remind us again of the extent to which Blake shared the traditions and techniques of the period from which he appears in some ways to deviate so vigorously.

II

EARLY

POEMS

TO judge from the introductory picture of "Gray writing his Poems," Blake regarded these early poems as the products of vigorous youth. In fact Gray, like Blake, was rather a late starter, and even at the time of writing his "early" poems bore little physical resemblance to the young, athletic-looking poet pictured here, although the profile is strikingly similar to Gray's as it appeared in the Basire engraving done while Blake was Basire's apprentice, and also to Blake's later pencil sketch of "The poet, Gray."[1] But the body and stance are offered less as portrait than as vision: not "this poet," but "this kind of poet."

The lines are firm, simple, energetic. The writer shows his right profile, his seat and gown indicated by bare curves of line. Above his back, extending from the lower left to the upper right of the page, is a double curved line arching over a large circular window, through which blue sky may be seen. The window admits a flood of yellow light, pictured as a broad, bright ray surrounding the seated poet. There is, then, a minimum of movement in the picture, but what there is, is vivid and intense, connoting a spirit of bold eagerness and lively inspiration. We already know from the illustrations to the Eton ode that Blake did not consider Gray's judgments sound; but like Milton, Gray was sometimes more of a "true Poet" than he knew. These early poems Blake examines closely for both truth and error.

"ODE ON THE SPRING"

The "Ode on the Spring" has four illustrations, although the two introductory illustrations already described are listed along with these (numbered 1 and 2), making a total of six in the list. The page listing the titles of the designs to this

---

[1] Reproduced in Keynes, *Pencil Drawings by William Blake, Second Series* (Holland, 1956), plate 37. Keynes dates the sketch "about 1820."

poem is unique in that below the titles Blake has added a couplet and signed his name:

> Around the Springs of Gray my wild root weaves
> Traveller repose & Dream among my leaves.
>
> —Will. Blake

The "Springs" referred to here are presumably "Helicon's harmonious springs," which Blake depicts in "The Progress of Poesy" as brilliantly and luxuriously life-giving; the root that is nurtured by this rich liquid Blake rightly sees as "wild," in that it does not always follow the implied dictates of its host, and it "weaves" "around" in a way that seems sometimes to capture and overpower. But Blake does not see the conjunction as a violent one, or a violating one, as is clear from the invitation of his second line. The traveler who visits here is not to be amazed or overwhelmed; rather he is to "repose" and "dream." That the dreams will not always be restful we already know from the discussion of the Eton ode: the important thing is that dreams are an activity of the mind. Blake's first title page for *Vala* (dated 1797 and thus close to this design in time) calls that ambitious poem "A Dream of Nine Nights." And one recalls the conclusion of Blake's Epilogue addressed "To The Accuser who is God of This World," in which he tells Satan that though worshiped by the names of Jesus and Jehovah, he is still only "The lost Traveller's Dream under the Hill" (771), the product of confused and weary minds. We are invited, then, to repose not "under the hill," weighed down by earth and shadow, but rather among Blake's leaves which spring to glorious life about the Helicon of Gray's poetry; and our dreams are not to be those of "The lost Traveller," but rather the visionary experiences that these two minds united can offer us.[2]

The opening ten lines of the "Ode on the Spring" comprise the first page of the text, and although Blake marked only the fourth, all are pertinent to his drawing:

> Lo! where the rosy-bosom'd hours,
> Fair Venus' train appear,
> Disclose the long-expected flowers,
> And wake the purple year!

---

[2] Compare Blake's Notebook verse: "In your pleasant dreams/Of reason you may drink of Life's clear streams." This is the "reason" of Jesus, not Newton, as Blake immediately takes pains to point out: "Reason says 'Miracle': Newton says 'Doubt'" (536). These "dreams of reason" are the visionary glimpses one may achieve in this sleep of death which is vegetative existence.

The Attic warbler pours her throat
Responsive to the cuckow's note,
The untaught harmony of spring:
While, whisp'ring pleasure as they fly,
Cool Zephyrs thro' the clear blue sky
Their gather'd fragrance fling.

Blake illustrates each step of this description, working more or less clockwise from the bottom. There lies the dominant figure, the waking year, an unrealistically purplish young man whose air of vitality and eagerness make him nonetheless a powerful and healthy figure. He pushes himself up from the root-covered ground with a gesture that implies an incipient burst of action. About his head is a nimbus, perhaps the rising sun (compare the penultimate line of the poem: "Thy sun is set, thy spring is gone—"), and about him swarm the hours, young women who "disclose" the flowers by gently drawing from each a tiny human infant. These women float up the page, gracefully lulling and nursing the infants. Toward the top, at the left, one floating-robed woman plays her lyre, apparently Blake's representation of the "Attic warbler," though she seems oblivious of the "cuckow" who sits on a spiraling flower stem at the center of the top of the page.[3] Below the little "cuckow" hangs a large six-pointed star not mentioned in the text. To the right, balancing the lyre-player and other figures, descend two parallel figures, apparently the Zephyrs, each reaching down with her left arm extended toward the head of the young year, who watches the two (and beyond them, the star) with apparent amazement and delight.

Blake takes liberties with the text at the same time that he takes pains to include every detail mentioned by Gray. It is not Gray who personifies the flowers, but Blake, and it is Blake who sees them as the children of the hours; his title to the design supports his illustration of it: "The Purple Year awaking from the Roots of Nature. & The Hours suckling their Flowery Infants." Whether or not he was aware of it, Blake might have found some justification for part of his iconography in the ancient view of the Hours (Horae) as goddesses of the elements and seasons, fostering the growth of flowers, fruits, and vegetables. Certainly Gray had some such view in mind when he says they "wake" the year. But it is in Blake's

---

[3] The "Attic warbler" is presumably the nightingale (Philomela, daughter of Pandion, King of Attica), which sings on its return from the south after winter and is therefore a springtime bird.

notion of the year's waking "from the Roots of Nature" that Blake departs most from Gray and descends deepest into his own private symbolism.[4]

The striking thing about this illustration, however, is not the liberties that Blake takes with details such as the added star and roots, but rather the impact of the illustration taken as a whole: Gray is talking about the arrival of spring, personifying not spring itself (traditionally feminine) but the Greek Horae and Zephyrs.[5] Personification of the year is only hinted at in the verb "wake," a hint that would normally be offset by the adjective "purple" that for Gray seems to carry its original sense of dark, presumably from the night of winter, aligning the sequence of seasons with the sequence of night and day—see again the penultimate line in which the setting sun and departing spring are set in apposition.[6] But Blake's design is alive with human forms: with the small swirling and floating ones, but most forcefully with the large male figure at the bottom, whose impossible posture and purplish color make him distracting as well as powerful. Becoming "awake" here means for Blake the assuming of human shape. Indeed a glance through the illustrations to these early poems reveals that almost everywhere Blake looked he sought out the *person* in the personifications and elaborated visually what language suggests through this humanizing metaphor: namely, that where the eye is man's, every object is human.

In this poem it is Gray's personification of the summer insects that most caught Blake's attention, and it is on this personification that the designs seem mainly to comment. The poem itself derives from the venerable topos comparing man's fate with the fly's fate, though here Gray concerns himself specifically with the moralizing poet and the frolicking flies about which he moralizes. Blake is, of course, only too happy to regard "the poet" as representative of "man." But poets differ, as we shall see.

The year is awake to spring, then; and while the Hours and Zephyrs go about their lively business, Gray himself withdraws to the shade to think and poeticize,

[4] Compare this figure with that of Orc in *America*, emerging from among the roots to sit above the earth with its litter of death-tokens.

[5] Cf. Bentley's design, which shows flies like Blake's (though larger, like plump life-sized children) and three "Hours" pictured as traditional nude young ladies.

[6] The use of the word "purple" is problematical and has an interesting history that suggests my reading of Gray's meaning may be wrong. See Arthur Johnston, "The Purple Year in Pope and Gray," *RES*, XIV (1963), 389-393. Blake, for his part, doubtless recalled the line from Milton's "Lycidas": "And purple all the ground with vernal flowers."

observing in that state of peacefulness the "insect youth" at play in "the peopled air." Blake shows Gray as he describes himself:

> With me the Muse shall sit, and think,
> (At ease reclin'd in rustic state). . . .

The page is heavily filled, rather dark, with almost no movement: the poet and his muse recline across the bottom of the design, the poet facing toward our right (as he does in each of the designs I have taken to mark the division into three groups), the muse looking down and to the left. The huge tree-trunk against which the poet leans his arm and shoulders roughly echoes in the stretching of its two heavy branches across the top of the page the shapes and postures of the figures beneath. This rather barren tree trunk and the position of the muse—her eyes are closed and she floats in a cloud, leaning against her unused lyre—combine to suggest that Blake may not think much of Gray's inspiration, at least in the lines to which the illustration pertains, for his "Muse" is be-clouded (a constant pun in Blake's work) and idle, apparently put right to sleep by this posturing of "rustic state."

Blake's next illustration comes from the next stanza. Having described the busy delight of the insects, "their gaily-gilded trim/Quick-glancing to the sun" as they skim through the air "Eager to taste the honied spring," Gray shifts his attention to the brevity of their pleasures and uses this darker view of their lives as a way to moralize the human condition:

> To Contemplation's sober eye
> Such is the race of man:
> And they that creep, and they that fly,
> Shall end where they began.

That is, both man and fly shall return to dust:

> Brush'd by the hand of rough Mischance,
> Or chill'd by Age, their airy dance
> They leave in dust to rest.

Gray is, then, no longer personifying the insects, but rather asserting an analogy between them and man: in the opinion of "Contemplation" a common fate awaits them both, one that man will more readily assign the fly than himself. For Blake the entire scene is human-formed. Dominating the page are two mas-

50

sive figures: "rough Mischance," with a brutish head and bushy hair, crushes two little winged insect-humans, one with each hand, and leaves another draped lifelessly over a branch behind him; "Age," wrapped in a long hood and robe, his eyes downcast and his white beard flowing down his chest, has little figures dropping from his robe, apparently "chill'd" to death on contact; one little figure huddled up against his hood appears to be on the point of expiring. But in the air above, a circle of little figures have joined hands and are dancing in the light, and a similar figure flies nimbly up toward them, blowing a gracefully winding horn that makes one suspect Blake had Milton's gray-fly on his mind, although the little figure is colored lime green and winds a bright red horn.

The tiny figures in this illustration are of two kinds: those in the circle are little humans, some in human dress, some naked, but all wingless; the rest, including the one who approaches the circle with his horn, have human figures but also lovely transparent wings. If, as this distinction may suggest, the winged creatures are personified flies and the others flying humans, or human spirits, it is worth noticing that every dead or dying creature has wings; the only winged creature to survive is the one with the horn, who flies up to join the human circle, perhaps to become in some way one of them. In a later design—to Milton's "Il Penseroso"—Blake shows a very similar circle of dancers and calls them "The Spirits of Air." Clearly Gray's flies are "Spirits of Air" in at least two ways: not only do they fly there, but their life is—as pictured by Gray—an "airy dance" in the sense Blake intends in *Milton* when he compliments the flies' powers of dancing and calls them "the Children of Los" (512). I will return to this passage shortly.

Blake's final illustration is to the final stanza:

> Methinks I hear, in accents low,
> The sportive kind reply;
> Poor Moralist! and what art thou?
> A solitary fly!
> Thy joys no glitt'ring female meets,
> No hive hast thou of hoarded sweets,
> No painted plumage to display:
> On hasty wings thy youth is flown;
> Thy sun is set, thy spring is gone—
> We frolic while 'tis May.

51

Blake's title for the illustration reads "Summer flies reproaching the poet," and the marked line—the fifth, above—emphasizes the point of the reproach: the flies and the poet may come to similar ends, but the flies meanwhile at least have a better life, since they are met by glittering females; they enjoy and multiply, taking advantage of the time given them, while the poet sits contemplating alone.

The poem ends with the tables turned on the moralist; having first asserted that man's life is no better than the fly's, being brief and destined to end in dust, he is now left with the assertion that it is indeed worse than the fly's because the short time allotted is poorly used. Blake's design shows a number of frolicking winged creatures, among them two mothers with infants. Two of these winged creatures, in parallel gestures, point down at the poet—evidently his rebukers. Interestingly, these paired figures echo, in position and gesture, the Zephyrs flinging fragrance at the waking year in the first illustration. But if the flies think the poet is one of them, Blake does not picture him so; rather, he presents a figure much like that of the waking year. But in contrast to the personified year, the poet rests firmly against the ground—indeed, directly against the "Roots of Nature"—and he is surrounded not by whirling and blossoming tendrils that spring to human life but by the heavy and largely bare trunk of the tree against which he leans, whose branch curves over him, and whose coloring matches that of his clothing. In a web suspended between the far end of the tree's branch and the box surrounding the text hangs a tiny black human figure wielding a tiny sword. He has a curiously insectlike head, though his small size makes it hard to verify such details. Clearly, however, he is a spider, and a villain in the world of flies. It would seem that neither world is without its losses and dangers, though Blake, like Gray, appears to leave the flies with the advantage.

One might suspect, judging from the plate that shows the poet engaged with his cloudy, sleeping muse by the barren tree trunk, and from the connection of poet and heavily rooted tree in the final design, that it is the theorizing of the poet that Blake rejects, rather than his role as representative of humanity in the opposition Gray sees between the values of human and the values of insect lives. In Blake's drawing of Old Age and Mischance only the winged creatures are falling; and the last illustration would seem to offer, among other things, another variation on the ancient theme of "Et in Arcadia Ego": for death comes from within the insect kingdom as well as from such externalized abstractions as "Old Age" and "Mischance." Moreover, Blake does not comply with Gray in suggesting that the two stations—human and insect—are interchangeable, or that they

52

may profitably be viewed so: rather he chooses to follow an alternate suggestion, implicit in the personifications of the insects and even of the abstractions "Mischance" and "Old Age," that the really meaningful matter here is the possibility of defining the essentially human qualities in all of these. It is not that humans are like flies (only better off, or worse off, depending on the point of view), but rather that flies, and Mischance—and even spiders—are to be seen as in some sense "human."

This view of **Gray**, and this commentary on him, are related, I think, to Blake's poem "The Fly" from the *Songs of Experience*:

> Little Fly,
> Thy summer's play
> My thoughtless hand
> Has brush'd away.
>
> Am not I
> A fly like thee?
> Or art not thou
> A man like me?
>
> For I dance,
> And drink, & sing,
> Till some blind hand
> Shall brush my wing.
>
> If thought is life
> And strength & breath,
> And the want
> Of thought is death;
>
> Then am I
> A happy fly,
> If I live
> Or if I die.   (213)

As suggested in the Introduction, above, Blake's language in the drafts as well as the final version of this poem intimates that he had Gray's poem in mind as he wrote. Gray's "gaily-gilded trim" and "painted plumage" combine in Blake's first draft to form "thy gilded, painted pride," and whereas Gray's flies are "Brush'd by the hand of rough Mischance," in Blake they are "brush'd" by the speaker's "guilty" hand in the first version, then "thoughtless" hand, making it in a sense literally true that "the want of thought is death." And of course the topos is the same in both poems. Initially the poem seems to have concerned guilt and for-giveness—along with "guilty hand" Blake deleted the lines in which

> The cut worm
> Forgives the plow,
> And dies in peace,
> And so do thou.

(The lines "The cut worm/ Forgives the plow" he used instead as a proverb of hell in *The Marriage of Heaven and Hell*, on which he was working at the same time.) But then, dropping the question of guilt from "The Fly," he seems to have shifted his interest to the relationship of thought to life, a relationship first expressed as an equivalence:

> Thought is life
> And strength & breath;
> But the want
> Of thought is death.   (183)

Then, in the final version, it becomes a postulate: "If thought is life. . . ."

In his long poem *Milton*, Blake had more to say on the relationship between man and fly:

> Seest thou the little winged fly, smaller than a grain of sand?
> It has a heart like thee, a brain open to heaven & hell,
> Withinside wondrous & expansive,: its gates are not clos'd:
> I hope thine are not: hence it clothes itself in rich array:
> Hence thou are cloth'd with human beauty.   (502)

And still later in the same poem occurs the passage to which I referred earlier:

> Thou seest the gorgeous clothed Flies that dance & sport in
>   summer
> Upon the sunny brooks & meadows: every one the dance
> Knows in its intricate mazes of delight artful to weave:
> Each one to sound his instruments of music in the dance,
> To touch each other & recede, to cross & change & return:
> These are the Children of Los.   (512)

That Los is Blake's figure for poetry, or the poet-creator, ties the passage even more closely to the complex of ideas running through his reading of Gray's poem and the writing of his own. In both instances Blake asserts analogy not to teach man about his death, but rather to teach him about his potential for life and for spiritual freedom.[7]

It is the human capacity to understand and react that seems important to him, a capacity put to limited use in most human beings, though human potential is infinite: the fly's gates "are not closed: I hope thine are not." The move in Blake is always from nonhuman to human. Gray's solitary moralist is not a fully developed human in Blake's eyes, as he is a fellow who tends to seek barren trees and isolation or the company of a sleeping, cloudy muse, and to focus his contemplations on death rather than life. That does not, however, make him more a fly, as Blake's picture clearly shows. One might merely wish that he was as "wondrous and expansive" in relation to his capacities, and as knowledgeable of his "intricate mazes of delight," as are the flies in the lines from *Milton*. Perhaps this is precisely the reason "The Fly" is one of the *Songs of Experience*, whereas its cheerful conclusion would make its tone seem more in keeping with the *Songs of Innocence*: the speaker is not "A fly like thee," nor should he be "A happy fly" in life or death, that is, whether he thinks or not. Rather he should busy himself about opening his "gates," and they are human ones.

"ODE ON THE DEATH OF A FAVOURITE CAT"

In the illustrations to Gray's next poem, this humanizing habit combines with Gray's own technique to make a counterpoint of great wit and brilliance. When

---

[7] Perhaps also pertinent to these passages is one from *The Marriage of Heaven and Hell* in which a "devil" (who, the context implies, may be Blake himself) writes with corroding fires (as Blake engraves with corrosives) the following lines:

> How do you know but ev'ry Bird that cuts the airy way,
> Is an immense world of delight, clos'd by your senses five? (150)

The lines parody Chatterton's:

> How dydd I know that ev'ry darte
> That cutte the airie waie
> Myghte nott fynde passage toe my harte
> And close myne eyes for aie?

but reject Chatterton's fatalistic inclinations. (See Max Plowman's note, p. 22, in the Dent facsimile of *The Marriage*, published in London in 1922.)

Walpole's cat, Selima, met her appointed fate, Gray commemorated the occasion poetically, offering at the same time a whimsical cautionary tale for the ladies. The humor and point derive from the proverbial similarities between the two species: their self-love and their self-indulgence. The cat, enamored of her reflection in the water, spies a pair of goldfish and plunges after them, to her death; just as the ladies may be similarly beguiled, through wantonness and complacency, to seek what glitters and fall to dishonor. It will be obvious that Gray's tone and double purpose present special problems to the illustrator.

The little allegory amuses as it instructs, teasing fun out of the beast fable and the moralizing elegy. Where Blake found in Gray's elegiac banter not only humor but also intimations of the kind of "vision" that transcends "allegory," Dr. Johnson simply found himself critical of the way the fable is related to the moral, complaining that some lines are applicable only to the cat, others only to the ladies. Gray apparently had a good deal of fun in confusing the distinctions, making the fable and the moral compete for the reader's attention by allowing the ladies to serve as a vehicle for the cat even as the cat serves as a vehicle for talk about the ladies. The cat, exposed to temptation, appears as that "hapless nymph"; her "feet"—not paws—are beguiled, and she falls a "Presumptuous maid"; as she stretches for the prize, the poet asks parallel but separate rhetorical questions, one each for moral and fable:

> What female heart can gold despise?
> What cat's averse to fish?

And the last stanza makes the moral amusingly explicit:

> From hence, ye beauties, undeceiv'd
> Know, one false step is ne'er retriev'd,
> And be with caution bold.
> Not all that tempts your wand'ring eyes,
> And heedless hearts, is lawful prize,
> Nor all that glisters, gold.

Logically considered, the last line remains, in Dr. Johnson's uncompromising words, "a pointed sentence of no relation to the purpose"; for, as Johnson resolutely maintained, "if *what glistered* had been *gold*, the cat would not have gone into the water; and, if she had, would not the less have been drowned."[8]

---

[8] "Life of Gray," *The Works of Samuel Johnson, LL.D. in Nine Volumes* (Oxford, 1825), XIII, 483.

Indeed, the sententious close will do for neither the fable nor the moral. Dr. Johnson is, as usual, right in asserting that cats do not dive for gold; and we may go on to observe that only very literal-minded, or very immoral, ladies take the plunge entirely for gold. Those "wand'ring eyes" and "heedless hearts," that "one false step" that is "ne'er retriev'd"—all these unmistakenly represent the usual cautions against sexual indiscretion; but they open the truism "nor all that glisters, gold" once again to the kind of objections Dr. Johnson directed against the fable. Addressed to the ladies, rather than the cat, the truism in the context of the whole poem would have to mean something like: "Indeed, what glisters may turn out to be of no more worth than a fish (—and prone to be as elusive too)!" As we pursue these distinctions the delicate parallel between feline and feminine becomes obliterated, and the poem begins to fragment into fable and wholly detachable moral.

From his illustrations we may infer that Blake was struck not only by the sexual connotations of Gray's moral but also by the shifting relationship between fable and moral. Blake in fact appears to have perceived the richest meanings of the poem in just those wavering distinctions that Johnson found logically reprehensible. For here, amid these shifting interrelationships, lay the "vision" within the "fable." If all this seems excessively solemn when placed next to the cat ode, perhaps we need to remind ourselves that for Blake, no less than for Freud, levity has its own weight and seriousness, a fact that does not so much undercut the humor as complicate and enrich it. Blake's illustrations are delightfully comic: it would be as much a misreading of them not to laugh as only to laugh.

The six illustrations depict the cat and the paired fish of the fable in progressively shifting shapes, extensions of the little allegory itself and of hints in Gray's language. The first two designs are in effect general, or introductory. The first appears on the title page, setting the tone and preparing for the action of the fable. Blake titles the picture by quoting from Gray's third stanza: " 'midst the tide/ Two angel forms were seen to glide"; as we learn in the next line, these angelic goldfish are the "Genii of the stream." What Blake actually chooses to show, however, is a leering, beckoning exchange between forms neither human nor animal but rather a kind of mocking, demonic perversion of both. Across the top of the box reserved for the text (in this case for the title) reclines Selima, a sort of comic gargoyle with a furry, catlike body but slyly human face, pointed ears located down the side of the head where human ears belong, arms furry but human in shape, and lower legs that end in wispy claws neither human nor quite feline; she sports both corset and shawl, and gestures with a coy wickedness, intensified by the glint in her red eyes, toward the two goldfish swimming beneath. The goldfish also combine human forms with attributes of the subhuman: scaly torsos and finlike wings make them resemble menacing goblins; their wide-flung arms seem almost to invite Selima to join them while at the same time they are swimming rapidly away. In this ribald, mischievous exchange Blake manages to parody specifically the animals of the mock elegy and the ladies toward whom the moral is directed.

Even a monochrome reproduction conveys some sense of the enormous visual energy of this design; it is one of Blake's best, most vigorous and appealing. But the colors are an even greater source of power—they are at once brilliant and dense, beautiful and a little terrible. These colors—as a glance at the frontispiece to this book will demonstrate—intensify the sense of perversity, of an entire world violent and misshapen in its metamorphoses. The whole is a splendid comic creation, and it demands our laughter; but it is by no means the laughter of self-approving joy. The gargoyle violence, the coy thrust of the gestures, prepare us for what will prove to be Blake's overall view of the action of the poem, and for his visionary interpretation of it.

The second introductory illustration surrounds Blake's list of titles, and the title of this particular design is "Demurest of the tabby kind," a line from Gray's first stanza. Here Selima—for the only time in Blake's sequence a wholly catlike cat—again reclines on the inserted box, though this time in a position roughly the reverse of that in the preceding design, and below her in the water swim two wholly fishlike fish. All three figures are relatively small and huddled close against the text box, leaving the rest of the page an undecorated expanse of yellowish air and blue water, perhaps to suggest a special connection here between figures and text. The curiosity of the illustration is that astride each animal figure sits a human one. A naked "nymph" with an elaborate hairdo rides the cat, leaning demurely and rather self-consciously on her arm and looking out at the reader. Two less distinctly drawn, more conventional nymph-figures ride the fish. This design illustrates not so much Gray's gently ironic judgment of Selima's character—her "demureness"—as it does the sense in which she is "of the tabby kind." For what we see is a comic literalizing of the poetic technique of layered meanings, a visual parody of the allegorical method in which the "real subject" is made to "ride" astride the ostensible one, the two combining as they do in this poem to point the moral for the ladies. As the cat-lady receives fuller treatment by Gray, so Blake also draws her as a recognizable character; the fish-figures remain less distinctly individual in poem and picture alike.

Each of these first two designs, then, seems largely self-contained, each a general comment on the poem—the first on the theme of hunter and prey implicit in the cat and fish story, the second on the literary method of allegory that would have us read a fable and find a moral. Illustrations 3, 4, and 5 form one movement to which the sixth and final illustration stands as conclusion: the titles for all these are lines quoted from the poem, but all depend more broadly on the whole poem than the technique of quoted single lines would imply. They finally depend upon the "vision" in the "fable."

This is of course a handling of the poem quite foreign to Gray and to his contemporary illustrator, Walpole's friend Richard Bentley, who joined Gray in regarding the whole affair with amused detachment. (This design is reproduced in Erdman and Grant, *Blake's Visionary Forms Dramatic*.) A glance shows Bentley's details to be at once realistic and more elaborately "arty." His cat is thorough cat; his bowl even reflects the windowpanes that light our view. But that little domestic scene is overwhelmed by the elaborate inventiveness, and indeed the sheer mass, of its decorative surroundings. The scene is framed—the word "framed" is insufficient—by a decorative entablature supported by caryatids of a river god stopping his ears to Selima's cries (so phrased in the accompanying "Explanation of the Prints") and Destiny cutting the nine threads of her life; and the whole structure is further embellished by a mandarin cat seated in a pagoda, fishing in a Chinese vase, another cat drawing up a massive net from another Chinese vase, various elegantly festooned flowers and draperies, and a number of jubilant mice. At the foot of the entire structure, and displayed with conscious pomp, are the signatures of Gray and his illustrator, the poet's initials inscribed on a lyre, the artist's on a palette.

Bentley, like Blake, worked up small hints from the language of the poem, making from the mention of Chinese vase a complete Oriental setting with costumed cat, and of the "wat'ry God" and "malignant Fate" robust imitations of Greek architectural statuary. The picture itself is a paradigm of Bentley's technique: the household cat surrounded in mock solemnity by the rich culture of fashionable eighteenth-century England, its deference to classical tradition, its vogue of chinoiserie, its decorous but pervasive accolade to the artist as gentleman-maker.

But if the two illustrators worked from some of the same hints, it was to wholly different effect. Bentley, perfectly catching Gray's stylish irony, returns the poem all the more forcefully to the public world of its social and literary context; we are safely located in time and space. One may notice that just as the cat's bowl faithfully reflects the light that illuminates our view of it, so too the framing figures are faithfully shaded for us, emphasizing our role as observers of a fixed scene; it is our familiar world, however fancifully played upon, and we are reassured in our sense of the reliability of reality. Flights of fancy take off from the ground, but like the thrown stone they return there too.

Not so with Blake. Gone is the picture frame, gone even the social frame of the parlor, and we are alone among those shifting shapes whose continual metamorphoses suggest that whatever reality is, it is no matter of stable physical structure. In this world of more than Ovidian mutability it is the imaginative form that asserts itself visually, not the physical form. And he who watches these mutual metamorphoses of eye and object within the six designs must ask what stretch his own eyes have made in response to the "objects" that are these designs.

We recall that Blake usually associated allegory with fable, finding both "totally distinct and inferior" to "Vision or Imagination," and that his distinction is based on his contention that what he calls "vision" or "imagination" must be "a Representation of what Eternally Exists, Really & Unchangeably," whereas allegory is topical, that is, applicable only to a given time or set of ethical principles. In literature it is the difference, say, between the Bible (which Blake called "Vision itself") and Dryden's "Absalom and Achitophel." The meaning and suggestiveness of the Bible expand as man's knowledge and understanding expand, whereas Dryden's poem contracts a Biblical episode to fit a passing set of facts, which explains why without fairly thorough footnotes much of Dryden's poem escapes a modern reader, and partially explains what Blake meant by asserting that allegory "is Form'd by the daughters of Memory" (604).

To find "vision" in Gray's fable, Blake would have us look for what "eternally exists" in the story—for the ways in which Gray's allegorizing of Walpole's cat suggests pervasive truths of human experience. And to discover with Blake what "eternally exists" we must attend not to Bentley's chinoise cat about to drown in eighteenth-century mock splendor, not even to the cat of Arlington Street whose death called forth Gray's playful elegy, but rather to the cat who is woman, the feline feminine who becomes the object of Gray's moral and who is the subject of Blake's "vision."

The final four illustrations complete a sequence that follows the action of Gray's fable, but with important shifts in emphasis. The first of the four, which surrounds the first page of the poetic text, shows, in the words Blake uses to abridge the first two stanzas,

> The pensive Selima
> Her ears of jet and emerald eyes
> She saw and purr'd applause.

In this, the first stage of the action, we view Selima, a dainty lady with a rather catty face, cat ears, and a tail protruding from her long skirt, absorbed in admiration of her reflection. The mirror image, which reveals only the face and torso, is just sufficiently distinct so that we can remark the startling fact that it reflects none of the catlike attributes, only those of the pretty young lady. What we see in part is another illustration of Gray's literary technique: the lady-like cat of the fable appears on the verge, the lady of the moral is mirrored in the water. But the reflection also prefigures Selima in what Blake sees as her essential, or perfected form, as we will see her in the final design. Here, as in all but the final illustration, there is no suggestion, as there emphatically is in Bentley, of a world outside the water and the air immediately above it. Air and water, most often barely differentiated by their pale coloring, are divided only by the horizontal halving of the page. Gray had described the scene from somewhere across the parlor:

> 'Twas on a lofty vase's side,
> Where China's gayest art had dy'd
>   The azure flowers, that blow;
> Demurest of the tabby kind,
> The pensive Selima reclin'd,
>   Gaz'd on the lake below.

Whereas Bentley had complied with Gray's sense of physical and ironic distance, in Blake's illustration we are invited to join a world of cat and fish: the flowers seem to be growing in an actual lake, no longer the purely metaphorical "lake" of the poem, and nestled among them, tenderly embracing in an echo of Selima's loving self-admiration, are the goldfish, the "Genii of the stream," depicted as "humanized" male and female figures, each with softly yellow, finlike wings folded against his side. What is imaginative or figurative in Gray tends toward the literal in Blake, and the goldfish bowl has become the world.

The following illustration shows the second stage of the action: Selima now has the head, shoulders, and forepaws of a cat—but she is draped from the waist down with clothes that reveal beneath them human feet, ready in Gray's phrasing to be "beguil'd." Hovering close, and drawn with an elaborate seriousness that echoes Gray's mock-epic tone, sits Fate, scissors in hand, preparing to slit the thick-spun thread of Selima's life. In the water below we see the Genii, their forms still much as they were in the preceding illustration but displaying in flight more of their finny wings, which are now a more vivid orange in color. Whereas the preceding illustration seemed relatively static, this design, more violent even in its coloring, begins the cycle of action between hunter and prey hinted at in the first of the two introductory illustrations.

The climax follows in the next design, which Blake significantly conceives as a clockwise circle of movement: at top center sits Fate (or Fortune, who traditionally dominates circular motion),[9] her arms extended over Selima, whom she has just shoved into the water; Selima, here depicted entirely as a human girl, falls headlong down the page on the right. Across and up from the bottom rise the Genii, their position almost the same as in the preceding picture but their figures completely transformed. Their metamorphosis may be traced to a cue in Gray, but it is a slight one and by no means suggests Blake's elaborate extension of it; three stanzas earlier Gray had described the glittering scales of the fish as "scaly armour," and now Blake again literalizes the figurative talk of eighteenth-century poetry, showing the Genii as human male and female costumed for war, brandishing long fish spears. The male—now harsh gold-green—grimaces fiercely at the viewer, while the female looks back over her shoulder, apparently regarding Selima's fall with feminine alarm. The cycle of action is complete also in its reversals: the fish, dressed for attack, have become the fishers, as they take on the fully human forms they do not possess for Gray; the warriors of a fallen world of humans, they wear the lineaments of destruction. In this

---

[9] Blake seems to have confused the functions of Fate and Fortune, but at least he has respectable precedent for the inaccuracy in "Lycidas," where Milton appears to have confused the Fates with the Furies:

> Comes the blind Fury with the abhorred shears,
> And slits the thin-spun life.

Moreover, if we take Gray's "Malignant Fate" to refer with precision to the classical Atropos (the text does not so insist, it seems to me), then Bentley also errs, for his "Explanation of the Prints" calls her "Destiny."

climactic metamorphosis the hunter becomes the hunted, and the countering aggressiveness of the prey stands revealed.

This reversal of roles is not noted directly by Gray, though his poem does ape the theme of the fall from greatness. The ode begins with the "favourite," Selima, atop a "lofty" vase, purring applause at the sight of her own "fair round face." But then she spies a new object of desire and, in stretching to capture it, falls, losing her friends with her footing and affording the occasion for the moral to the "beauties." The fall from greatness may of course be taken to represent one half of the wheel of fortune, and this is apparently what Blake invites us to see in the illustration. In the poem "Fate" passively "sits by" in a parenthetical line, whereas Blake lends his goddess a wider, far more active role: she figures prominently in two of the six illustrations, and here she occupies the central position at the top of the page, thus taking Selima's place on the wheel after having actively pushed Selima to her death. The circular pattern is completed by the fish, who fling themselves upward—human-shaped, armored for battle—as Selima falls. Although Blake, in his own role of creative illustrator, seems to have taken us far from the poem as written by Gray, we have to realize that Blake is not misunderstanding Gray—rather, he is attempting to draw out the "visionary" implications, that which "eternally exists," in the little beast fable, whether it exists as a result of Gray's intentions or in spite of them.

In the sixth and final illustration we are shown Selima as a young woman "emerging" from the water, her hands folded in prayer. Again Blake may seem to have misunderstood Gray. Blake's title to the picture, "Nine times emerging from the flood/ She mew'd to every wat'ry god," amplifies Gray's "eight times emerging," arriving at the number beyond which cats proverbially do not emerge from water. Whereas Gray's "eight times" allows for the ninth and fatal submersion, Blake's "Nine times" dismisses the feline point, making explicit in the ninth submersion the death only anticipated by Gray, then raising the "spiritual body"[10] for a tenth—and new—life. And in the distance one can just make out the form of a shore with trees, the first sign in Blake of a world outside the deadly circle of this drama. Blake, then, carries his conclusion beyond that of Gray's poem; at the level of fable what we see emerging could be read as the feminine soul of the cat. But at the level of vision the cat has died within the woman to release her into her fully "human form." Put another way, the literal death of the cat

[10] Blake used this Biblical phrase in his plate "To Tirzah" (reproduced in the Keynes edition, p. 220), whose theme is closely related to Blake's in these designs to the cat ode.

becomes for Blake the figurative death of the fable: the fable dies with the cat, leaving the "moral level" to survive alone both in text and in illustration. The cat is gone from Gray's final stanza; and Blake's title and design both suggest that the cat, become woman, may survive with a tenth and new life—her own, this time, as she is freed from the destructive cycle of hunter and prey and emerges from the watery world of generation and death which is for Blake always a symbol of the fallen universe, the sea of time and space, this present dispensation in which we all live somewhat less than fully human lives. Beneath her in the picture, and swimming off to the right, are her former prey and adversaries, now seen to be two flatly realistic fish who depart glassy-eyed and oblivious.

Fable and moral have finally split, then: no one rides the fish, and there is no cat beneath the girl. Instead, one realistically portrayed figure remains from each "level"—an extraordinary denouement for an allegory. Also gone are the parallel shifts in the relationship of cat to fish; the oscillation between them has ceased. They are completely separate at last, and as one would expect with a supplicating girl and two fish in water, they pay no attention to each other.

It seems to have been more than anything else the allegory—the relationship of fable to moral—that attracted Blake to the poem, and that makes his illustrations to it provocative and interesting. Remember that for Blake "Fable or Allegory is seldom without some Vision," that is to say, some awareness of those pervasive shapes that human experience assumes again and again, however different the reasons and circumstances in each case. In taking Walpole's drowned cat and giving her human dimensions Gray released a "fable" with wider implications than perhaps he realized or intended. Part of what Blake found there, buried in such words as "armour," "bold," and "prize," was a story about woman as predator, whose relationship with her prey is a cyclical and mutually dangerous one. "As the eye, so the object," Blake constantly maintained, and where the eye is man's, every object should be fully human. But in these illustrations we see the eye and object of Gray's story—the cat and fish, woman and the object of her desire—shifting to fit one another in grotesque and subhuman ways.

Blake regarded as disastrous the view of sex that sees lovers as antagonists and the sexually experienced woman as "fallen," a prey, by revealing metaphor, to the man who made love to her. A society that demanded coyness of the woman, or that regarded the beloved as a possession rather than a partner, was for Blake the type and result of humanity's real fall. Thus the degraded half-human parodies of the title page demonstrate how each party in the relationship of hunter to prey draws the other into a scheme of malicious coyness. And thus the parallel shifts of cat and fish throughout define their interdependency. Where Selima is the object of her own self-love, the fish are their own lovers too. As she prepares her attack they become fleeing and vulnerable "angels," their long webbed wings betraying nonetheless a telling relationship to that master of hypocrisy, Satan. In Selima's fall, when she exchanges in herself the preying cat for the vulnerable woman, the fish become human attackers, seeming to find strength in her weakness. The final illustration brings us full circle, and out: the hunter-prey exchange on which Selima had engaged was invoked, it suggests, by her faulty view both of herself and of her object. Man's view of the universe is self-regarding, according to Blake: see yourself as a predator and you will be likely to find yourself preyed on as well. "As the eye, so the object" means, in other terms, "as ye sow, so shall ye reap." By dividing off the "levels" of the allegory in this final illustration Blake seems to be allowing the fable to swim away with the fish, leaving a clearer-eyed young woman free of her entrapment.

In visionary terms this has been the story not of the lamented Selima who died in Arlington Street, but rather of a coy, terrible, and piteous Selima who grows—like the tree of Mystery—in the human brain, whenever it mistakes love for war or the objects of love for possessions. The Selima of Blake's reading is a partially misguided woman struggling to find her humanity. Her cat-ness is interesting to us only negatively, that is, insofar as she must rid herself of it, "cast" her "Spectre Into the Lake,"[11] and assume in spiritual self-fulfillment the human form that Gray gave Walpole's Selima by way of moralizing allegory. Whereas Dr. Johnson had found in Gray's wavering distinctions between feline and feminine the source of poetic illogic, Blake discerned there the vision that transcends fable.

We appear to have come a long way from the poem printed on the page, and yet the two areas of Blake's visionary interpretation are surely central to Gray's poem: these are the analogies between the temperaments of cat and lady, and the analogies between their aggressiveness in the hunt and their downfall. Thus, for example, the metaphor "scaly armour," which alludes to the war games of cat and fish, expands for Blake to become one of the central images in the poem, paralleling as it does his own constant use of scales to symbolize forces of domi-

---

[11] The phrase appears in *Jerusalem*, in mirror writing on a scroll beside a figure self-enclosed "in his Spectre's power" (669).

nation and evil. And the water in which Selima struggles is the fallen world, depicted as a sea of time and space by Blake and the Neoplatonists before him. As for Gray's confusions of identity, they must have seemed to Blake the proof of Gray's poetic genius: in Blake's reading the poem is precisely about the problem of identity, the movement toward humanity, the mutations of form along the way. In this view we are right as readers to feel the language appropriate to cats and to ladies—and incidentally to warriors—competing for our attention, as this very competition illuminates the meaning of the poem. We are left to hope that Selima will be ready for dry land and a truly human life, no longer a subject of "Fate" because no longer a believer in her wheel, on which all human relationships are necessarily those of up and down, oppressor and oppressed.

For Blake, however, the story of Selima assumed an even wider perspective, offering an even more private, though corollary, way to understand the visionary meaning of the tale. Blake saw the fish in designs 3, 4, and 5 not only as the objects of Selima's lust but also as embodiments and examples of a mutual love that she lacks and desires to experience. We first see Selima narcissistically admiring her own reflection (her face and bonnet are suggestively heart-shaped), in contrast to the "angels" who lie below in mutual embrace. Her plunge would then be in envy of such a love, her death the death of "selfhood," her redemption her new capacity for selflessness. The progress is not explicitly explained in these designs, and so remains decidedly private—as it is also decidedly foreign to any intention of Gray's. But readers familiar with Blake's other work can trace the connections throughout. A loose but suggestive parallel to design 3, in which Selima admires her own image as the fish embrace below, may be found in the 1808 illustration to *Paradise Lost* entitled "Satan Watching the Endearments of Adam and Eve."[12] There Satan, at the top of the design, regards and embraces a serpent (the extension of himself) in interesting analogy to the self-contemplating Selima. Below Satan lie Adam and Eve, encircled by a flowery bower and clasped in mutual embrace like the fish of the Gray design. Milton's lines tell us that Satan envies

[12] Reproduced in Marcia R. Pointon, *Milton & English Art* (Manchester, 1970), p. 149. This valuable new book offers a generous anthology of reproductions of Blake's illustrations to Milton's poems. The author concludes her survey of these designs with the judgment that "It is an astonishing phenomenon that an artist of Blake's individuality and vividness of imagination *and* a poet in his own right should have been one of the greatest illustrators of Milton's verse" (p. 166).

their bliss, "Imparadis'd in one anothers arms," since he can feel only "fierce desire . . . still unfulfill'd," a phrase that echoes throughout Blake's pronouncements on the fallen human condition.[13]

Clearly Blake's vision of Adam and Eve under the envious watch of the self-loving Satan is not in all respects parallel to his vision of Selima and the fish; the connection lies in the sterility of the self-loving figures and their envy of the flower-encircled mutual lovers below. The psychology of envy operates in Satan and Selima alike, making predators of both. But there the similarities between their two stories end; the next step in Selima's progress is to be understood not from the story of Satan but rather from the visionary meaning Blake saw in the fish.

Gray had called the fish "The Genii of the stream" by way of polite eighteenth-century periphrasis. But Blake had observed in *The Marriage of Heaven and Hell* that "The ancient Poets animated all sensible objects with Gods or Geniuses, calling them by the names and adorning them with the properties of woods, rivers, mountains, lakes, cities, nations, and whatever their enlarged & numerous senses could percieve" (153). Blake himself exercised this poetic prerogative constantly, and treated Gray's use of it with respect. Almost twenty years later, again illustrating Milton, Blake's mind returned to the figures he had used in response to Gray's phrase. In the "Il Penseroso" design entitled "The Spirit of Plato unfolds his Worlds to Milton . . ." Blake pictures Milton in his chair beneath "the Circles of Plato's Heavens" and surrounded by "The Spirits of Fire, Air, Water & Earth." The Spirits of Water are a pair of spread-armed fish-humans closely analogous in both form and gesture to those of Blake's design to the title page of Gray's cat ode. These later figures lack the gargoyle faces of the Gray title page (they resemble in this the figures of design 4), but they perform much the same function as those fish-turned-fishermen, for in the Milton design Blake shows them catching in fishnets a plunging human similar to the plunging Selima of design 5. Even the coloring is similar to that of the Gray designs, combining the bright gold-orange finny wings of the fish in the Gray title page with the pallor of the falling human form in design 5. These fish-humans are "Spirits of Water" in Blake's visionary sense, where water means what it did in plate 10 of *The Gates of Paradise*: there only the hand of a drowning man remains stretched

---

[13] Note that this is a composition on which Blake exercised some thought, as it is an alteration of the 1806 version in which the serpent lies at Adam's feet.

above a sea of water, and the caption reads "Help! Help!" (767); Blake later added to this the explanation "In Time's Ocean falling drown'd" (771). The spirits of this water are indeed captors, their nets those in which Blake's prophetic figures are seen so often to struggle; but it is revealing that after almost twenty years Blake should again return, in a picturing of watery entrapment, to the rather comic little fish of these Gray designs. That he did is, I think, an indication of their original meaning and importance to him.

Finally, even casual readers of Blake can recognize the falling Selima of design 5 as similar to the countless lost figures who plummet downward in Blake's pictures; they clasp their heads in fear, as distinct from those who dive or float fearlessly, connoting a state of spiritual freedom in which no direction is really down. And Selima's final rise, in prayer, is again a familiar one in Blake designs: an analogy may be found close at hand in the last of the 116 Gray illustrations, which shows one spirit conducting another heavenward, the conducted spirit in an attitude of wonder.

This is, then, a prophetic sequence in which all the stages are familiar to those well acquainted with Blake's designs, however far afield such a reading lies from Gray's intent. Yet this quite private Blakean reading is not in all ways foreign to some recent interpretations. William Empson rightly observes that in Gray's poem both nymph and cat are the main subject, but adds that "the clash is not only between *nymph* and *cat* but between two metaphorical nymphs; between snatching at a pleasure, real but dangerous . . . and mistaking a false love for a true one . . .—believing that happiness to be permanent which will, in fact, be fleeting."[14]

The distinction is an interesting one, and something like it may surely be found in the poem. Gray's final stanza offers three compact and separable warnings: what you ladies seek, he says, may be too dangerous ("one false step is n'er retriev'd"), immoral ("Not all . . . is lawful prize"), or deceptive ("Nor all that glisters, gold"). The central tie in the poem between lady and cat, moral and fable, lies in a punning split of the word "goldfish": "gold" applies to the desires of ladies, "fish" to cats. Yet the word "gold," used alone only twice in the poem, is there used in two different ways. In the line "What female heart can gold despise?" it is used literally to mean money, implying in the ladies an equation of sexual and financial acquisitiveness that reduces love to lust and Gray's satire to unwonted savagery. But in the final line, so trying to critics from John-

[14] *Seven Types of Ambiguity* (New York, 1957), pp. 139-140.

son to Gosse,[15] the word "gold" is used figuratively to mean "of true worth." Thus Gray's turn on this pivotal word allows the literal distinction between real gold and fool's gold to enter by metaphor the moral realm of the poem and suggest that of his three warnings (against danger, immorality, and deception) the last is actually the inclusive one, implying not an audience of ladies to be deterred only by threats of danger or the wagging of tutorial finger, but of ladies who seek true value (read also "love") and need only to be taught to distinguish it from false. We are thus returned to the second of Empson's "two metaphorical nymphs" and to that gentler satire that readers have always found in Gray's poem.

Blake's idosyncratic reading has important and interesting alliances, then, with Empson's, for Blake, too, saw something like two distinguishable nymphs, but he saw them as two states of the individual. One is the fallen woman who "seeketh only Self to please" with a love whose method is "To bind another to Its delight" (211), who snatches her prey with lustful possessiveness, and who dies the death of the cat, drowned in the sea of time and space. The other is the struggling daughter of Albion within her, who dies to "rise from Generation free" (220) in the final design, human-formed at last in her repudiation of "self-love that envies all" (194). The first is the woman who is cat, "snatching at a pleasure real but dangerous" in Empson's words; the second is that milder lady who seeks "true gold," whom Empson elsewhere calls "the more spiritual nymph" and Blake "the Human Form Divine."

That the same plunge should bring death to one and life to the other is to be understood from Blake's early views about sex. Love in the fallen world is never uncomplicated by jealousy, possessiveness, and cruelty; these are the motives of the cat, and they drown her.[16] But "fierce desire" is in itself a mark of life; the effort to gratify desire (rather than repress it) is a movement toward salvation as it is both a partial repudiation of selfhood and the expression of an energy. These are the motives of the woman, and they drown her cat-ness to save her humanity. In pictorial terms, plunging is a movement toward life, away from self-restriction; but self-contemplation is self-enclosure, and deadens the soul.

---

[15] Edmund Gosse in *Gray* dismisses the final line as "a specious little error" (English Men of Letters Series, London, 1882), p. 81.

[16] There is a provocative and altogether curious alliance between the cat ode designs and Blake's later designs to Milton's "L'Allegro" and "Il Penseroso." I have already alluded to the reappearance of Gray's fish as "The Spirits of Water," but his cat may be found as well. The first "L'Allegro" design, entitled "Mirth," personifies "wanton wiles" as a young lady with fine catty face and whiskers—she is the dainty Selima of design 3, even down to her heartshaped bonnet. (Both designs are reproduced in *Blake's Visionary Forms Dramatic*.)

Gray's tone and double purpose do indeed present special problems to the illustrator, enormous ones if like Blake he aspires to be critic and interpreter as well. As we saw, Bentley brilliantly caught the tone, but ignored the double purpose. Blake carried the tone rather beyond its limits, yet he did not, I believe, intend to violate it. Rather, he intended to expand the comic proportions of the poem until they reached those of a miniature divine comedy, concluding with a visionary glimpse of paradise. Thus he extended the double purpose even more forcefully. Ignoring the cautionary purport of Gray's moral, Blake felt he recognized in its elusive suggestiveness a visionary truth about love in the fallen world. Within the confines of that world it is grotesque and destructive and deserves satiric treatment. Interestingly, the same "Il Penseroso" design that yielded "Spirits of Water" analogous to those of the Gray designs also yields a tiny study of that love here satirized. At the top of the Milton design sit "The Three Destinies," each positioned over one of the "Circles of Plato's Heavens." According to Blake, "these Heavens are Venus, Jupiter & Mars." The heaven of Venus—placed, perhaps significantly, beneath the cutting Destiny—depicts the love goddess presiding with voluptuous grace over two pairs of tiny figures, a male and female bound back to back with serpents or thorny vines (their bonds are unclear in reproduction, but in any case are a version of those "iron threads of love & jealousy & despair" mentioned in plate 31 of *Jerusalem*, Stirling copy), and on the other side two paler figures, a shunned and weeping female and a male departing from her, his left arm pushing her away behind him. The scene is of course again a vision of the love that binds and grieves.[17]

But where human love exhibits a desire to break the confines of the fallen world, to transcend selfhood and seek "true gold" like the gold of that burning bow with its arrows of desire celebrated at the outset of Blake's *Milton*—in short, where it is redemptive love—then it is no longer a subject for satire, but rather for jubilant prophecy.

Gray had divided his poem into a fable and a moral for the eighteenth-century ladies; looking far beyond Gray's moral, Blake sought to reveal in the story of Walpole's cat both a satiric view of the fallen world and a prophetic glance toward eternity.

[17] Compare the plate of *Visions of the Daughters of Albion*, which shows Oothoon and Bromion bound back to back on the shore of the sea of time and space, while near them sits the self-enclosed Theotormon, shunning Oothoon's offers of love.

"A LONG STORY"

Since the "Ode on a Distant Prospect of Eton College" has already been discussed, let us turn directly to the poem that follows it—a humorous little tale illustrated with twelve designs. Gray wrote "A Long Story" as a playful compliment to two distinguished ladies who had called on him and, finding him not at home, left their cards that he might return the visit; this small incident he enlivened with some of the machinery of romance and fairy tale, never intending it, he insisted, for public view. He would not have published it, he claimed, but "because of Mr. Bentley's designs, which were not intelligible without it."[18] The poem was first published in the Bentley edition, in 1753.

Blake has caught the mock-romance spirit of the poem in some of the wittiest and most playful designs he ever made: indeed this sequence displays a whole range of playful and satiric humor that I find nowhere else so clearly revealed: there is something of the spirit of "An Island in the Moon" or of the Notebook epigrams, but visually conceived, and executed with a somewhat lighter hand.

The title page shows "A Circular Dance," a ring of five dancing, flying figures encircling the text box; it is strongly reminiscent of the lively human dance above Old Age and Mischance in Spring 5, and like that dance offers a vision of what Blake will later call "The Spirits of Air." It seems a fitting introduction to this rather airy set of designs, particularly to the next two.

The text box of the second page contains a brief printed account of the source of the poem and Gray's hesitation at publishing it. On the top of the box stands a tiny mother holding the hands of two children, while two others vigorously play musical instruments—one a pipe and the second a drum or cymbal. At the side and bottom of the page are two little creatures in flight: the one at the side is astride a butterfly and points toward the text; the other is apparently herself a butterfly, with bright wings at her back and her arms spread wide with delight. Evidently this design is not the one originally conceived by Blake for this page, as faint traces of a large earlier design have been whited over but not entirely obscured; a fuller and busier page was originally planned, then altered in favor of the minute simplicity of the present design. Blake's title is "Fairies riding on Flies"—which would seem to hark back to the "flies" of the spring ode, with

[18] *The Complete Poems of Thomas Gray*, ed. W. H. Starr and J. R. Hendrickson (Oxford, 1966), p. 284.

perhaps a squint at the visualized allegorical method of the cat ode. But in fact only one figure does ride a "fly." It may be relevant to observe that this fairy indicates those lines of the printed text that emphasize the need for a proper awareness of Gray's tone: "Although this performance certainly possesses great humour," the text reads, "yet it is not immediately perceived; and has not been *universally* relished." There were several aspects of its humor that Blake relished thoroughly. The entire poem makes fun of various popular notions of "The Poet." In his manner of narration (and explicitly in the title and joke at the conclusion) Gray affects to be one in a long line of stuffy bores, not unlike Chaucer in his characterization of himself in the *Canterbury Tales*; on the other hand the narrative itself makes fun of that other "popular view" of the poet as a rather dangerous character, to be associated with black magic and perhaps even bad morals. Blake draws fine comic portraits of both poets, as we shall see.

In the opening lines Gray offers with mock pretentiousness to begin at the beginning by recounting some of the history of the building in which the action of his poem will take place:

> In Britain's isle, no matter where,
> An ancient pile of building stands;
> The Huntingdons and Hattons there
> Employed the power of Fairy hands
>
> To raise the ceiling's fretted height. . . .

Blake pictures an ornately embellished Gothic window and the arches rising above it, with eight tiny fairies variously busied in hammering, polishing, and carrying materials among the frets of the ceiling. It is noteworthy that they are actually creating: the sculptor really works on a niche, the painter is painting a spot yellow to match the surrounding area. The window, described by Gray as one of those "Rich windows that exclude the light," in Blake's picturing admits brilliant light at its center, where a radiant dove hovers over the suspended figure of Christ in glory. The entire scene is one of delicate vitality and appears to suggest that fairies are better builders than Gray supposed.

The next lines offer some rather wicked irony at the expense of Queen Elizabeth and her court, hinting at the superficiality of her trifling and the dizzying visions of power it invited:

Full oft within the spacious walls,
When he had fifty winters o'er him,
My grave Lord-Keeper led the Brawls:
The Seals and Maces danc'd before him.

Gray's note identifies the Lord-Keeper as "Hatton, preferred by Queen Elizabeth for his graceful person and fine dancing." This rather snide comment Gray elaborates, with a glance at English political history, in the verse:

His bushy beard, and shoe-strings green,
His high-crown'd hat, and satin doublet,
Mov'd the stout heart of England's Queen,
Tho' Pope and Spaniard could not trouble it.

Not surprisingly, Blake appreciated this aspect of Gray's humor as well, and responded in kind. Startling green bows decorate the pink shoes of Blake's Lord-Keeper, a foppishly elegant fellow who sniffs a rose; the seal and mace, personified by Gray, are given by Blake subhuman forms—one with a seal inscribed "Elizabeth Rex"[19] for its body, the other the crown-topped head of a mace for its head. This dancing mace in turn brandishes a mace, and so implies a comic regression that is its own comment on political power. Its figure is moreover reminiscent of fat "Folly" as pictured in Eton 9, and "Vice" as it will appear in Poesy 8. The touches are comic but sinister: peaked ruffs, like the Lord-Keeper's here, may usually be read in Blake's iconography as something like a gentlemanly version of devil's or bat's wings, and Elizabeth's seal sports a red devil's tail. "It was a Common opinion in the Court of Queen Elizabeth that Knavery Is Wisdom," Blake wrote in 1798 in his annotations to Bacon's *Essays*; he affirmed elsewhere in the same annotations that "The Prince of darkness is a Gentleman & not a Man" (399). Blake must have pictured him, in such a context, as a knavish fellow very much like "my grave Lord-Keeper," that favorite of stouthearted queens.

The fifth design shows the "brace of warriors," by whom Gray means his elegant lady visitors. Blake eschews the metaphor and displays the women, visions

---

[19] Eglington, "Blake Illustrates Gray," p. 47, mistakenly deciphers the writing on the seal as "Lambeth," suggesting that this might help date the designs. In fact the seal does bear a "date," but it appears to be composed not of numbers, but rather of lines intended to suggest numbers.

of gracious, modish elegance with fans and bonnets and swirling scarves; he has clearly borrowed from fashion prints of his day, or possibly from Fuseli (who was sometimes a wicked commentator on the world of fashion) or from Bentley, who sees the ladies in terms not dissimilar to Blake's.

Design 6 is Blake's comic masterpiece. Word had it, Gray says, that there was prowling the countryside "A wicked Imp they call a Poet," who

> Bewitch'd the children of the peasants
> Dried up the cows, and lam'd the deer,
> And suck'd the eggs, and kill'd the pheasants.

Off to one side of the page flap three honking geese, their necks comically extended; three little pigs hump off in the other direction squealing in dismay; to the front rush a mother hen and her chicks, their wings hunched high in speed and fear. Two children flee, clasping one another for protection, and a third runs forward toward the reader, his hands before his face and his hair standing straight out on all sides. Behind these, strolls the unwitting cause of the commotion, the gentle poet, chin on hand, his book dropped momentarily from the line of his quiet gaze, his long flowered gown brushing softly against his ankles: such the terrifying creature from whom the "brace of warriors" have set out to rescue the countryside.

The next two designs show the lovely "warriors" invading the poet's home, first sweeping by the "trembling family," past whom they "up stairs in whirlwind rattle"; then "out of the window, whisk," flying amid the cracklings of their own lightning, having left behind them "a spell upon the table"—their calling cards.

The ninth design is again marvelously funny, a joke at the expense of the race of Gothic ghosts and visions that Blake elsewhere uses soberly. The "spell" has drawn the poet up to the "great house," where he is to be judged by "the Peeress," historically the Viscountess Cobham, who had sent the two distinguished ladies to call on Gray at his home. In the poem, Gray prepares the scene for this "judgment" on the poet by imagining that the ghosts of all the old sour-faced "High Dames" from "the drawing room of fierce Queen Mary" come forth from "their gloomy mansions" to be present at the trial. Gray describes them:

> Such as in silence of the night
> Come (sweep) along some winding entry
> (*Styack* has often seen the sight)
> Or at the chapel-door stand sentry. . . .

In Blake's picture, rendered almost entirely in shades of dark gray, Styack (the Peeress' housekeeper) flees gasping from a ghostly sentry with bayonet, shroud, a grin of jack-o'-lantern teeth, and hollow eyes from which shoot forth horns of fire that glow fiercely in the dark. Barely visible through the dimly seen folds of the bottom of the shroud are weblike feet that cling to the doorsill like claws. This is what remains of some fashionable court lady!

The next two illustrations depict the trial itself: first the Peeress sits above a row of these sour-faced "High Dames," who now look like their tight-mouthed selves rather than Gothic apparitions; then she descends, to their horror and dismay, and invites the poet—to dinner! Blake's drawing of the "High Dames" reveals another borrowing from the illustrations by Bentley, whose sour-faced snappish gossipers are clearly close relations of those in Blake's two trial scenes.

The final illustration to this poem returns us from the action of the poem to the characterization of its ceaselessly droning author. The grim biddies are left exclaiming indignantly at the sight of a Peeress speaking "to a Commoner and Poet," upon which we are given the joking editorial insertion: "[*Here 500 Stanzas are lost.*]" Gray concludes with the prayer:

> And so God save our noble King,
> And guard us from long-winded Lubbers,
> That to eternity would sing,
> And keep my Lady from her Rubbers.

Blake pictures the "Lubber" classically garbed in tunic and laurel wreath, his papers in one hand, the other hand extended in a regal request for silence. He is, by the way, an unmistakable parallel to the Virgil of Flaxman's Dante designs, first published in 1793 (e.g., the eleventh design to the *Inferno*). Before him at the card table sit two ladies, one lost in her cards, the other looking up with an expression of helpless discomfort; the third member of their party is a chubby fellow, swathed in foppish collars, half-rising to protest the impending deluge. Gray's lines suggest that the poet will cease and the card game continue; Blake's comic view implies that the players may well have a 499-stanza wait ahead of them, since they look quite impotent before the stern determination of the unmoved poet.

In this sequence of designs Blake appears to have had in mind no single line of unified commentary, no special argument; what does unify the series is the sense of Blake's delight in Gray's fairies and ghosts, his brief but grainy political satire, and his broader jokes at the expense of the poetic role where it threatens to become pompous or too self-regarding. The designs, in short, illustrate Gray's intelligent and finely varied humor rather than forming a sequential argument among themselves.

"ODE TO ADVERSITY"

The "Ode to Adversity" is the last poem of this group, one that picks up Gray's earlier theme concerning the inevitability of hardship and sorrow, but goes on to argue—as the Eton ode had not—that these are desirable, that they build and reveal strength of character. Blake, who believed that moral strength came not with abstinence but with "The lineaments of Gratified desire" (178), reacts predictably to such a view of character. In his Notebook some years earlier he remarked in a little verse that he never engraved:

> Abstinence sows sand all over,
> The ruddy limbs & flaming hair,
> But Desire Gratified
> Plants fruits of life & beauty there.   (178)

And his view that virtue accompanies delight, fulfillment, and affluence is expounded again and again in his work. As Blake wrote Hayley in November 1800, "Happinesses have wings and wheels; miseries are leaden legged, and their whole employment is to clip the wings and to take off the wheels of our chariots" (807). This view is explicit in "The Little Vagabond" (216), implicit in "The Garden of Love" (215) and in the Proverbs of Hell of *The Marriage of Heaven and Hell*, and is indeed his constant premise. (One of the most moving statements of it is found in Eno's song, which opens *The Book of Los* [256].) Blake's outrage at Gray's stated position, and his rejection of it, are evident in his designs to this ode.

Joseph Wicksteed in his study of Blake's illustrations to the Book of Job[20] made public his important discovery that Blake used in these designs a right-left symbolism in his positioning of feet and hands, right indicating a spiritual and left a material attitude or orientation. The Job illustrations were, of course, a very late work, executed after Blake's "system" had been elaborately worked out in the late, long prophecies and a lifetime of illustration. S. Foster Damon claims to see the symbolism operating as early as the designs for *The Gates of Paradise*

[20] *Blake's Vision of the Book of Job* (London and New York, 1910).

(completed by 1793),[21] but generally critics have found relatively little evidence of such early use. In his illustrations to Gray's "Ode to Adversity," however, left is indeed sinister. The technique is used here with disarming simplicity: every time a foot sticks out it is the left one, is unwontedly large and obvious, and accompanies a scene of some kind of destruction. This set of illustrations is the earliest I know of in which this symbolism—later much elaborated—operates repeatedly and consistently; and even in the Gray illustrations the use is confined (at least with this kind of force and certainty) to the designs for this one poem.

The title page offers a rather stylized design depicting a father and his two children mourning beside a gravestone. The father has his hands crossed over his chest and looks upward with an expression of piety and grief. At his knees stand the two children: the girl, at his left, shows nothing but gown and hair, her face and hands being muffled by her garment, into which she appears to be weeping; the boy clasps his father's left leg—both his left foot and his father's are prominent—and looks down with a kind of stolidly sullen expression. The motionless stoicism of the group gives an impression of sterile hopelessness.

The second design, surrounding the list of titles to the illustrations, has no direct source in Gray's poem, but rather seems to offer a general commentary on it. Blake entitles it "Grief among the roots of trees," and it is a stirringly powerful design. The main body of the picture consists of three massive tree stumps, their gnarled and heavy roots extending down almost savagely to encircle a kind of cave or nest beneath them. The axe that felled the trees remains in view, poised uneasily between a root and a stump. Inside the cave below— it is pictured as a sort of womb of earth formed by the spreading roots—sits a fierce woman in striking green dress; her spreading hair joins with the lines of the bare roots and seems finally to become part of them. She bends over an infant that lies in her left arm, regarding it with grim ferocity as she points her breasts at it for nursing. But the child, whose form is the center of the generally circular, enclosing shape of the design, hangs limp and motionless—quite dead. Blake's point is made with visual brilliance: grief is no proper nurse, but rather kills the life it attends. Rather than allying us with the forces of spiritual growth it binds us in the roots of nature, inhibiting our powers and destroying the infant joy.

[21] *A Blake Dictionary* (Providence, R.I., 1965), p. 140.

The next design illustrates Gray's lines telling how the proud, in chains, "are taught to taste of pain":

> And purple tyrants vainly groan
> With pangs unfelt before, unpitied and alone.

A huge crowned tyrant, chained in his dark cell, clutches at his throat with grief and what looks to be proud despair. His left foot is thrust forward, his right hidden; left foot and hand are both bound by heavy chains. The design is potentially a symmetrical one, with the tyrant seated at the center of a heavy stone-arched prison cell, beneath barred windows. The entire unit of arch, window, and tyrant is, however, placed off-center, to the right of the text box; and the effect is powerful, for it engages the margin of the page to make the tyrant seem all the more crushed and crowded, the more heavily weighed down by his oppressive surroundings.[22]

The fourth design offers another version of adversity as nurse, this time in response to Gray's own language. Adversity is addressed:

> When first thy Sire to send on earth
> Virtue, his darling child, design'd,
> To thee he gave the heavenly birth,
> And bade to form her infant mind.
> Stern rugged nurse!

A giant woman half-squats upright on a low bench, her sad eyes staring out from a gaunt, wrinkled face; her dress is the same striking green as that of Grief in Adversity 2, further associating her with that deadly nurse. Her arms are draped over her raised knees: the left hand holds a large closed book, the right holds Urizenic compasses; both objects rest on the ground, and projecting out between the two is her huge left foot. In her lap sits a miniature young lady with hair pulled back in a neat bun; she bends over a closed book on which she is writing, absorbed in concentration. This is Virtue, still a pretty child, but clearly in the process of formation by her nurse. This design finds a fascinating counterpart in the Young designs, for there, illustrating the line "Virtue, kept alive by

[22] I find this purple tyrant faintly reminiscent of the Richard II of Gough's *Sepulchral Monuments in Great Britain* (London, 1786-1796), that Malkin attributes to Blake—the wispy moustaches and broad nose particularly. There is of course also the supposed historical circumstance of Richard II's having been starved to death in prison, an event which Blake renders allegorically in Bard 9.

care and toil,"[23] we see Virtue grown up—into the same gaunt, stern woman who had "nursed" her. Clearly the nurse has done her job in forming the "infant mind"! This virtue bred of adversity ("care and toil") is austerity itself: and so—completing the line of association—she is shown also in another Young design, this one illustrating "How knits Austerity her cloudy brow."[24] There the same gaunt woman walks against a background of stormy clouds and rain. We know, then, the lineage and power of Adversity as she exists in Blake's imagination, and we know what to expect of her tutelage.

Design 5 shows Adversity in "Gorgon terrors clad," as she is seen by the "impious." Blake, who had had considerable private experience of this view of Adversity, drew her with animation. A menacing serpent-haired monster lunges at the reader, flanked by her "vengeful band" of "Despair, and fell Disease, and ghastly Poverty." Despair raises two short daggers pointed at his own breast, poverty wields whips, and "fell Disease," her greenish skin again reminiscent of the clothing of Grief in design 2 and Adversity in design 5, above (and her face a more worn and sickly version of that of Adversity in the fifth design), pours from an urn a yellowish plague. The Gorgon's large left foot is thrust forward at the bottom center of the design, and poverty's is also visible.

The final design surrounds a page of text marked at the line "Thy form benign, oh Goddess, wear," though Blake's list of titles identifies this design by quoting two lines from the page before:

> Oh, gently, on thy suppliant's head,
> Dread Goddess, lay thy chast'ning hand!

Both titles are pertinent, for here we see Adversity in a "benign" form, a gravely woeful floating creature draped in a hooded robe like a Gothic *pleurant*, that frequent figure in tomb decoration; she closely resembles Night in a later design (Elegy 3) and is an almost exact redrawing of Darkness in design no. 536 of *Night Thoughts*, though her expression here is sterner than that worn by either of these two. The "suppliant" mentioned in the lines of Blake's title is receiving the admonitory attentions of this "benign" Adversity, but seems entirely unresponsive, lying stiffly across the bottom of the page and similarly enveloped in a hooded robe that reveals only the profile of his face, and on it an expression of sulky resentment and withdrawn isolation.

The six designs to this poem are, then, united in their one aim: to argue against

---

[23] *Night Thoughts*, no. 294.　　　　[24] *Night Thoughts*, no. 376.

the notion that adversity in itself has any constructive effects. All his life Blake believed that abstinence is a destroyer. In December 1795 he wrote his friend and fellow artist George Cumberland: "Now you will, I hope, shew all the family of Antique Borers that Peace & Plenty & Domestic Happiness is the Source of Sublime Art, & prove to the Abstract Philosophers that Enjoyment & not Abstinence is the food of Intellect" (790). And years later he was still affirming in *Jerusalem*: "No one bruises or starves himself to make himself fit for labour!" (639). The design entitled "Grief among the roots of trees" thus epitomizes Blake's entire argument; here Blake administers his corrective in microcosm. Grief is opposed to the forces of life as the roots of nature are to the waking year, as "abstinence" is to "the fruits of life and beauty." Adversity, as teacher, inculcates only a gaunt and weary wisdom; as afflicter she terrifies the mind and wounds the body; as benign "softener" she must perhaps be borne, but fosters at best no more than a self-enclosing resentment. She is never a fruitful goddess, though Blake knew her intimately enough to know that one must sometimes bear one's fruits despite her.

In each of these illustrations Blake may be seen to take Gray's figurative language and build it out visually, making it reveal not only Gray's paraphrasable meaning and the less easily paraphrased suggestions that surround it, but also certain congruent suggestions not actually present in Gray and not necessarily noticeable to someone who did not know Blake's other work and some of his other opinions. He would seem in this regard to be a remarkably apt illustrator of Gray's work, pointing enthusiastically to the surprising power of some of Gray's "poetic diction," yet permitting himself the right to interpret—as indeed any reader must—on the basis of his own experience and interests and at many points to condemn what he felt to be Gray's perilous misconstruings of the truth.

Distant as the poems seem in some ways to be, they are all in a sense personal poems—they are Gray's intimacies, however formalized by decorum and humor, and the reader who allows Gray his period, temperament, and genre will sense his person in them. Blake did so, and his illustrations are kinds of personal response, ranging in tone from pleasure at shared wit and insight to indignation at the discovery of vastly destructive error in the one place where it may least be suffered: art. But the ensuing warfare of design against text Blake saw as humane and constructive, a form of Milton's "Wars of Truth."

For the Soldier who fights for Truth calls his enemy his brother:
They fight & contend for life & not for eternal death. (672)

Blake explains in his poem *Milton*:

As the breath of the Almighty such are the words of man to man
In the great Wars of Eternity, in fury of Poetic Inspiration,
To build the Universe stupendous, Mental forms Creating. (519)

His designs are, then, to be understood as the correctives of a brother poet, central to the salvation of both artists, and of all readers.

But the personal immediacy of the contention in these early poems—the sense of Gray's own presence in Blake's designs and of a dialogue between the two—becomes more fragmented and various in Blake's treatment of the poems that follow.

III

LATER

POEMS

"THE PROGRESS OF POESY"

THE opening piece of this second group is, fittingly, a poem about poetry, one that allows to Gray's mind—and even more to Blake's—a wide critical range. "The Progress of Poesy" is "A Pindaric Ode" offering first a general account of the power and place of poetry, then a history of its development from Greece to Rome to England and within England from Shakespeare to Milton to Dryden to Gray himself. Blake's design for the title page of the poem shows a figure not mentioned in Gray, "The Beginning of Poesy. The blind begging Bard," whom he represents as a large, robust man with a lyre led by a young boy. On the chance that the right-left symbolism mentioned in connection with the "Ode to Adversity" might once again prove to be relevant, one ought to observe that the bard plays his lyre with his right hand, and is shown with his right foot forward in a large, striding walk. The boy who leads him also has his right foot forward, and extends his right hand to guide the blind poet. We see in this design the first step in poetry's historical progress, beginning with the blind Homer; but it may also be read as a more general commentary on the nature of poetic vision, which sees—as Milton also knew—"not with but thro' the eye."

Poesy 2 is the second of a sequence of three designs showing the poet at work; this design "introduces" the later poems, and again tells us something of Blake's attitude toward the group, and toward Gray's apparently changing view of his role as poet. He is now to be addressed in visionary confrontation less as "brother poet" than as chronicler, translator, and—in "Ode for Music"—an official author of official praise. The picture is entitled simply "Study," and the poet, somewhat leaner and more mature than the eager young man of the first version, bends

82

thoughtfully, almost wearily, over a book in his lap. George Sherburn's observation that "After 1751 Gray derived poetic stimulus from his reading of books rather than from life itself"[1] might almost serve as a caption for Blake's picture, and the poems Blake groups together—headed by this design entitled "Study"—are precisely those Gray wrote after 1751.

Certainly this second group of poems reflects clearly Gray's immense learning: the Pindaric odes have been criticized both in Gray's time and later for their obscurity, and Gray's notes (available to Blake in the 1790 edition that was used in this project) hint at the wealth of scholarship that lies behind this group. Less than two pages of notes covered all Gray felt he was obliged to explain about the poems discussed above in Chapter I; but it took more than fifteen to cover the poems Blake placed in this second group. (Gray's notes to the "Elegy Written in a Country Churchyard" take less than a page.) Blake's "Study" appears to allude—at least indirectly—to this academic weight, as well as to the derivative nature of Gray's inspiration.

The poet in this design sits in almost the same position as he did in the earlier one, and, as has already been observed, the makeup of the two pages is virtually the same, although the present design is generally darker. The arch above the poet reveals in this case not a clear opening in the wall, but rather a Gothic window through whose stained-glass designs the light radiates. Filling the upper central portion of the window is a bright six-winged creature with light flowing in all around it, holding in its hand a fiery red dove and clearly representing divine inspiration. At the bottom of the window (perhaps part of the window's design, but more likely a separate figure sitting on the sill, since her skirt slightly overlaps it) is a muse with a scroll across her lap and a pen in her hand, looking up to receive dictation from the divine spirit. It may be that she will then impart her received glory to the studying poet—perhaps she is the subject of his study—but as he is pictured he is oblivious to her and to the light of inspiration that flows in above her. As the blazing light is yellow, so is the muse's scroll and, though dimmed, the poet's book.[2]

The third design illustrates the opening lines of "The Progress of Poesy," and here Blake adds a kind of gratuitous felicity that takes off from Gray's suggestion

---

[1] "The Restoration and Eighteenth Century," *A Literary History of England*, ed. Albert C. Baugh (New York, 1948), p. 1014.

[2] In his pictures Blake frequently opposes books to scrolls: books, squared off and hard, symbolize knowledge measured and contained (cf. Adversity 4); scrolls more often bear the products of inspiration.

but does not strictly support his meaning: it is basically the technique of Spring 3. The "Progress" begins with the following six lines:

> Awake, Æolian lyre, awake,
> And give to rapture all thy trembling strings.
> From Helicon's harmonious springs
> A thousand rills their mazy progress take:
> The laughing flowers, that round them blow,
> Drink life and fragrance as they flow.

Blake has marked lines 5 and 6 for illustration, but his drawing takes account of all the lines just quoted, for the lyre is shown, and plucking it is a large, robed lady, presumably a muse, who approaches gently from the right. Balancing this figure, on the other side of the inserted text, falls Helicon's spring, which swirls past her feet, its movement blending with the movement of the hem of her gown and their blue colors merging. Bordering the stream is a soft tangle of flowers that bend and curl, releasing tiny, living figures in flowing gowns rather like that of the muse: some figures emerge from the centers of buds and flowers, others seem themselves to be the leaves or buds of the plants on which they grow, and all are gathering water from the stream in pitchers or cups, or drinking it from goblets. Behind the lyre-player, seeming to emerge from the folds of her dress, are two long-stemmed blossoms without living creatures in them—the only two in the page: possibly as she passes they too will reach the water and spring to life, though I think it more likely that the hunched shoulders, vacant stare, and rather unresponsive-looking lyre of the muse intimate a Blakean criticism of some of the assumptions of her poem, in which case the two flowers may be supposed doomed, blighted by an intruder in Helicon.

Gray does personify the flowers—they laugh and drink—but his chief concern in this opening section of the poem is with the sound and music of Helicon's springs; line 7 continues, "Now the rich stream of music winds along," and the remaining five lines describe the stream's progress, an implied epitome of the larger subject of the poem—the progress of poesy—in keeping with the traditional association of the muses' stream with man's verse. Blake, however, is stopped by the notion of life that he interprets quite literally in his visualization of the scene. Indeed, Blake's interpretation goes beyond the literal, for Gray's "life" need mean no more than nourishment, especially as it is paired with "fragrance," a word that carries us back to the literal flowers and away from personification, whereas to Blake "life" meant something like "incarnation," the taking of human form. His remarkable drawing, then, distracts from Gray's intended emphasis, pointing instead to Blake's own view of the poetic vision behind the choice of expression; when we recall how in Spring 3 becoming "awake" had meant the assuming of human shape, as here becoming "alive" does, we see how even Gray's tentative and partial uses of personification brought to Blake's mind fully human-formed scenes.

The next design illustrates Gray's statements about the power of poetry, how it tames even the "Lord of War" and brings "the feather'd king" down to perch "on the sceptered hand/ Of Jove." Blake's eagle looks like a drugged, malevolent vulture, slumping on the wrist of the huge, pleasant-faced Jove who sits, head on hand, enchanted by the magic of poetry; but the effect of the design is carried by the bold and brilliant yellow that washes almost the entire page. This effect is problematical, for its splendor seems also rather heavy, or airless. And although Jove's present expression is peaceful and generous enough, his right hand rests on a scepter whose top is a cluster of oak leaves and acorns, traditionally sacred to Jove but a frequent symbol of sacrifice and oppression in Blake's work; and (for what it may be worth) Jove leans on his left arm, extending his left foot forward. As Blake remarked elsewhere with what sounds like a smack of satisfaction, "Every Body hates a King" (400). If we can abstract a "statement" from the design, it would probably be—roughly—that even the powerful, tyrannical king of the gods may be lulled and gentled by the power of poetry.

Design 5 is one of Blake's several, and varying, early studies for the kind of symmetrical and repetitive design that he used with greatest force and beauty in the Job design known as "When the morning stars sang together." Here we see the "loves" frisking on Cytherea's day: on the left four figures advance, floating lightly over the grass and shaking timbrels high in the air; on the right five similar figures retreat, making identical gestures; at each side in the foreground two flutists advance, almost mirror images of each other; in the center, beneath the text, a flying cupid plays the violin; the leafy branches of two trees on either side of the page (only the slender trunk of the tree on the right is visible) intertwine in front of a large six-pointed star that has the effect of pinning the entire design together. The symmetry is almost perfect, and would be dull if it were not just off center: five timbrel players advance and four retreat, one trunk is visible and one is not. The design offers a delicate and gracious vision of what Blake came to call the daughters of Beulah.

In the lines illustrated by design 6, Gray writes that Jove lets Night with her "sickly dews" and "spectres wan" range the sky "Till down the eastern cliffs afar/ Hyperion's march they spy, and glitt'ring shafts of war"—that is, until morning. The context of the poem suggests also that Hyperion's approach is the approach of poetry, night's specters the ills of man's mind and body.[3] So morning ends night, and the language tells us that the shift is a violent one, the sun's approach being seen as a march, his rays as "glitt'ring shafts of war": the enemy Night apparently flies in fear at the sight, since the lines say that she and her dews and specters range "Till" Hyperion is seen; we are told nothing more, since the two lines quoted above end this section of the ode.

A paraphrase of the passage might go something like this: as day ends night, so poetry eases the sufferings of man. But what Gray chooses to talk about when he presents his point is the approach of a mythological god of youth, beauty, and brightness, the sight of whom overwhelms personified Night and her company of sickly and fearsome creatures. And this is what Blake chooses to illustrate, though he personifies in addition Gray's "sickly dews" and "birds of boding cry," apparently returning for his figures to the earlier lines in which Gray enumerates the ills awaiting "Man's feeble race":

> Labour, and Penury, the racks of Pain,
> Disease, and Sorrow's weeping train,
> And Death. . . .

We see, then, a glorious and surprisingly gentle-faced young man surrounded by a bursting circle of golden yellow, spearlike flames; he dominates the page, the text of the poem being centered over his torso almost as though he were wearing it. Below him, across the bottom of the page, are the dark heads of the downward-hurtling creatures whom he has put to flight.

This picture does illustrate Gray's language: it shows us Hyperion and his glittering shafts of war purging the "dreary sky" of Night's creatures. Just as Gray's Hyperion stands for the sun, rising over "the eastern cliffs afar," so Blake's young man is a sungod with the flames of the sun about him. And to the extent that Hyperion's rout of the night creatures may be understood to suggest also the way poetry can rid man of his sufferings, Blake's vision of brilliant youth driving away a band of menacing and horrible creatures suggests the same.

Gray's particular context does not carry these implications farther; but a later

---

[3] Gray makes this connection explicit in a note.

version of this same picture shows at least one other way in which Blake "read" his own vision. In 1807 Blake illustrated in watercolor the fall of the rebel angels, from Milton's *Paradise Lost*, Book VI, lines 835ff., using a somewhat more stylized version of the same design.[4] In this version Christ kneels in a nimbus, surrounded by six angels rather than by flames, shooting an arrow straight down into a mass of writhing, falling figures who are received into flames that reach up from below. As in the Gray illustration the god shoots one arrow from his own bow and others issue from about him, though in the Milton version there are only six other arrows, and they are neatly spaced, three to a side. In both illustrations the figures fall headfirst, though in the Milton illustration there are several complete bodies as well as a crowd of falling heads, whereas in the Gray illustration there are only heads. C. H. Collins Baker notes in the description of the Henry E. Huntington Library copy of the Milton design that "In the falling rebels reminiscences and adaptations of Michelangelo's 'Last Judgment' in the Sistine Chapel can be traced."[5]

One sees, then, at least part of a line of associations in Blake's mind: Gray's traditional connection of sun and Hyperion and poetry as visualized by Blake takes on a shape that is later able to assimilate his vision of Milton's lines about Christ and the rebel angels. And in his borrowing from Michelangelo, whom Blake greatly admired and whose works he had studied and copied since his years as an engraver's apprentice,[6] we see Blake's visual association of the scenes from Gray and Milton with Michelangelo's treatment of the Last Judgment. Thus Blake's rendering of Gray's brief personification not only picks up the threads of Gray's latent or suggested meanings, but carries them further into the realm of Blake's own visual ideas, hinting at connections not actually present in Gray's poem but not inconsistent with it. We will see this happen again.

Design 7 illustrates the line "Where shaggy forms o'er ice-built mountains roam"; even in such a place "The Muse has broke the twilight gloom" and the influence of poetry is felt, according to Gray; Blake shows a young man warmly

[4] There also exists a sketch, sometimes called "The Bowman and the Spirit of Inspiration" (reproduced in Raine, *Blake and Tradition*, I, 228) that makes clear again the visionary significance of this figure with his "Bow of burning gold" and "Arrows of desire."

[5] *Catalogue of William Blake's Drawings and Paintings in The Huntington Library* (San Marino, Cal., 1957), p. 21.

[6] See Blunt, *The Art of William Blake* (New York, 1959), p. 4, for evidence of Blake's early copying of Michelangelo; praise of Michelangelo is of course scattered throughout Blake's prose.

dressed in leggings and a wolfskin, playing a pipe as he walks. It is an icy-quiet scene, the whole stark background done in cold, light blues. But the vision of the man within the beast—his face emerges from the wolf's gaping mouth—is a faintly disquieting one. One recalls Blake's dictum that "Savages are Fops & Fribbles more than any other Men" (468), yet this primitive boy quietly playing his pipe seems a generally sympathetic figure in Blake's view. A possible gloss on this design returns us once more to Blake's borrowings from Michelangelo. On an engraving marked "Michel Angelo Pinxit" that Blake entitled "Joseph of Arimathea among The Rocks of Albion," Blake inscribed: "This is One of the Gothic Artists who Built the Cathedrals in what we call the Dark Ages, Wandering about in sheep skins & goat skins, of whom the World was not worthy; such were the Christians in all Ages" (604). Apparently such are the artists who break "the twilight gloom," as well, though here a wolf's skin replaces the goat skin or sheep skin. In his list of illustrations to "The Descent of Odin" Blake notes that "The Serpent & the Wolvish Dog" are "two terrors in the Northern Mythology." Perhaps we may take it that this young piper of the North has subdued at least one of his people's terrors, though a hostile—if unobservant—critic might claim he embodied it.

In design 8 we see another example—and a particularly subtle and elaborate one—of Blake's taking fire from the kind of language to which Wordsworth had objected. Celebrating England's position as a virtuous and proper home for the arts, Gray relates how the muses fled Greece for Rome and then Rome for England, scorning each of their earlier homes as each became unworthy. The muses demand an appropriate culture in which to thrive, Gray says:

> Alike they scorn the pomp of tyrant Power,
> And coward Vice, that revels in her chains.

Blake illustrates these two lines by showing a sweep of muses disappearing out the top of the page, leaving behind two female figures: a regal woman clothed in the pomp of robe, crown, and scepter directs with her outstretched hand the other figure, a mindless, slovenly, fat, horned creature who fingers aimlessly the keys of an organ and is clearly not at all discomfited by the heavy chain that binds her to her ruler; she is an alternate version of the pestilence-flinging, ignorant Folly of Eton 9. Gray's point, stated in abstract rather than figurative language, is that art does not flourish under conditions of tyranny and corruption. But his figurative language also alludes to related matters: that the corrupt

create their own bondage in preferring payment to liberty, and that this preference is a cowardly one. Finally, being cast in the form of personification, Gray's
statement invites the reader to see the three abstracts—art, tyrannic power, and
vice—as a human triangle with the feelings and relationships of individual
human beings: the muses feel scorn; power is pompous; vice is weak and undis-
cerning. Blake responds vigorously to the invitation, incidentally laying out his
design in a clearly marked triangular shape that extends from the apex down
one side through the fleeing figures of the muses to Power's scepter, and down
the other through the printed text to the horns of Vice. The chains of Vice,
predictably, form the base of the triangle, the muses' disappearing heads its apex.
This is not so schematically presented as to demand a schematic reading, but in
the sense that one "gets the picture," the picture here is clear: the corrupt really
are chained to those they serve, and both *are* abased by that fact; vice really *is*
soft and mindless, almost bestial, and doubly disgusting because insensitive to
the degradation. And this mutually chained pair will obviously be shunned by
those who truly are free and can fly such a base conjunction.

Blake, then, takes Gray's personifications and makes them, if you like, more
personal—that is, he reminds the reader of Gray that when "Art" flies "Power"
and "Vice," it is ultimately a matter of revulsion experienced by individual men,
a revulsion the reader is likely to share as he regards these caricatures. And Blake
here adds a wry fillip of his own in showing Vice as herself a would-be follower
of the arts (she fingers the organ), and Power a would-be conductor of the arts
(her finger is raised to direct the music); this is a dimension not actually present
in Gray, though entirely consistent with his overall point. It happened, indeed,
to be a matter of great concern to Blake, who did not share Gray's optimistic
view of England as the home of freedom for the arts. Blake saw flattering portrait painters being flattered in return by the nobility, and lavishly paid, whereas
he himself was ridiculed or ignored, and was at times too poor to buy the sheets
of copper he needed for his engraving. He later commented bitterly in the
margin of his copy of Reynolds' *Discourses*: "The Enquiry in England is not
whether a Man has Talents & Genius, But whether he is Passive & Polite & a
Virtuous Ass & obedient to Noblemen's Opinions in Art & Science. If he is, he is
a Good Man. If Not, he must be starved" (452-453). We can sense, then, particular animus in his portrait of this "Virtuous Ass" at the organ, playing to please
Power. In fact Vice's "horns," if scrutinized closely, are furry and brown and a
little too wide to be real horns—they are the ass's ears that were conferred by

Phoebus Apollo upon Midas for his presumption and bad taste—and mixed in her hair is a shaggy laurel band. If Apollo has not approved, nonetheless patrons have.[7]

The next stanzas, and Blake's next three designs, trace the development of poetry through several of its great figures: Shakespeare, Milton, Dryden, and finally, with disclaimers, Gray himself. Speaking first of Shakespeare, Gray says: "To him the mighty mother did unveil/ Her awful face"—lines that Blake illustrates by showing the "mighty mother," Nature, in a swirl of cape or veil that surrounds her almost like a nimbus; she half-emerges from a sort of yellow, open sphere, regarding benevolently the infant Shakespeare who rises in her embrace and reaches up to her face with his arms. If—as seems probable—Nature is here emerging from a moon, this would be Blake's way of emphasizing the mutual lovingness of Shakespeare's relationship with Nature: "Beulah" (Hebrew for "married") became Blake's name for the moony and restful state of gratified love, a state that is also a source of poetic inspiration. In that Gray speaks of Nature as giving Shakespeare the "golden keys" that unlock emotion, he seems very close to sharing Blake's view of Beulah, if not his idiom, for Beulah is also the subconscious and the land of dreams in Blake's developing mythology.

This picture stands in remarkable contrast to that other picture of nurse and infant, the one from "Ode to Adversity" entitled "Grief among the roots of trees." There, in almost exactly the same attitude as Nature, sat the fierce young woman bending over a dead infant. This striking parallel underlines the emotional force of each of the pictures: the grim barrenness of one offsets the rich lovingness of the other, and reminds us of the differing effects of adversity and the warm wealth of a nature lovingly seen. The one is a "real world" of nature red in tooth and claw; the other a visionary poet's nature, alive with the rich vitality that his own spirit imparts to it. In a poem recounting his spiritual biography Blake says that "Shakespeare in riper years gave me his hand" (799), and we see in this design Blake's gratitude for the gift.

The next poets considered by Gray in his "Progress" are Milton and Dryden;

---

[7] Compare the third verse of Blake's early "Imitation of Spenser": Midas, like Vice, has not even the wit to sense his degradation.

> Midas the praise hath gain'd of lengthen'd ears,
>   For which himself might deem him n'er the worse
> To sit in council with his modern peers,
>   And judge of tinkling rhimes, and elegances terse. (14)

there is insufficient space to illustrate both, however, and perhaps because Blake will show Milton elsewhere (Music 4), or because Dryden was more to his critical purpose, he chooses Dryden here. The illustration shows the poet seated, like the figure of Gray in earlier illustrations, but Dryden regards a swirling vision and gently strums a lyre. His vision is "the Muse's ray," a term Gray uses some lines later in reference to his own poetic vision, but which Blake borrows here for use in the Dryden design as well. Typically, Blake's version of the ray is quite literal: from the arc of a brightly colored rainbow bends a muse pouring from an urn, illustrating Gray's description:

> Bright-eyed Fancy, hov'ring o'er,
> Scatters from her pictur'd urn
> Thoughts that breathe, and words that burn.

From the urn tumbles a rush of flames ("words that burn") and small human figures ("thoughts that breathe") bearing laurel, two snakes, an egg, a grasshopper, and a bird. The tiny "picture" on the urn shows one figure crowning another with laurel, and the lip of the urn is decorated with laurel. The laurel, of course, pays deference to the position Dryden held as poet laureate. But what of the other details added by Blake to Gray's description?

We know what Blake thought of Dryden as rhymer of Milton:

> Dryden in Rhyme cries, "Milton only Planned."
> Every Fool shook his bells throughout the Land. (595)

And he clearly considered Dryden's own poetry as imitation, at best: "While the Works [of Imitators *deleted*] of Pope & Dryden are look'd upon as the same Art with those of Milton & Shakespeare . . . there can be no Art in a Nation but such as is Subservient to the interest of the Monopolizing Trader" (595). That is, there can be no art that is not in the service of moneyed power. Elsewhere Blake's terminologies of contempt for bad poetry and bad engraving blend in one devastating attack on malpractice in both in arts: "Now let Dryden's Fall & Milton's Paradise be read, & I will assert that every Body of Understanding must cry out Shame on such Niggling & Poco-Pen as Dryden has degraded Milton with. But at the same time I will allow that Stupidity will Prefer Dryden, because it is in Rhyme & Monotonous Sing Song, Sing Song from beginning to end. Such are Bartolozzi, Woolett & Strange" (600). This puts Dryden in pretty bad company. One can further deduce what Blake would have thought of Dryden as abhorrer of religious enthusiasm in *Religio Laici*; if Blake read it, it must have seemed to him beneath either pity or contempt. It is not, then, difficult to know the general—if not always the particular—significance of the snakes and grasshopper, and to understand why the bird, the same who perches and sings in other illustrations to Gray, should here be shown returning in protest to the urn from which he has just emerged. It was noted that one figure carried an egg—the same who brings the two snakes. In Blake's own mythology the "mundane egg" is the three-dimensional world of time and space, the fallen world of physical as opposed to imaginative reality. Blake's sixth design for "The Gates of Paradise" shows the spirit breaking out of the enclosing shell that has been his "world" until now, and design 13 for *Night Thoughts* repeats the figure, using it to illustrate Young's lines about man's dual nature as "Heir of Glory" and "frail Child of Dust." The snakes are of course a universal symbol. In short, Dryden's vision of Fancy is Blake's comment on Dryden: it is a Fancy that presents images of the mundane world and its attendant evils, and that therefore, not surprisingly, appeals to that world, being subservient to its interests. Fancy makes her presentation, and Dryden seems impressed; but Blake leaves us to judge for ourselves the merits of a poet who accepts so undiscriminatingly the gifts of his fancy. Like the bird, we may well wish to return the way we came.

The eleventh illustration comments on Gray's lines about himself—the last lines of the poem. Gray depreciates himself in comparison with the "Theban eagle" Pindar, who sailed "with supreme dominion/ Thro' the azure deep of air," but concludes, in the lines that Blake here illustrates, that he has nonetheless seen something of the muse:

> Yet oft before his infant eyes would run
> Such forms as glitter in the Muse's ray,
> With orient hues, unborrowed of the sun.

Again we are shown "the Muse's ray," but the muse herself hangs in it almost invisible, with two near-transparent children clinging to her. Her expression is woebegone, the children's apprehensive. Regarding this "Muse's ray," whose "orient hues" Blake depicts with wavering lines of white light that descend from the ray to the scene below, stands a young man with his back turned to us, his hands spread out to his sides in an expression of what appears to be mild wonder. On the ground below and to the right, stretched upon a bed of cut wheat, lies a dead infant. A similar dead infant lies in a wheatfield in *America*, having been fed on war rather than mother's milk; another appears in *The Marriage of Heaven and Hell*, the counterpart of a delighted living child at the top of the same plate. The living child there is being taught by its mother to see as the "ancient Poets" saw: all "sensible objects" animated "with Gods or Geniuses." The child stretches up its arms like the infant Shakespeare of Poesy 9, and behind its mother we see what the child sees—vigorous animated "gods" of sun and water. Below, the mother and bright gods of the upper scene are replaced by Urizen, his arms stretched out over dark waters on which the dead infant floats: his is the "system" that was formed when men began "Choosing forms of worship from poetic tales," forgetting that "All deities reside in the human breast" (153).

Blake's illustration to Gray's lines about himself seems to imply that the muse-seeing "infant" part of Gray is now dead, leaving the grown man to see only blurred and troubled muses. The clinging infants in the muse's ray are perhaps some of the products of Gray's muse—that is, his poems—and in their haziness and her distress may be seen Blake's judgment of the danger that besets Gray's inspiration. Gray should seek to revive in himself his "infant eyes" and see as the "ancient Poets" saw, with the bold immediacy of bardic power. As an admirer of Dryden, Gray is in danger of becoming, like him, "Subservient to the interest of the Monopolizing Trader." As Blake observed, "Where any view of Money exists, Art cannot be carried on, but War only" (776). War, systematized worship, and commerce: all blend in Blake's vision to become the "mundane" enemy, the destroyer of that infant joy through which the spirit grows, and with it the creative capacities for art and poetry. Thus an infant dead on a bed of wheat is human waste epitomized:

> Is this a holy thing to see
> In a rich and fruitful land,
> Babes reduc'd to misery,
> Fed with cold and usurous hand? (211)

In this illustration the waste is the loss of the "infant" inspiration of Gray.

This picture, clear in its adverse judgment of Gray, seems particularly strange in view of Blake's clear admiration of Gray elsewhere—even elsewhere in this same poem. I think the answer lies in the assumptions that appear to lie behind Gray's "Progress," namely that the British Establishment is unimpeachable, its patronage of the arts generous. Blake believed neither to be the case, and found

Gray's "song" too eager in its self-stated goal: to "justify the Laws of Jove" (see stanza II.1, line 6).

The final design to this series is entitled simply "A Muse," and shows a large female figure in a sunny yellow gown curving upward in flight around the text box, which here gives the list of designs to the next poem. It appears to be a transitional picture, since the muse seems to be handing her lyre up to someone else—perhaps to the poetic vision of the next poem, "The Bard."

"THE BARD"

The next four poems form a kind of group within this larger group, since all four have grandly legendary themes that carry a greater sense of violence and action than is present in any of the earlier poems. In Blake's designs we see, likewise, a new turn: the designs less often illustrate half-obscured implications of the language, more often draw on the subject matter itself; and the composition is correspondingly more daring and advanced, with new and exciting uses of angle and perspective and of the allotment of space on the page.

The first of these poems is Gray's famous Pindaric ode "The Bard," which we recall had early interested Blake, and whose conception he later admired publicly in his *Descriptive Catalogue*.[8] The ode is, as the accompanying "Advertisement" explains, "founded on a Tradition current in Wales, that Edward the First, when he completed the conquest of that country, ordered all the Bards that fell into his hands to be put to death." The poem tells how a bard, standing on a rock high over the River Conway, accosts Edward's victorious army as it returns from battle and addresses Edward prophetically, telling him of the future downfall of his family and the subsequent return of Welsh power (the Tudors) to the English throne, a return that will be followed by a renaissance in English poetry. Having confounded Edward with this vision of the future, the bard plunges to his death in the water below.

The first design, that surrounding the poem's title page, is stately and serene: entitled simply "A Welch Bard," it shows this tall, imposing figure standing beside his harp, wearing a blue starred robe that alludes to the occult knowledge and power attributed to the bards of old. His huge harp is decorated with a small

[8] For discussions of Blake's borrowings from "The Bard," see Miner, "Two Notes on Sources" and Erdman, *Prophet Against Empire*, 47, 66 (rev. edn., 49, 65). Mark Schorer, *William Blake: The Politics of Vision* (New York, 1959), p. 352n, further finds some interesting possible borrowings by Blake from "The Descent of Odin."

winged golden muse or angel playing a tiny gold harp similar in shape to the bard's. The figure is an idealized—or visionary—portrait of "the poet" in his days of greatest authority.[9] It is presumably he who speaks most of this poem, though he is joined in the long denunciatory prophetic song by a "grisly band," the spirits of the murdered bards. Gray does not number them, but Blake pictures them as three, for reasons I will discuss later.

Design 2 is entitled "The slaughtered Bards" and is taken, as Blake adds in his title, from the line "The famished eagle screams and passes by." Across the top of the page hovers a terrible spread-winged bird, below him lie broken harps and three outstretched bards, their heads toward the reader, the rest of their bodies foreshortened by the extreme perspective so that the viewer sees only the hair, chests, and knees of two and the hair and back of the third, who lies on his stomach. The center figure dominates: his closed eyes are the only eyes visible at all, and his long white hair and beard spread out on each side to blend visually with the contours of the other two bards, both apparently younger men. This central figure resembles by virtue of his streaming white hair and beard the bard who appears to speak the poem—the stately one just described and later seen alone in designs 3 and 13. As we will see, the three outstretched bards with their differing features are forebears of Blake's "Ancient Britons," the Strong, Ugly, and Beautiful men whom he discusses in 1809 in his *Catalogue*. The screaming bird and a lurid red light gleaming from the distance behind him emphasize the ominousness of the scene, and the carnage out of which the bard's bitter vengeance has arisen. The eagle is for Blake a figure of inspiration, or intellect, here perverted from its original magnificence by a "starvation" expressed also in the death of the bards. The whole is a vision of inspiration persecuted to the brink of catastrophe—poetry dead, intellect famished—which the poem seeks to cleanse by a sort of furious catharsis (in the terrible prophecy) in order to open a way for the return of the "genuine Kings" and the resulting renaissance in poetry. Gray here writes English history from the bardic viewpoint; Blake's illustrations not only emphasize the viewpoint, but imply in the death and return of the bards the efficient as well as the final cause of the course of history. As we will see, however, Blake's notion of "genuine Kings" differs from Gray's.

In the facing illustration—design 3—we see "The Bard weaving Edward's fate": the tremendous figure crouches before us, his eyes wide with agitation, his hands gripping several huge, blood-dripping ropes that appear to be the

---

[9] Compare the majestic figure in the "Introduction" to the *Songs of Experience*.

strings of a gigantic harp and, in the poem's imagery, the threads of the "winding sheet" for "Edward's race" that is woven by the bard's song. It is a remarkable conception on Blake's part, for the bard, even crouched as he is to put the full weight of his body into the moving of his enormous harp strings, takes up nearly the entire page: his head and streaming hair alone are larger than the text box, and his huge limbs seem to crowd against the margins of the sheet on which he is drawn. There are none of the niceties of background to "set" him in a location; rather, he and his gory ropes comprise the entire universe of the picture, and seem to threaten to burst out beyond it. Blake admired Gray's conception, and clearly sought to match it with his own.

We are then shown Edward's reaction to this stupendous sight: "Edward & his Queen & Nobles astonished at the Bard's song." The king cowers low on his bowed horse, his head turned to look back and up at the bard (now no longer visible to us); behind him crouches his frightened queen, on the other side two nobles. The lines of the picture all emphasize the sense of downward pressures on the king's body: the spears echo the line of his forward-bent back, and the other three figures and the horse also bend with him. The horse alone seems undismayed, but kneels peacefully under its burden.

It was noted above that in this poem and the three that follow Blake illustrates Gray's figures of speech less often than the actions they describe; but design 5 is a deeply striking and curious variation on the earlier technique of illustrating the figures themselves. At this point in the bard's prophecy he calls on the king to hear how the very forces of nature vow revenge for the death of the Welsh poets:

> Hark, how each giant-oak and desert-cave
> Sigh to the torrent's awful voice beneath!
> O'er thee, oh King! their hundred arms they wave,
> Revenge on thee in hoarser murmurs breathe;
> Vocal no more, since Cambria's fatal day,
> To high-born Hoel's harp, or soft Llewellyn's lay.

Blake marks the first two lines of this passage and illustrates them with three massive, intertwined figures representing the oak, cave, and torrent. The oak is a huge, muscular man whose crouched body and flowing leafy beard combine to appear somewhat like a tree trunk, while his outstretched arms form branches; clustered about him, and seeming to grow out of him, are smaller, more realistic

96

branches, green leaves, and acorns.[10] Behind him may be seen the head of another such oak-man and the faint trace of one of his outstretched arms, the forearm represented by several separate, thin branches, with a shape like a man's hand drawn at the end. Beneath their feet, which stream out in rootlike wisps, crouches the dark, moaning figure of a woman; her hunched shape and darkly indistinct mossy-green robe show her to be the cave. To the left, in a winding fall of water, is the face of a man whose blue-white features and hair blend him into the pictured movement of the torrent. No one of these is at all realistically human, yet the human form of each is at least as readily discernible as its "natural" form; and while only the tree is unmistakably both a tree and a man at first glance, this explicit suggestion makes the identity of the other two figures immediately clear. This design is one of the most striking examples in Blake's art of this way of seeing the "human form" of nature, for we have here by no means an ordinary personification. (The Father Thames of Eton 4 is a borderline case between ordinary personification, such as Bentley's "Father Thames" or Blake's own "purple Year," and the mixed human and natural forms of this design.)

Rather, we have here a version of the "double vision" of which Blake speaks in the well-known poem addressed to his friend and patron Thomas Butts:

> For double the vision my Eyes do see,
> And a double vision is always with me.
> With my inward Eye 'tis an old Man grey,
> With my outward, a Thistle across my way. (817)

Another double encounter offers an alternate example of this expanded capacity of sight:

> Then Los appear'd in all his power:
> In the Sun he appear'd, descending before
> My face in fierce flames; in my double sight
> 'Twas outward a Sun: inward Los in his might. (818)

The poem concludes with Blake's famous description of his fourfold vision:

> Now I a fourfold vision see,
> And a fourfold vision is given to me;

[10] For contrast, compare Flaxman's design 14 for Dante's *Inferno*. Blake also uses the tree-humans elsewhere, notably as the "Spirits of Earth" in design 9 to "Il Penseroso."

'Tis fourfold in my supreme delight
And threefold in soft Beulah's night
And twofold Always. May God us keep
From Single vision & Newton's sleep! (818)

This poem is taken from a letter dated November 1802—that is, toward the end of his Felpham stay. I do not think that Blake had clearly developed his theory of fourfold vision even then, and certainly not by the time he illustrated Gray. In any event, it is chiefly in the visions of his own prophetic books that we find threefold and fourfold vision exemplified, though perhaps also in his late illustrations. But in the Gray designs he is almost always concerned with twofold vision, with the vision that sees the visionary in the natural, the creative imagination of another mind—here Gray's—tangled in its cant and "corrupted vision." In fact, I am tempted to believe that "threefold" and "fourfold" vision are only roughly applicable to Blake's art, that he used them to make intellectual distinctions not always traceable in the pictures. Like Dante's advocacy of the fourfold method, it affords splendid if often futile exercise for scholars—clear as theory, difficult in application.

We are familiar with Blake's answer to the self-posed question: " 'What,' it will be Question'd, 'When the Sun rises, do you not see a round disk of fire somewhat like a Guinea?' O no, no, I see an Innumerable company of the Heavenly host crying 'Holy, Holy, Holy is the Lord God Almighty.' I question not my Corporeal or Vegetative Eye any more than I would Question a Window concerning a Sight. I look thro' it & not with it" (617). But the oak, cave, and torrent of this picture still cling to their attributes of "single vision" with an effect strangely powerful and ominous. The cave here recalls the weeping figure of Eton 6, and both are related, as observed in the discussion of that design, to the expression of the Greek tragic mask that is frequently a symbol of oppression for Blake. The oak's connection with tyranny we already know, and while here Blake could be simply obeying his source in presenting an oak where one is called for, he intensifies the connotations of oppression by showing the massive figure as itself bent down in an expression of weariness and sorrow. Finally, the torrent has a brutal face, and accosts the reader with a sort of vicious snarl. As the lines from the poem show, these figures are oppressed by Edward's tyranny in depriving Wales of "Hoel's harp" and "soft Llewellyn's lay"; but like the eagle they have further been transformed by that tryanny into something ugly and menacing, breathing revenge in "hoarser murmurs."

The sixth illustration again shows the three bards—Blake's response to the following lines:

> On yonder cliffs, a grisly band,
> I see them sit, they linger yet,
> Avengers of their native land:
> With me in dreadful harmony they join,
> And weave with bloody hands the tissue of thy line.

The three enormous bards cling perilously but with evident strength to the side of a cliff that, on closer inspection, proves to be a mass of thick bloody ropes that are the clustered strings of a gigantic harp—and hence the threads that will be woven into the "tissue" of Edward's winding sheet. The composition is another of Blake's daring ones, for the lines sweep diagonally across the page, the lines of rope being echoed in the sideward-spread hair, beards, arms, and robes of the bards and in the lines of the streaked sky. Offsetting these is the single, bulky line of the foremost bard's shoulder, leg, and foot, which are braced against the perpendicular ropes. Since the basic lines are of course the simple vertical and horizontal of the drawing sheet and the inserted text box, these diagonals that dispute and finally overwhelm the viewer's expectations are visually powerful and very unsettling, giving one a sharp sense of the supernatural bardic power.[11]

Design 7 is interesting less in itself than for several curiosities that attend it. First, it is a return to Blake's simplest literalism, in that Gray's lines about Edward the Third—

> From thee be born, who o'er thy country hangs
> The scourge of Heav'n. What terrors round him wait!
> Amazement in his van, with flight combin'd,
> And Sorrow's faded form, and Solitude behind.

—are illustrated by a soaring king wielding his whip over four figures representing respectively Amazement and Flight, faded Sorrow, and Solitude (fallen well behind). Second, the terrors of the second line quoted above were first sketched

---

[11] Compare to this the *Night Thoughts* design showing the unprepared soul asleep as if "on a *Precipice*/ Puff'd off by the first Blast, and lost for ever" (reproduced in Keynes, *William Blake. Illustrations to Young's Night Thoughts* [Cambridge, Mass., 1927]). There, head down, knees and shoulders drawn together, balances a figure about to tumble down the page—a hunched, indrawn man barely poised over the void. He forms a useful contrast to these sinewy bardic spirits, who are well in command of the situation.

"waiting" around the king, as Gray's line prescribes, then rejected in favor of a simpler design: their forms remain faintly visible, however, in the original manuscript, and one of them was quite clearly what is now the center beast (a "vulture of the mind") at the bottom of Eton 6. The shift in design carries a shift in point as well. In Gray's line, "Amazement," "Sorrow," and the others are the terrors loosed on England by that "scourge" Edward III. Blake, however, shows the terrors themselves terrorized, four fleeing victims of the scourge. The result is a rather naturalistic view of punishment, corporeal rather than spiritual, and so stands in marked contrast to Eton 6, whose beastlike inner "terror" has here been rejected. We have in this vision of Edward III not a study of the warped soul, but (in effect) a political cartoon.[12]

The eighth design is a splendid vision of Gray's "Whirlwind":

> In gallant trim the gilded vessel goes;
> Youth on the prow, and pleasure at the helm;
> Regardless of the sweeping Whirlwind's sway,
> That, hush'd in grim repose, expects his evening-prey.

In the distance a tiny ship rides toward the sun, it and the sun forming a center of bright light encircled by dark clouds. In the foreground the Whirlwind reposes on the water, a peaceful giant curled in buoyant sleep within a sort of floating nest of white wind-wings, his golden horn wound around his folded arms. From the left corner of his mouth protrudes a tiny uncolored object that I am unable to identify, though it might be a thin snakelike tongue. No one could doubt the power of Blake's giant Whirlwind, but in him we see no present sign of the expected destruction, unless the object at the corner of his mouth be one.

Blake knew from Gray's note, however, that the ominous lines refer to the ending of Richard II's magnificent reign, an ending portrayed in Gray's next lines and Blake's next design. Gray's notes remind the reader that "Richard the Second . . . was starved to death," an event his poem describes by personification:

> Fell thirst and famine scowl
> A baleful smile upon their baffled guest . . . ,

and that there followed the "Ruinous civil wars of York and Lancaster." The wars are alluded to in the next pair of lines:

[12] For commentary on this design in connection with Blake's own early play about Edward III, see Erdman, *Prophet Against Empire*, pp. 61-63 (rev. edn., p. 65n).

Hear ye the din of battle bray,
Lance to lance, and horse to horse?

Blake's ninth design incorporates both these sets of lines from the poem, employing a technique he was often to use in later years, that of the layered picture. Seated on a throne at the center of the page is Richard, thin and agonized; at his feet, obedient to the text, sit the figures of thirst and famine—thirst with an inverted goblet and famine pointing to three bare stones that remind Richard of his inability to turn them into bread. In a kind of arc over all their heads may be seen Blake's vision of the din of battle: highly symmetrical groups of figures on horseback encounter one another "lance to lance" before a red sky whose color is further dramatized in the horses' bloody hooves. At the right, as if emerging from the battle and spreading its spirit to the regions outside, a glaring dragon descends from the arc, snorting fire. The two scenes of course refer to different times in history, and occupy different spaces on the page; but as Gray has juxtaposed them in his lines, so Blake does in the design, and the effect is to telescope the terrible history.

And so the long sequence of murder and war is summarized in the stanzas that follow, until the bards conclude:

Now, Brothers, bending o'er th' accursed loom
Stamp we our vengeance deep, and ratify his doom.

Here they prophesy the death of Edward's queen, Eleanor, who died (as Gray remarks in a note) a few years after the conquest of Wales:

Edward, lo! to sudden fate
(Weave we the woof. The thread is spun,)
Half of thy heart we consecrate.
(The web is wove. The work is done.)

Seizing on the line "Half of thy heart we consecrate"—a line that avoids all human detail—Blake shows the three bards hovering electrified as the stricken Edward mourns over the limp body of his dead queen. The bard's brilliant yellow hair is in strong contrast to the white or grayish hair of all the earlier bards, and as it streaks out straight up and forward from their heads it resembles rays of light or lightning. The vengeance of art upon tyranny has begun, and it is indeed electrifying. But it is also a strikingly pitiful sight: Edward is pictured here not as a tyrant getting his just desert, but as a bereaved husband bent in grief

101

over a frail young wife. (Blake had also gone beyond his text in representing Eleanor beside her husband in Bard 4.) Gray observed of Eleanor in his note that "The heroic proof she gave of her affection for her lord [she is said to have died of poison sucked from his wound] is well known. The monuments of his regret, and sorrow for the loss of her, are still to be seen at Northampton, Geddington, Waltham, and other places." One of Blake's earliest watercolors, done shortly after his apprenticeship with Basire ended, illustrates this incident, displaying in it, as Sir Anthony Blunt remarks, "a theme of self-sacrifice and heroism."[13] While still an apprentice Blake had executed two views of Eleanor's monument, showing her full face and in profile, for Richard Gough's *Sepulchral Monuments in Great Britain*.[14] It is noteworthy that the crown, shape of nose and face, and hairstyle of the Gough Eleanor are similar to those of the queen of the Gray design (though not to those of the earlier watercolor). Blake could have read in Gough a long disquisition which denies the story of her death by sucking poison, but gives her a character Blake would have admired. After noting (to add emphasis to this special case) that "our old historians do not deal in characters," Gough quotes the historian Walsingham as saying, "She was a woman of great piety, moderation, and tenderness. . . . In her time foreigners did not pester England, nor were the subjects opprest by the king's officers, if the least complaint came by any means to her ears. She administered comfort to the distresst every where as her rank enabled, and reconciled to the best of her power all who were at variance." Blake's apparent sympathy for the unfortunate queen must have complicated his feelings about the historical royal couple, as they complicated, I think, the tone of this curious design. Gray, however, does not pause to consider Edward as a private man. His concern is with the terrible vengeance of time upon tyranny: it is the theme of his poem, and an important theme in Blake's approving response.

The bards' prophecy concludes with the promise of a renaissance to accompany the reign of Elizabeth I, one of the line of Britannia's "genuine Kings."

> Girt with many a Baron bold
> Sublime their starry fronts they rear;
> And gorgeous Dames, and Statesmen old

[13] *The Art of William Blake*, p. 9.

[14] See the discussion of this work in G. E. Bentley, Jr. and Martin K. Nurmi, *A Blake Bibliography* (Minneapolis, Minn., 1964), p. 119. The quotation from Walsingham occurs in the first volume of *Sepulchral Monuments*, p. 65.

In bearded majesty, appear.
In the midst a form divine!

The "form" is Elizabeth, whom Blake pictures at top center of the page (wearing, incidentally, a peaked ruff similar to that of the Lord-Keeper of "A Long Story"). Below her and to the left is a magnificent "Baron bold" in gold armor with a huge plume adorning his helmet; beneath him, and completing the dominant curve of movement, are reared the "fronts" not of those "genuine Kings" to whom Gray's syntax refers, but of quite another kind of "genuine" king: the three bards we saw outstretched beneath the screaming eagle in design 3. The bard on the left still has his head turned away, the middle bard's long white hair now streams in the wind, and the bard on the right—whose head had rested against his broken harp—now plays his harp and "rears" the "starry front." In Blake's vision, renaissance really is rebirth, as the ancient bards return from death.

Blake's twelfth design takes its cue from the line "And Truth severe, by Fairy fiction drest," a reference to the poetry that will follow from this renaissance. Gray notes his own poetic allusions to Spenser, Shakespeare, Milton, and "the succession of Poets after Milton's time," but it is "Spenser creating his fairies" (in the words of Blake's title) that Blake chooses for illustration. This aspect of Spenser's art had long captivated Blake, as one of his earliest poems shows: the "truth" to be found in "fairy dreams" is the subject of his "Imitation of Spenser" in the *Poetical Sketches*:

> Golden Apollo, that thro' heaven wide
>   Scatter'st the rays of light and truth's beams!
> In lucent words my darkling verses dight,
>   And wash my earthy mind in thy clear streams,
>   That wisdom may descend in fairy dreams.   (14)

The role of Arthur in *The Faerie Queene* might have added to Blake's sense of its pertinence to "The Bard," since Arthurian legend forms the background, or mythic context, of the Welsh story on which Gray's poem builds. "No more our long-lost Arthur we bewail," say the bards as the vision of the "genuine Kings" comes upon them, to which Gray adds a note that "It was the common belief of the Welch nation, that King Arthur was still alive in Fairy-Land, and should return again to reign over Britain." But although Blake found Arthurian legend pertinent to a proper understanding of "The Bard," it is not Arthur's part in

The Faerie Queene that he chooses to illustrate. In the center of Blake's design is Spenser himself, regarding a tiny figure in the palm of his hand—evidently a freshly created "fairy." Above him and to the right are two smaller figures that I take to represent "Truth severe" and "fairy Fiction." "Truth severe" stands primly to the left, gazing down at a book in his hand; "fairy Fiction" stands to the right, dressed in what appears to be a theatrical outfit, a loose scroll in his hand, his gaze upward. The contrast of scroll and book in Blake has already been alluded to—the book implying rigidity of doctrine, the scroll a creative product. Moreover, lest we should miss the virtues of this excellent fairy figure, two cherubs with horns play over his head.

Yet there is still something disturbing about "fairy Fiction." For one thing, he bears a strong resemblance in face and manner, as well as collar, to the Lord-Keeper of Story 4, Elizabeth's favorite. Further, he resembles the Spenser of Blake's series of "Heads of the Poets," done for Hayley's library while Blake was in Felpham from 1800 to 1803.[15] Blake's model was an engraving by George Vertue, which he followed quite closely with two exceptions: Blake's Spenser has an expression of supercilious elegance not present in his source, and whereas Vertue's Spenser wears no decoration, Blake's has about his neck a medallion containing a portrait of Queen Elizabeth. Encircling Spenser's head is a ring of five dancing fairies—more "Spirits of the Air"—and at either side of the portrait a small background figure. On the left Elizabeth, in regal dress, sits in a crescent moon and lifts her hand in a gesture of royal command; to the right stands a large, venerable man with staff—the shepherd-poet, apparently the recipient of her command. I believe the design synopsizes Blake's view of Spenser: the center portrait shows what Hayley wanted shown, a likeness of the "natural" man, as nearly as possible correct in historical detail. But imposed on this is the suggestion that Spenser was in real life too much the queen's man, a courtier quick with polished praise, and of insufficient poetic independence. The ring of fairies alludes to Spenser's real strength as a poet, his ability to build and people visionary worlds, to offer "wisdom" (again quoting Blake's "Imitation of Spenser") in

[15] These "Heads of the Poets," rarely reproduced, are all available in small monochrome reproductions (with brief and extremely interesting commentary by Mr. William Wells) in a booklet published by the William Morris Press Ltd., Wythenshawe, Manchester (n.d.). This booklet served as catalogue for a fine exhibition of Blake's heads (along with samples of the sources he used, where available) at the City Art Gallery of Manchester in 1969. I was fortunate enough to be able to see this exhibition, and wish that Mr. Wells's catalogue and commentary might be made more widely available.

"fairy dreams." Like the fairies at the beginning of "A Long Story," Spenser's fairies are "good builders"; they are good storytellers, like the fairy who dictated Blake's *Europe*. The pair of outer figures, Elizabeth and the shepherd-poet, expand the suggestions of the portrait into their visionary significance. The shepherd, an allusion to Spenser's alias Colin Clout and his use of the pastoral genre, is a visionary portrait of Spenser, just as the center picture is his natural portrait: he is calm, imposing, a recognizable cousin of Blake's other venerable bards. Elizabeth's moon alludes at once to her virginity—"chaste Cynthia," as she was depicted by her poets—and to the state called Beulah in Blake's mythology, associated with sexuality and femininity. As royal patroness Elizabeth encouraged the arts generously and successfully; but as maiden queen she imposed her will unhealthily, demanding a flirtatious attentiveness that impelled Spenser to address her in *The Shepheardes Calendar* ("Aprill") as "fayre Elisa, queene of shepheardes all" or, demeaning himself, to approach her, in "Colin Clout's Come Home Againe," as Godhead:

> But vaine it is to thinke, by paragone
> Of earthly things, to judge of things divine:
> Her power, her mercy, and her wisdome, none
> Can deeme, but who the Godhead can define.
> Why then do I, base shepheard bold and blind,
> Presume the things so sacred to prophane?
> More fit it is t'adore, with humble mind,
> The image of the heavens in shape humane.

Women always make poor rulers, in Blake's opinion; as inspiration they can enrich the poetic vision, but as dictators they can only divide the man and deaden the poet. Spenser's vision Blake certainly respected, but I think he felt that the greatest danger to that vision might be epitomized in the figure of a coyly demanding virgin queen.[16]

This view, then, would explain the implications of the slightly feminized "fairy Fiction." But the rest of Bard 12 seems to be devoted to those areas of Spenser's strength most admired by Blake—the "fairies" themselves. Blake illustrates two small scenes from *The Faerie Queene*, neither of them obviously perti-

[16] Compare Byron's opinion of Elizabeth, in *Don Juan*, Canto IX, stanza lxxxi:

> Her vile, ambiguous method of flirtation,
> And stinginess, disgrace her sex and station.

nent to the other or to Gray's poem. One scene shows Sir Guyon in the cave of
Mammon, stalked from behind by the "ugly feend":

> So soone as Mammon there arrivd, the dore
> To him did open and affoorded way;
> Him followed eke Sir Guyon evermore,
> Ne darkenesse him, ne daunger might dismay.
> Soone as he entred was, the dore streight way
> Did shutt, and from behind it forth there lept
> An ugly feend, more fowle then dismall day,
> The which with monstrous stalke behind him stept,
> And ever as he went, dew watch upon him kept.
>
> *(Faerie Queene*, II, vii, 26)

Blake is faithful in his details, showing Mammon, who indicates a pile of gleaming yellow gold; Sir Guyon advancing fearlessly; and the "feend," a diabolical
black creature with gold horns and batlike wings, stalking behind with hands
held ready to shove the knight forward. It is a fine little scene in itself, and
though by no means the center of the design, yet—partly because of the fine
coloring—it is the center of attention. The other pictured group shows that "man
of hell, that calls himselfe Despayre" (*Faerie Queene*, I, ix, 28). Blake again
follows Spenser's description of the scene:

> And him beside there lay upon the gras
> A dreary corse, whose life away did pas,
> All wallowd in his own yet luke-warme blood,
> That from his wound yet welled fresh, alas!
> In which a rusty knife fast fixed stood,
> And made an open passage for the gushing flood.
>
> *(Faerie Queene*, I, ix, 36)

And he further adds the later climax, in which Despair tempts the knight:

> He to him raught a dagger sharpe and keene,
> And gave it him in hand: his hand did quake.
>
> *(Faerie Queene*, I, ix, 51)

Blake shows all three figures: Despair handing the dagger to the knight, who
stands before him, his face buried in his hands; and the freshly bleeding body

106

of the man already fallen. The dagger is still in his chest, and bright blood gushes from the wound.

These two groups of figures represent a peculiar imaginative excursion on Blake's part. The episodes to which they refer are certainly powerful combinations of "Truth severe" and "fairy Fiction," but why did he choose these particular episodes, and why did he conflate episodes from two different books, risking possible confusion between the caves of Mammon and Despair and between Redcrosse and Guyon? That they are variously temptations to wealth and to despair might be a comment on Blake's own recent history—say, his encounters with Edwards. But more likely he wished merely to indicate that these are the stuff of Spenser's poetic art, indications of the variety of his visionary knowledge.

Design 13 illustrates Gray's conclusion, the bard's suicidal leap:

> . . . headlong, from the mountain's height,
> Deep in the roaring tide he plung'd to endless night.

But although Blake's figure is shown descending headfirst, he seems to be not so much falling as floating. A telling parallel may be seen in the figure of the resurrecting angel on the title page of Blake's illustrations to Blair's *Grave*,[17] which, as Damon notes, is itself a repetition of the resurrecting angel of *Night Thoughts* no. 19. The bard Blake shows us is not a mortal man in the act of suicide, but, as his posture and attitude reveal, a spiritual form to whom "the roaring tide" is irrelevant. He will be—indeed, already is—resurrected.

The final design of this long series is a complete departure from the text itself, and, as we shall see, acts as something of a conclusion and commentary. Blake entitles it "A Poor Goatherd in Wales," and shows the goatherd seated beneath a drooping tree, his downcast face paralleling that of one of his goats; he gazes absently before him, and in his hand, dropped limply by his side, is a pipe for music. The grass beneath him, while green, is trodden down; the distant hills are brown and bare. The total effect is of oppressed weariness and inactivity, of art and human life held still in a deadening sleep.

In Blake's hands, Gray's poem takes on a political theme much wider than that of the history of the English royal houses. I observed earlier that in at least two designs the spirits of the dead bards, who join "in dreadful harmony" with the speaking bard to "weave, with bloody hands, the tissue of [Edward's] line," are represented by Blake as a trio reminiscent of his three "Ancient Britons,"

---

[17] Reproduced in Damon, *Blake's Grave, A Prophetic Book* (Providence, R.I., 1963).

the subject of a picture Blake displayed at his exhibition in 1809 and discussed in his *Descriptive Catalogue*. The picture has long been lost, but Keynes notes that "Seymour Kirkup, who visited Blake's exhibition and afterwards wrote his memories of it for Swinburne, regarded this painting as Blake's masterpiece" (913). By 1809 these three had taken their places in Blake's still developing mythology, as a glance at Blake's discussion of them in his *Catalogue* will show (577-581). I doubt that one could ascertain exactly what place they had in Blake's thought in the late 1790's—one of the tasks of the *Vala* revisions was to work out the fourfold division of man—but a residuum of an earlier connection in Blake's mind with Gray's bard remains in the *Catalogue* discussion.

In the *Catalogue* "the three general classes of men who are represented by the most Beautiful, the most Strong, and the most Ugly" are associated with the reign of King Arthur: *"In the last Battle of King Arthur, only Three Britons escaped; these were the Strongest Man, the Beautifullest Man, and the Ugliest Man; these three marched through the field unsubdued, as Gods, and the Sun of Britain set, but shall arise again with tenfold splendor when Arthur shall awake from sleep, and resume his dominion over earth and ocean"* (577). Arthur's return is, of course, a vision in local historical terms of the Second Coming, or what Blake variously referred to as a return to the Golden Age (605) or a return to Eden (578). These three Britons were not, of course, living physical men, but rather representatives of mankind: the "small remnant" that failed to be "overwhelmed by brutal arms," escaping instead to "remain for ever unsubdued, age after age" (577). "Four Mighty Ones are in every Man," Blake writes at the outset of *The Four Zoas*, and their unity forms "The Universal Man" who is the subject of the long prophecy and whose "fall into Division & his Resurrection to Unity" (264) forms its argument. The *Catalogue* alludes to this poem, saying of the "Three Britons" (and one other) that their history "is a subject of great sublimity and pathos. The Artist has written it under inspiration, and will, if God please, publish it" (578). "In the mean time," Blake continues, he has painted this picture of the ancient Britons, "which supposes that in the reign of that British Prince, who lived in the fifth century, there were remains of those naked Heroes in the Welch Mountains; they are there now, Gray saw them in the person of his bard on Snowdon; there they dwell in naked simplicity; happy is he who can see and converse with them above the shadows of generation and death" (578). The history of King Arthur, then, is an alternate "vision" of that sublime and pathetic history of the divided Albion, which is in turn an alternate version of man's fall from happiness as variously told in Christian, classical, and countless other terms. "The stories of Arthur are the acts of Albion, applied to a Prince of the fifth century" (578).

The point here is that in Gray's story of the murdered bards and their prophesied return at a time of great artistic (and thus human) renaissance, Blake found a powerful analogue to the same history that he was developing in his own vision. The three bards of the Gray designs are not the three "Ancient Britons"—the Gray bards are often more like punishing furies—nor am I certain that when they do parallel those three Britons they take on the same special meanings each had in 1809;[18] but a connection is there by context, and it is important to Blake's reading of Gray's poem. In Bard 2 and Bard 11 the traits of strength, beauty, and ugliness (as Blake explained these traits in his catalogue) are perhaps roughly discernible, especially if we view the turned head as the "ugly" one; but the tempera painting displayed in 1809 shows four bards, and the "Britons" are treated in an altogether separate picture. As Blake's own thinking shifted and developed over the years, so did his reading of Gray's poem.

It is in terms of the fall into disunity and the hoped-for return that we can best understand the mixed vision—"single" and "double"—of the oak, cave, and torrent, and the point of that final picture of the weary goatherd. As oak, cave, and torrent are nature deprived of human voice and song, so he is mankind "asleep" like Arthur and Albion, mankind after the time of the "naked heroes" and before the time of the great bardic return, weary of war but not yet at peace. When the goatherd is ready—and able—to raise the musical instrument at his side and use it for prophetic song, he will awake from sleep and return to life; and in his individual existence, his own variation of the "eternal" story, the renaissance will have come, and nature around him will spring to life because he will see the life in it: "As a man is, So he Sees" (793). But until that time he permits and shares in the oppression and death which has for so long been the story of English history, and therefore remains, like his animal, bent down toward the earth. That Blake could not agree with Gray about the date and form of the great renaissance (it did not come when Elizabeth ascended the throne) was of secondary concern; it was much more important that Gray understood in this

---

18 For Blake's source in the *Welch Triades* see Damon's *Dictionary*, p. 443. It is worth noticing that the *Myvyrian Archailogy*, Blake's source for the descriptions of his strong, ugly, and beautiful survivors, did not begin publication until 1801, though presumably Blake's friend Pughe (the *Archailogy*'s main editor) might well have shown the passage to Blake long before publishing it.

poem the fundamental truth of the matter, for he understood who the bards were, what their importance was, and that they must return in their first glory. In depicting the bards, not the Tudors, as those returned "genuine Kings," Blake has simply pressed Gray one stage farther toward full vision.

"THE FATAL SISTERS"

In line with the growing interest in things ancient, with the erecting of artificial ruins and the popularity of the poetry attributed to Ossian—indeed, with the broad preference for the "sublime" over the regular—Gray wrote "The Bard" and translated a series of three medieval poems, two from the Norse and one from the Welsh. Blake, who admired Ossian and had himself been educated as a student by the Gothic of Westminster Abbey, might be expected to find these poems particularly attractive; and in fact, as observed in the commentary on his illustrations to "The Bard," some of his most daringly conceived designs occur here, though some of his least finished as well. Aside from "The Bard," the poem that seems to have most struck his imagination was "The Fatal Sisters," one of the translations from the Norse.

When Gray first mentions the Bards as weavers ("With me in dreadful harmony they join,/ And weave . . ."), he notes, "See the Norwegian ode that follows," referring to his translation of "The Fatal Sisters."[19] This poem takes its subject from a battle in eleventh-century Ireland, and from the legend that on the day of battle, as Gray recounts in his preface to the poem, "a native of Caithness in Scotland saw, at a distance, a number of persons on horseback, riding full speed toward a hill, and seeming to enter into it. Curiosity led him to follow them; till looking through an opening in the rocks, he saw twelve gigantic figures resembling women: they were all employed about a loom, and as they wove, they sung the following dreadful song." The poem is that song. Gray added a note explaining the myth of the valkyries: "The *Valkyrieur* were female Divinities, servants of *Odin* (or *Woden*), in the Gothic mythology. Their name signifies *Chusers of the slain.* They were mounted on swift horses, with drawn swords in their hands; and in the throng of battle selected such as were destined to slaughter, and conducted them to *Valkalla*, the hall of *Odin*, or paradise of the Brave; where they attended the banquet, and served the departed Heroes with

---

[19] *Complete Poems of Gray*, ed. Starr and Hendrickson, pp. 211-215, give the history of the poem, a literal translation from the Latin that Gray used, and some explanations of Gray's procedures.

horns of mead and ale." Whereas Gray leaves the number open—when he does mention a number, it is twelve—Blake almost always pictures the sisters as three, perhaps conflating them in his mind with the three Norns, or Fates. Only once do there appear to be more, and that is in the illustration to the opening lines of the poem. Paul Miner, in "Two Notes on Sources," calls attention to the many ways in which the sisters—sometimes as "twelve"—entered Blake's later symbolism, with their "shuttles," "black Woof of Death," and "webs of war." Certainly the poem had powerful visionary significance for Blake, and his dark reading of it is delineated in the designs.

The design for the title page is heavily schematic: three tall, handsome women, almost identical in features, posture, and dress, stand close together, hand in hand, and stare somewhat emptily out at the reader; a tall spear stands at each end of the group, enclosing it. Crossing all these vertical lines and further unifying them are two lines of color: the yellow of the scalelike mailed vests and of the sandals. The effect is one of formidable discipline, of woman dehumanized in military review. Here, as in each of their appearances, they act in severe martial unity.

A simple design surrounds the "Advertisement," in which Gray explains that these translations had originally been intended as part of a now-discarded *History of English Poetry*. But the simplicity, on this occasion, is of a special order. One large figure of a retreating muse fills the entire page, her wings spread to the two upper corners of the page, her feet and gown trailing out at the lower left. The inserted "Advertisement" crosses her back from shoulder to hip as if she were carrying it. The design is entitled simply "A Muse," and is brightly colored: the entire background is a sunny yellow, the muse's gown pink and her wings pinkish-blue. There are two similar designs in the illustrations to Young's *Night Thoughts*, one of which (no. 127) depicts the risen Christ soaring "Triumphant past the Crystal ports of Light"; the other, even more similar (no. 428), depicts "A swift Archangel, with his golden Wing," who "sweeps the Stars and Suns aside." We have what must have been for Blake a vision of enormous power and glory, and his incorporation of it into this series of designs for "The Fatal Sisters" would seem to be a compliment to the vision of the poem.

I think there is further significance to be found in this design, however, when it is viewed in conjunction with the next, "Sigtryg with the silken beard," a figure identified in Gray's Preface (which the design surrounds) as one of the participants in that eleventh-century Irish battle. He strides forward, a gigantic and powerful man in gold armor, with a pale yellow beard that streams to his knees. The massive spear in his right hand is rude, almost like a club, and his crown is of the primitive, spiked form that Blake often gives to rude, ancient, or tyrannous royalty.[20] Yet his bearing, clear eyes, and flowing beard are more closely related to those of the stately Welsh bard in Bard 1; the background against which he is shown consists simply of a strip of green ground and a wide blue sky, and indeed the total effect of the design is less terrible than beautiful. Sigtryg is a warrior, but like the ancient Britons who *"marched through the field unsubdued, as Gods, and the Sun of Britain set"* (577) he is part of Britain's "ancient glory." Both he and the muse of the facing design are single giant figures, brightly colored, drawn to comparable scale; the one departs as the other advances, for with the ravaging wars that led to Arthur's "death, or sleep" (577) the *"Sun of Britain"* did set—the bards were killed, the muses "left the antient love/ That bards of old enjoy'd" (11); in the yellow radiance of the departing muse we see that sunset. That she should bear with her a projected and rejected *History of English Poetry* adds gratuitous corroboration of the point.

With design 4 the mood begins to change, for here Blake stages our entry into the vision of the native of Caithness—a kind of "lost Traveller's Dream under the Hill" (771), and indeed a satanic vision. A young man stands astonished as two figures on horseback appear to ride full speed into the side of the mountain next to him. We see only the backs of the horses and one rider (the other is hidden by the text box), but it is interesting that the coloring of the native's tunic catches in its stripes the rather bloody red of the riders' outfits, arguing a subtle union of watcher and scene.

Design 5 was mentioned earlier as the one illustration in which there appear to be more than three "Sisters." The opening lines of the poem are those illustrated:

> Now the storm begins to lour,
> (Haste, the loom of hell prepare,)
> Iron sleet of arrowy shower
> Hurtles in the darkened air.

Blake shows a dark sky filled with hurtling arrows that are directed to their unseen targets by a row of almost identical seated women disappearing into the right margin. Parts of the design are only roughly finished, and so emphasize Blake's

---

[20] See Eton 7, 8; Adversity 3; Bard 7; Sisters 8.

visual point: the meaningless, random cruelty of the rain of the arrows, and the monstrousness of female forms reduced to a monotonous curve.[21]

Design 6 illustrates the lines on which Fuseli commented in 1800, saying that if they were vividly pictured "We should equally loath the fancy that bred, and the work that exposed them to our eye." Blake's picture is vivid enough: the three women bend forward with fierce vigor over their weaving, using swords "dipt in gore" as shuttles and winding about them the entrails of the battle's dead. Below, making a row of moaning weights, are four inverted, disembodied warriors' heads. The whole illustrates the following lines:

> See the grisly texture grow!
> ('Tis of human entrails made,)
> And the weights that play below
> Each a gasping warrior's head.
>
> Shafts for shuttles, dipt in gore,
> Shoot the trembling cords along.
> Sword, that once a monarch bore,
> Keep the tissue close and strong.

At the bottom right are the bare sketches of what appear to be three other heads, perhaps those of onlookers, perhaps replacements for the weights. They are, however, unfinished and uncolored.

Design 7, too, appears to be unfinished at the bottom, where we see a group of half-drawn figures being trampled by the hooves of the sisters' horses. The most finished of these heads is a close study of a larger, more fully worked head in the next design; this is, so far as I have observed, the only time in the Gray designs that such duplication occurs. Above, forming the main movement of the page, the same three sisters spring down to the earth on their horses; the horses' back hooves are still high in the air, indicating that this is the end of a swift descending flight. About the group swirl reddish clouds of war, bearing the form of dust but the color of blood.

In design 8 the same three sisters ride forward on horseback, their arms raised

[21] In "Two Notes on Sources" Paul Miner points out (p. 205) the verbal echo of Gray's "Iron sleet of arrowy shower / Hurtles in the darkened air" in *The Four Zoas*, Night the Seventh (b), line 159; but the whole of the passage containing this line has a bearing on Blake's understanding of the theme of war both in this poem and in "The Triumphs of Owen."

as they point straight ahead, oblivious of the carnage beneath them. Blake's title says they are "The Fatal Sisters riding thro the Battle" and reminds us "they are called in some Northern poems 'Choosers of the Slain.'" Their pointing fingers may, then, be taken to be indicating the next to die; Blake has marked the line "Soon a king shall bite the ground," and shows him literally doing so beneath their horses, savage with fury and pain. His is the head Blake had also worked into the preceding design, and a close look at the original manuscript reveals that he still had trouble with details of the mouth, for it has been erased and redrawn several times. The final effect is chilling in its bestiality.

The ninth design is reminiscent of the first, for again we see the three sisters in parallel action, this time in identical stride mounting identical horses. As they are seen from the back, there are not even the slight variations of face to distinguish them, though (as always) the shade of hair differs from one to the next. Again the main lines are vertical, though again the gold mail cuts across the page in a horizontal line of color.

The final design Blake entitled simply "A Battle," and it is a vision of ruthless carnage. Warriors on horseback rear over unhorsed figures beneath them; swords on both sides are arched back in powerful swing. All humanity and discrimination are lost in the passion of bloody opposition, which seems to offer neither hope nor purpose. Blake left the design entirely uncolored like an engraving, except for faint blues in the metal and very faint buff coloring in some of the skin.

It is for this composition that Blake borrowed most heavily from his friend Flaxman, for the two major figures in Blake's design reveal their parentage in two of Flaxman's line engravings illustrating Homer's *Iliad*, published by J. Mathews on January 12, 1795 (although Flaxman's title page is dated 1793). Plate 11 of the *Iliad* shows Ajax with his sword swung back over his head in a gesture parallel to that of the attacker of Sisters 10; the victim of Sisters 10, a striking backward-bent figure, parallels another victim of Ajax in Flaxman's twentieth design. The handling of the mouth in Blake's and Flaxman's victims is remarkably similar as well, and in each the ugly regression of carnage is emphasized by bracing the foot of the victim, apparently soon to die, against the prostrate body of one already dead. Flaxman's compositions are on the whole lucid, restrained, almost serene in their dancelike quality; but Blake chose his models from two of the sculptor's most violent designs, renderings of that Homeric glorification of prowess in battle that made Blake reject Homer as one of those "silly Greek & Latin slaves of the Sword" aligned with all who would "depress Mental & prolong Corporeal War" (480). As he wrote bitterly in his copy of Bacon's *Essays*, "What do these Knaves mean by Virtue? Do they mean War & its horrors & its Heroic Villains?" (400). Blake's own mental war with misdirected art was part of what lay behind his judgment that "it is the Classics, & not Goths nor Monks, that Desolate Europe with Wars" (778), by which he meant—at least in part—to repudiate the notion that physical courage exercised in human slaughter had anything whatsoever to recommend it. So-called "Holy wars" are no better: "God never makes one man murder another, nor one nation" (388). The allusions to Flaxman's work suggest that by this time at least—if not earlier—Blake knew his volume's ultimate destination. I take it that he is at once complimenting his friend and reminding him "how to see," reminding him by telescoped allusions that corporeal war is never glorious; it is always a reduction of the Human Form Divine into "what is truly Ugly, the incapability of intellect. . . . The Ugly Man acts from love of carnage, and delight in the savage barbarities of war, rushing with sportive precipitation into the very jaws of the affrighted enemy" (580).

It has been noted that Gray, where he suggests numbers at all, indicates an entire "band" of murdered poets in "The Bard" and a full twelve "Fatal Sisters"; but for Blake both bards and sisters are three. And as it was Gray's figure of the bards as weavers that most caught Blake's imagination in the former poem, so it is the association of weavers with the three fates that seems to have dominated his vision of these valkyries. In his later borrowing of this weaving imagery for his own poems, Blake associated it with blood, evil, and destruction; and aside from the reappearing triads, it is the focus on blood and carnage that seems most to have united Blake's visualizations of the two poems, as these visualizations are communicated in his designs. Certainly the two poems were closely associated in Gray's mind as well; his note points to the association (see above, p. 110), and it may be seen also in the language and truncated tetrameters of the poems. Compare, for example, these lines from "The Bard"

> Half of thy heart we consecrate.
> (The web is wove. The work is done.)

with these from "The Fatal Sisters":

> Sisters, weave the web of death.
> Sisters, cease: The work is done.

Blake shared the association, and it explains in "The Bard" what the association with the "Ancient Britons" did not, namely the way in which the murdered bards seemed to be as much vindictive furies as vestiges of the union and greatness of former times. Something of both attitudes may be sensed in Gray's language, and Blake has picked up both and responded to both in his own terms as well as Gray's: this accounts in part for the vast uneasiness and grim power that some of the designs communicate, especially some of those to "The Bard." Where the associations are not active, as apparently in Sisters 2 and 3, the tone is entirely different: a soaring muse can be a reminder of the power of visionary insight, the handsome Sigtryg of the beauty and strength of which the human form is capable. However, that the man and not his occupation has the capability of beauty, the horror of the subsequent designs liberally attests.

"THE DESCENT OF ODIN"

This poem tells the story of the descent of the god Odin to "Hela's drear abode," which Gray identifies in a note as "the hell of the Gothic nations." At the "eastern gate" he stops and pronounces a "Runic rhyme" to summon "the prophetic Maid," whose identity the poem never makes very clear. Odin's questions and the prophetess' unwilling responses make up the remainder of the poem: Odin's son Balder shall die at his brother's hand, we learn, and another brother, a "wondrous boy" yet unborn, will avenge him. In the last lines the prophetess recognizes her questioner, who until now has called himself simply "A Traveller to thee unknown," and refuses to answer further. Odin in turn addresses her as "No boding Maid of skill divine/ . . . nor Prophetess of good,/ But mother of the giant-brood!" She sinks back into the earth vowing that she shall not again be disturbed "Till *Lok* has burst his tenfold chain"—that is, until the "Twilight of the Gods." Blake's illustrations to the poem again draw their subjects from its characters and action rather than its language.

The designs to the poem open with the title page illustration, a magnificent vision of "The serpent who girds the earth"; it coils splendidly, a grander and more terrible version of the serpent of *The Marriage of Heaven and Hell*, plate 20. One would expect it to be similarly vividly colored; but Blake has left the entire design in gray pen and brush on white, perhaps in deference to the restrained coloring of the designs around it, perhaps to intensify the sense of line that dominates the designs for "The Bard" and the three translations. (Another grotesque, barely visible, is sketched in pencil half inside the serpent's mouth—apparently the "Wolvish Dog" who accompanies the serpent in design 10.)

Design 2 offers Blake's list of illustrations, surrounded by a vision of three "Spectres," as Blake's title identifies them. One is a smaller, distant, butterflylike creature, another a moth with brilliant wings figured with stars and two rings of concentric circles. This second moth is ridden by a tiny female creature, mostly hidden by the moth's wings. The third spectre, the largest, is a weirdly collapsed version of a bat. Springing up and forward from its forehead is a naked girl, the same who flees across the waters on the title page of *Visions of the Daughters of Albion*, but it is unclear in this drawing whether she flees the spectre or directs it; in either case the pair convey a sexual meaning aligned with the images of earth and death, grave and underworld that pervade the designs to this poem.

Design 3 illustrates the opening lines and shows Odin approaching hell and being met by the "dog of darkness," who provides most of the visual interest and energy of the picture. In design 4 Odin sits before the "portals nine of hell" pronouncing "The thrilling verse that wakes the dead." The picture is dark and closely packed, and while it illustrates with fairly realistic fidelity the action of Gray's lines, a comparison of Blake's design with the parallel illustration published in the 1790 text[22] reveals how different two such "realistic" portrayals can be. By comparison the tone of the 1790 design is open and gentlemanly, the total effect almost gracious, whereas Blake's vision is dim and foreboding, the coloring heavy with dark mossy-greens that seem to bespeak long-damp earth. The one touch of light comes from the few flames that begin to emerge from the ground where the prophetess will arise, and which glint faintly on Odin's shield.

The composition of design 5 offers a daring and remarkable perspective: the page is largely blocked by the huge figure of Odin, who stands with his back to us, spear in one hand and shield in the other, with feet spread wide, the text box filling no more than a space on his back. Between his huge legs we see the prophetess who rises before him, only her head and shoulders above the ground. Her eyes are red, her face and the flames that spread around her pale blue. The design is otherwise largely uncolored, and it is perhaps unfinished as well. The horse, for example, is seen in the same posture as in the preceding design, and shows the same portion of head and neck; but here it has been barely sketched in. Blake may have felt that in view of the bold conception of the design a highly

[22] The picture is unsigned, and I have so far been unable to discover who executed it. There are in all seven illustrations in this edition, two signed "William Hamilton."

finished surface would be inappropriate, and so wished to leave rather the impression of a vigorous sketch. The "unfinished" designs are in general the most audacious.

The next two designs again follow descriptions ready-made in the poem: design 6 shows the goblet and shield to which the prophetess directs Odin's attention; Blake's one innovation is to add in a sweeping curve a female figure who carries the goblet and gazes at the shield, giving movement to the design and unifying it formally. Design 7 shows us the "wondrous boy" who shall avenge Balder. The prophetess foretells that he

> . . . ne'er shall comb his raven hair
> Nor wash his visage in the stream,
> Nor see the sun's departing beam,
> Till he on *Hoder*'s corse shall smile

—a reference to the legend that he killed his enemy before he was a day old.[23] Blake, presumably unaware of this legend (it goes unmentioned by Gray), shows a young man seated thoughtfully beside a river, combing his hair as the distant sun sets behind him. It is a rather dull composition; indeed, the effect is almost comic in view of the big comb and morose stodginess of the boy using it. Perhaps Blake wished to suggest that he was less marvelous than the prophetess believed him to be.

The next two designs return to the heroic manner and proportions of the earlier ones. Design 8 shows Odin with his hand raised over the head of the prophetess, now seen standing next to him, her robe and hair flung out flamelike. He is perhaps indicating something beyond, not depicted in the illustration but described in the poem by his question, "What Virgins these, in speechless woe,/ That bend to earth their solemn brow . . . ?" She does not answer, but suddenly recognizes her questioner for the god he is, and looks at him aghast. This appears to be the moment Blake is showing: question and recognition coming together; the two huge figures fill the page, again without a discernible background. In design 9 we see them for the last time, Odin departing on horseback, looking down on the prophetess as she sinks back into the ground, only her head and lifted arm visible as she warns the god that she will not be disturbed again. Odin's figure is dark, hers only lightly sketched, with a few flames of color about her hair.

The final design moves back outside the action of the poem in a return to the

[23] The legend is mentioned in *Complete Poems of Gray*, ed. Starr and Hendrickson, p. 215.

opening figure of the world-serpent, here joined by the demonic "dog of darkness" to make a kind of frame for the strange, dark story. Blake entitles the picture "The Serpent & the Wolvish Dog, two terrors in the Northern Mythology," and here we see them poised eye to eye, the fully coiled serpent above, the snapping dog's head below, both wrapped in tongues of flame. The frame reinforces the mythological context of the poem and adds to its strangeness: each culture has its own terrors, Blake seems to remind us, and each person his own vision of them.

"THE TRIUMPHS OF OWEN"

This poem is "a Fragment," and a short one, allowing for only six designs, of which the first, fourth, and fifth again depict the violence and human turmoil of war. The second and third, on facing pages, depict the banquet at which the story of the war is told, and the final design makes, as so often, a summary commentary. The title page shows "A Standard Bearer fainting in the routed battle": a figure of Blake's imagination rather than Gray's, he is a large, armored warrior who bears a vast, swirling, flame-colored flag and runs, falling forward, over the sketchily drawn prostrate bodies of his fellow soldiers. He and the one fallen figure whose face is visible wear expressions of grief, pain, and terror.[24]

The two illustrations that follow are quiet ones: design 2 shows "A Festal Board" at which a group of men sit quietly, served by another who carries a large pitcher; design 3, facing this, shows "The Bard singing Owen's praise," evidently the entertainment that follows or accompanies the feast of the preceding illustration. The two form a visual as well as thematic sequence. The bard himself is like the figure on the title page to "The Bard"—large and calm, dressed in his blue starred robe of office; but it should be noticed, in view of the song he sings, that Blake places this bard in a dark corner, with his eyes closed.

The next two designs return to the depiction of war and again form a kind of visual sequence, though each design is technically self-contained. Design 4 takes its title from two lines also marked in the text:

> Dauntless on his native sands
> The dragon-son of Mona stands.

---

[24] This standard-bearer closely resembles one in the background of Blake's 1809 "Whore of Babylon" (reproduced in Keynes, *William Blake's Illustrations to the Bible: A Catalogue* [London and New York, 1957]) also a scene of carnage. In *Milton* (plate 38, line 26) Babylon wears a "scarlet Veil woven in pestilence & war."

This is Owen, a helmeted and armed warrior who advances terribly toward the center of the page, waving shield and sword, while before him fall two grotesquely contorted naked victims who virtually fill the right side of the page. The design is done in gray and white, except for the fiery feather of Owen's helmet, which is a flaming blood-red reminiscent of the war colors of—for example—Bard 9, Sisters 4, and Owen 1.

Facing the warrior from the adjoining illustration (design 5) are a group of frightened warriors, terrified behind their shields, exhibiting "Fear to stop and shame to fly" before their mighty opponent. The composition of these two combined pages—designs 4 and 5—bears a strong resemblance to that of Flaxman's illustration of "Ulysses killing the suitors" in the *Odyssey* series (also, by the way, the depiction of a man who stands, like Gray's Owen, "dauntless on his native sands"). It is hard to establish borrowing in a composition such as this, yet the design does again suggest Blake's thorough familiarity with Flaxman's designs.

Significantly, the closing lines of the fragment[25] provide Blake with a particularly fine opportunity for the kind of visualized personifications that he so often delights in:

> There Confusion, Terror's child;
> Conflict fierce, and Ruin wild
> Agony that pants for breath;
> Despair and honorable death.

But Blake ignores them: he does not need them. We recall that in the past he turned to the figurative language of the poem only when its vision seemed to him to reside there rather than in the literal purport of the poem. But what could be more a vision of "Confusion," "Terror," "Ruin," or "Agony" than battle itself, and what could portray them more vividly than the sight of embattled men? Here the events themselves are their own terrible meaning; "vision" can take them no farther.

In view of this reading of Blake's intention, the final illustration to the fragment is particularly interesting, for there we see "The Liberal Man inviting the traveller into his house," a reference, apparently, to the liberality of Owen mentioned in the poem's opening lines but then lost in the praise of his warlike deeds:

[25] These lines are mostly Gray's invention, as he here goes outside his source (*Complete Poems of Gray*, ed. Starr and Hendrickson, p. 221).

Lord of every regal art,
Liberal hand, and open heart.

Blake's two figures seem, however, to be members of the banquet at which the song is sung rather than participants in the action of the song; for we see them— or men very like them—seated at the table in design 2, to the right of the text box. (The Liberal Man may almost certainly be identified there, and the travel- ler, though somewhat less heavily bearded, appears to be essentially the same man.)

This concluding design acts as a quiet but thorough repudiation of the human relationships and values implicit in the rest of the poem; in place of violence and fear, even in place of their poetic celebration, we see dramatized generosity to a stranger, the epitome of humane benevolence since Homer and the Good Samaritan. It seems pertinent that the Liberal Man is rather like Christ in stance and dress; a gentle, white-bearded man, he stands barefoot in a softly flowing robe and gestures gently with both hands toward the steps of his home. Approach- ing him is the traveller, a familiar figure in Blake's art: his hat is in one hand, his walking stick in the other, and he steps with equal gentleness toward the offered door.

The total effect of this closing composition is supremely restful, as in a world of peace: the simplified background shows only blue sky, green grass, and trees, so that the scene is generalized out of particular time or place; no detail of the architecture of the house is shown, only two completely plain steps that lead into it. Blake's illustration, with quiet irony, concludes the warlike poem by remind- ing the reader of its peaceful opening lines. We see not an event, but rather a state of being that stands in ironic contrast to the preceding pictures and lines.

"ODE FOR MUSIC"

We now leave the translations and come to the next to last poem of this middle group, Gray's "Ode for Music" (that is, an ode to be set to music) written for "the INSTALLATION of his Grace Augustus-Henry Fitzroy, Duke of Grafton" as Chancellor of the University of Cambridge in 1769, only two years before Gray's death. It is not a particularly inspired poem, nor did Gray have a very high opinion of it;[26] but he felt obliged to contribute to the installation ceremonies

[26] See *Complete Poems of Gray*, ed. Starr and Hendrickson, pp. 226-227.

because Grafton had obtained for him the Regius Professorship of Modern History at Cambridge.

Blake rightly regards this as Fame's poem, and accordingly his first and last illustrations to it show Fame first descending to earth, then at the end again ascending. The descent is an interesting one, for Blake alludes to the traditional goddess with double trumpets, characterized as follows in Milton's *Samson*:

> Fame, if not double-faced, is double-mouthed,
> And with contrary blast proclaims most deeds;
> On both his wings, one black, the other white,
> Bears greatest names in his wild aery flight.
>
> (*Samson*, lines 971-974)

The wings of Blake's goddess are both faint yellow, touched with gray, and while there is quite a bit of gray shadowing on the left wing, it is not enough to indicate in itself a "black" side to the lady.[27] She has, however, double trumpets—one in each hand—and as she descends she touches the earth with her right foot, perhaps pertinent here as the spiritual foot, indicating spiritual approach. The earth on which she alights is represented not as grass or dirt or otherwise "natural" ground, but rather as a series of uncolored buildings that line the bottom of the page. Those on her right are chiefly domes and spires; on her left are two pyramids (one rather narrower and taller than the other, and so perhaps an obelisk), almost always evil symbols for Blake. (A star hangs over Fame's head, and four others adorn the sky on her right, one shooting upward toward her.)

We may perhaps be able to say, then, that in Blake's eyes Fame descends to earth mainly through institutions: at worst, oppressive and evil ones like those out of which the pyramids were conceived and built, at best those that willingly support the imaginative art of a Gothic cathedral or public displays such as the

---

[27] The figure of Fame with double trumpets was of course widely available throughout the medieval period, as in Boccaccio and Chaucer; but Blake could have been reminded of it by Bentley's illustrations to Gray, where Bentley wittily depicts "Fame in the shape of Mr. Pitt" (from "A Long Story") puffing heavily on two long trumpets similar to the ones in this design.

Students of Blake's iconography should notice that the same ominous buildings that greet Fame as she descends also lie in the background of "The Virgin and Child in Egypt," a tempera painting done in 1810, now in the Victoria and Albert Museum. There, too, domes and spires stand on the Virgin's right, pyramids on her left.

portable frescos that Blake was to advocate a few years later. It is interesting, and perhaps significant, that for Blake Fame is neither good nor bad, nor does she have—of herself—a good or bad side, apparently. Rather she is a spiritual creature who, in her descent to earth, may be put to good or bad uses: the builder of pyramids seeks fame through stone monuments raised by the labor of an oppressed people; the creative artist welcomes fame as the rightful acknowledgment of his divine imagination.

The second design is brightly simple, showing only a long curled green tendril that curves in a "C" around the box of Blake's illustration titles, unembellished except for a colorful bird perching on it at center bottom, throat pointed straight up as it sings with all its might. The bare tendril would ordinarily be a rather ominously snakelike figure in Blake's symbology, but here it is clearly in the control of the lively little bird, as Jove was controlled by music in Poesy 4. Blake may wish to suggest a relationship between his art (the bird) and this ode (the tendril) if, as would seem to be the case, there was relatively little in the poem to attract his approval: the rather undiscriminating parade of the already famous, and the effort to raise Grafton to join their number, must have seemed to Blake a trivial occupation for any poet.

The ode opens with lines supposedly sung by Milton from "on high," whence he and Newton and other great former students of Cambridge admire their Alma Mater: Milton orders away "Comus," "Ignorance," and other evil creatures, then recalls his own early days at the college. As he concludes there appears a sanctimonious procession of "High Potentates, and Dames of royal birth,/ And mitred fathers"—the illustrious dead founders and supporters of Cambridge— who together intone lines asserting the strenuousness of their obligations:

> What is grandeur, what is Power?
> Heavier toil, superior pain

for which their "bright reward" is to be the sweetness of "The still small voice of Gratitude."

Last in this procession is "The venerable Marg'ret," Countess of Richmond and Derby, whose double claims, first as founder of two of the colleges and second through her family alliance with Tudors and Beauforts (from both of which lines Grafton also claimed descent), make her the appropriate speaker for the final stanzas welcoming the duke to his new position.

Design 3 is the first to illustrate material drawn from the poem directly, and shows "A Genius" driving away "Comus & his midnight crew." Surrounded by purplish flames and lightnings, she scatters before her a serpent-bottomed "Servitude that hugs her chains" and a pink "painted Flatt'ry" (Blake gives her heavy makeup), whose right arm and hand are shaped into the sketchy form of a snake. These are joined by two other less certainly identifiable figures from Gray's list.

Design 4 is divided through the middle by a roughly horizontal white cloud above which "Newton's self bends from his state sublime" to listen as "Milton struck the deep-ton'd shell" beneath. About Newton's head are four large stars; Milton sits on a chair between a bare tendril on one side and a disproportionately large yellow sunflower and white lily on the other. One may remember that these are two of the three flowers celebrated in the *Songs of Experience*, the lily for her delight in love, the sunflower for its aspirations toward that "sweet golden clime" of eternity after death.[28] The action of this picture, however, takes place in eternity, when a Newton might be supposed to listen appreciatively to a Milton, as in Blake's own version of eternity at the end of *Jerusalem*, when there appear reconciled in heaven "Bacon & Newton & Locke, & Milton & Shakspear & Chaucer" (745). The ominous tendril at Milton's side may allude to Milton's errors and offer advance notice of his return to earth—the subject of Blake's next great prophecy—to correct these errors through Blake's poetic voice.

The fifth design is an inconclusive one. The center of the picture is framed by uncolored sky above, water below, and a tree at each side, both bare of branches and one (at left) extending its branchlike roots into the water. The text box dominates the scene within this frame, with a yellow crescent moon above and a Gothic tower, perhaps from Cambridge, behind to the right. In front of the tower, in the foreground, Milton walks head down, folded arms wrapped in his gown. One assumes it must be Milton, since the lines on which the illustration is based are the lines of Milton's song, to which Newton listens in the preceding design. But the Milton shown here bears little resemblance to the one of the facing page: this is no spiritual Milton, no spiritual scene. Blake quotes in his own title to the picture two lines, out of order, from Milton's "song" in Gray:

---

[28] Note another interesting connection with the Young designs: in no. 87, where Young speaks of *lilies* drooping in the sunlight, Blake shows a *sunflower* with a tiny form emerging, its arms stretched out eagerly to Apollo, who nonetheless passes unnoticing through the heavens.

> I woo'd the gleam of Cynthia silver-bright
> Where willowy Camus lingers with delight.[29]

But as Gray himself had Milton's own lines in mind as he wrote this stanza in imitation of him (Gray's editor Mason notes that it is written in the "metre which he fixed upon for the stanza of his Christmas hymn")[30] Blake may in this illustration have had in mind also the lines from "Lycidas" in which the river Cam personifies Cambridge, Edward King's alma mater: "Next *Camus*, reverend Sire, went footing slow/ . . . Ah! Who hath reft (quoth he) my dearest pledge?" Blake would then be drawing together into one image Milton and the "Camus" of Milton's elegy.

There remain nagging inconsistencies: the moon, silver in Gray, is colored yellow by Blake—in itself not remarkable, since Blake never felt obliged to adhere to all the details of Gray's descriptions. On the other hand, the wooing of a chaste silver "Cynthia" would be questionable in Blakean terms, a taint that is eliminated by the yellow color Blake in fact chooses for her, so that one might conclude from this that Blake wishes to portray the "wooer" as contemplative melancholy in its best sense. Yet the bareness of the two trees on either side of the foreground would seem to belie this view. And the issue is further complicated in that the background "sky" that one would expect to see through the branches is uncolored, whereas the sky beneath them—surrounding the moon and extending down to the skyline—is colored a strong blue. Yet the answer cannot be that the foliage, though not colored or drawn in, may be assumed to be blocking the "sky," since the top of the Gothic tower, which extends above the branches, is fully drawn and colored. The picture remains in all a puzzling one.

In design 6 "Great Edward, with the lilies on his brow" sweeps through the center of the page, lilies adorning his hair and dropping from each hand; at either side are others of Gray's list of great men and women. In design 7 we see "the venerable Marg'ret" leaning from her "golden cloud"—Blake is faithful to the color—admonishing in motherly fashion a young man in academic robes who stands reverently before her. It is the great moment toward which the poem has built, but Blake's visualization of it seems somewhat deflating.

Design 8 shows personified "Granta" (the old name for the river Cam) pre-

---

[29] Blake varies Gray's "Oft woo'd" to "I woo'd," but I take this to have no special significance; rather, Blake has clarified Gray's syntax by giving "woo'd" its understood subject: "I trod your level lawn,/Oft woo'd. . . ."

[30] Quoted in *Complete Poems of Gray*, ed. Starr and Hendrickson, p. 227.

senting the "laurel wreath" to the duke: she stands still and large at the left of the page, he still and a little smaller to the right. Both their countenances are stony, and Blake's coloring—white robes for the river, black robes for the duke—emphasizes the rigidity of the design.

The poem's next to last design illustrates lines spoken by Margaret: in counseling the new chancellor to remain watchful and honorable through difficult times, Gray has her adopt the metaphor of helmsman guiding his ship with "watchful eye" through the "wide waves." He should

> Nor fear the rocks, nor seek the shore:
> The star of Brunswick smiles serene,
> And gilds the horrors of the deep.

Blake picks up the metaphor for his illustration, showing a man at the rudder of a small sailing vessel, the edge of whose sail the eye follows up the left-hand side of the page to encounter a yellow star (to gild the horrors), at which the man gazes. The "star of Brunswick" refers, presumably, to the Hanoverian succession—a closing compliment to the king—but Blake ignores the reference.

As already mentioned, the final illustration depicts the departing figure of Fame: this time she bears only one trumpet, which she vigorously blows, pointing it upward to form the peak of her ascent. Her large, curved body and widespread yellow wings give the page a movement of enormous energy, an energy restated in a design on her dress, where across her thighs sketchily drawn figures reenact a version of the dance of the tambourine-carrying "loves" on Cytheria's day in Poesy 5. As Fame had first touched earth with her right foot, she here departs right foot first. One is left with the impression that the subject, that docile fellow being lectured by Margaret and wreathed by Granta, scarcely deserves all the attention. Certainly the entire energy of the designs is directed elsewhere, though that direction—if it was intended as a unified one—remains unclear.

"EPITAPH ON MRS. CLARKE"

The final poem of this group is the briefest in the entire collection of poems and there is accordingly space for only two designs. The "Epitaph on Mrs. Clarke" tells of the death of a tender wife and mother, whose "infant image" (her young daughter) alone remains to comfort the bereaved husband; his future Gray depicts as a long straying "along the vale of days,"

Till time shall ev'ry grief remove,
With life, with Memory, and with Love.

Blake's first design is a traditional one showing the mourner at the tomb; it is done entirely in grays, except for the face and the one visible foot (the left one) of the mourner, a lady in drapery who stands, her eyes cast down and her hand at her bosom, next to a tall rectangular tomb with a burial urn on top. There is a faint sketch on the urn, too dim to make out with certainty even in the original manuscript, but it may be a rendering of a soul departing from loved ones left behind: one figure soars off from another, perhaps two others.

In Blake's second design we see the surviving father and daughter: the little girl looks up from a book and smiles gently at her father, who is muffled in a dark gown and stares at the fireplace before which they both sit. There seems to be no fire, though possibly a few coals glow in the upper grate—it is hard to be certain. Again the picture is done entirely in grays, except for faintly colored skin and for the fireplace hardware and the father's robe, both of which are grayish-blue. The one curious thing about the drawing is a set of three decorative objects on the high mantelpiece; they are hardly noticeable at first, but on closer examination it is clear that each is a kind of miniature tomb decoration. A memorial statue on a rectangular base stands at the left; an obelisk in the center; and at the right a thicker, blunt-topped sort of obelisk set on a base with ionic scrolls at the corners.

What are we to understand to be the point of these? Blake, who in May 1800 wrote as follows to Hayley on the death of Hayley's beloved illegitimate son, could not be expected to agree with the view of death implied in Gray's poem: "I know that our deceased friends are more really with us than when they were apparent to our mortal part. . . . [May you] be more & more perswaded that every Mortal loss is an Immortal Gain. The Ruins of Time builds Mansions in Eternity" (797). Gray's lines suggest a view of death in which the only relief for the grief of a survivor is his own death—which itself relieves not by permitting him to rejoin the beloved, but rather by extinguishing his "Memory" and "Love" together with his "life." Such a view leads to a cult of tombs, a fastening on the past rather than a confidence in present and future, a building of mansions in marble rather than in eternity. Blake accordingly shows us first such a sepulcher, then a family that decorates its hearth (of all places) with sepulchral monuments, indicating its ties to memory and that kind of earth which is less than life, the earth of roots and caves, and burial. Even the child seems tied by her open book to the past and its rigidities, though there is hope in the fact that she does look up, and is smiling.

In this second group of illustrations we have seen a wider variety of responses of illustrator to poet than was present in the first group: the designs to "The Progress of Poesy" and "Ode for Music" most often returned to the technique of the earlier poems, the technique of visualized personification, though the "Poesy" designs did so more richly, successfully, and often. "The Bard" appeared to touch on themes developing in Blake's own mythology, and must have seemed to him the most directly visionary of all Gray's poems. The translations I think Blake regarded *as* translations, considering himself to be the illustrator of ancient poets whose works appeared on Gray's pages largely through an accident of history: they were not necessarily better poetry for this, but they were somewhat closer to unspoiled vision; and Blake treated them accordingly, searching not for traces of creative insight hidden from Urizen's watchguards, but for bold and daring ways of exhibiting the visionary surface. Where the subject is war, Blake shows it at its most terrible. Where it is a trip to the underworld, Blake shows us the beasts that prosper there: they are not so different from the modern "vultures of the mind."

Finally, in the treatment of the brief "Epitaph" we see techniques that Blake will develop with more subtlety in the longer and more important "Elegy Written in a Country Churchyard," the last work of the series.

IV

"ELEGY WRITTEN IN A

COUNTRY CHURCHYARD"

THE first design to Gray's "Elegy" shows "The author writing," and is the last of Blake's three portraits of Gray. Like the other two it is set indoors, here inside a Gothic church whose vaulted ceiling rises in the now-familiar defining arch up the left of the page, over the seated poet. In the distance, through a vast doorway, we see the main hall of a church and a pulpit draped with purple cloth, evidently in preparation for a funeral. This picture is an interesting variant of the other two in that no source of light is shown—no window, no sun. The interior of the church is light and airy, painted in pale yellows and tans; but there is no direct source of brilliance (as there was in both earlier pictures) that might be supposed to be the poet's inspiration.

Indeed, this poet seems largely incapable of receiving inspiration anyway, for Blake pictures him bent almost double over his page, his face turned out toward the viewer, but his eyes cast down and his expression distressed. His robe, hand, and book are all left uncolored and his face shows only the faintest indication of living pink. The deep collar of his robe, which might be expected to hang down the back, has slipped forward over his head and face, entirely blocking his view outward. Were he able to look up he would see, as we do, the light interior of the church and in the distance the bright purple of the draped pulpit; but as nearly as can be gathered from the shadowing of the picture (or rather the lack of shadowing) he would not necessarily see a window or any other opening to the outside world.

It has already been remarked how often the illustrations to Gray betray significant connections with the designs from Blake's longer series illustrating Young's *Night Thoughts*, and there is a particularly curious example to be found among the "Elegy" designs. The sixth design illustrates Gray's observation about the peasants, that "Chill Penury repress'd their noble rage." Blake shows two figures bent in concentration on the ground; in the foreground a man bends over his shovel, regarding intently the earth he is digging; behind him a boy walks mopishly with arms folded, his eyes also intent on the ground. Around them, unnoticed, nature lowers with a kind of somber excitement: two trees in the background at the right fling their branches up as if whipped by wind, and from above left a forbidding light streaks through a thundercloud, down past the back of the man with the shovel. The fifth design of Night IX of *Night Thoughts* (no. 423) illustrates the lines:

> The spade, the Plough, disturb our ancestors;
> From human Mould we reap our daily Bread . . . ,

and the picture shows exactly the same shoveler in the same pose, except that he is working in a quiet graveyard and looks up with interest and concern at the inscription on a stone near where he digs: "Here Lieth Thomas Day," aged "100." There is no "Thomas Day" in Young; rather, Blake was in this way honoring a recently dead contemporary opponent of slavery and the American war.[1] But Day was no hundred years old when he died in 1789—he was in fact barely over forty. The round and generous age Blake gives him is a reminder that in the 1790's this ancestor was still quite "alive," whatever the facts of human mould. This shoveler, then, looks up to discover a "living" ancestor; but in the Gray design he is uncovering nothing but mould, and his head is bowed.

The implications of this contrast in two similar compositions are clearer when one considers design 8 for the "Elegy"—in one detail, at least, the most tantalizing and provocative of the set. Here we see a modest "unlettered Muse" standing before several half-fallen tombs, on one of which she traces letters with her finger. Blake entitles the design (quoting Gray's line) "Many a holy text around she strews." But this is an exceedingly fine joke, for when one scrutinizes the stone one can decipher beneath the "holy" words—"DUST THOU ART"—the further inscription "HERE LIETH Wm Blake," with scratches below to indicate an age in four figures, the first two "10," the second two faintly suggestive of two more zeros: inevitably it is at the very least 1000, the millennial figure. Blake's tomb-

[1] Erdman, in *Prophet Against Empire*, p. 27n (rev. edn., p. 28n), observes that "A Poetic response to the American War that presents several analogies to Blake's is that of Thomas Day, 1748-1789," and there catalogues the various resemblances. Day was also an opponent of slavery, authoring in 1773, with his friend John Bicknell, "The Dying Negro." He also wrote a tract titled "Fragment of a Letter," addressed to an American slaveholder; the "letter," written in 1776 and printed in London in 1784 (*Four Tracts* by Thomas Day Esq.), demanded vigorously, "What! are not all men naturally equal?" (p. 37).

stone in Gray's graveyard increases the interest of finding Day in Young's graveyard, and if Blake there gave Day a hundred years, he is here doing even better
by himself. But beyond providing his work with a wry signature, what is the
still-living Blake doing with a tombstone? And indeed one with that particular
"holy text"? Let us begin with a brief look at the argument of the "Elegy," and
then at Blake's illustrations to it.

In the familiar opening lines the poet imagines himself standing in a graveyard at "parting day": the plowman returns home wearily and the sounds in the
air are those of the night creatures, beetle and owl. In this setting and atmosphere
the poet turns to the graves in which the dead villagers repose, "Each in his narrow cell for ever laid," no more to be aroused by "The breezy call of incense
breathing Morn" or to feel the warm pleasures of family love. They were useful
toilers, says Gray, and "Ambition" should not mock them, for like the paths of
these simple men, the "paths of glory," too, "lead but to the grave." The dead
are dead, and no funereal pomp makes them less so. Moreover, the men buried
here, men whose "noble rage" had been "repress'd" by poverty, perhaps had as
much potential for greatness as their putative mockers; indeed, the repression
may have made them even more fortunate, for the same lot that circumscribed
"their growing virtues" also "confined" their "crimes." Yet "ev'n these bones"
have found "some frail memorial," though the rhymes be "uncouth" and the
sculptures "shapeless." Who does not want at his death "some fond breast" and
"pious drops"? Gray then turns around and addresses his own situation:[2] if some
kindred spirit "by lonely Contemplation led" should ask the fate of him who
relates this "artless tale," "Haply some hoary-headed swain" may tell how the
poet used to come in the early morning to "yonder nodding beech," "pore upon
the brook that babbles by," and rove through the wood, until one morning he
appeared no more; "another came" in his place, and on the next day he was
borne "with dirges due" to the grave, where one may read "The EPITAPH" that
comprises the final three stanzas of the poem. We learn in these stanzas that
"A Youth" here "rests his head upon the lap of earth," one who had been generous and sincere, and was rewarded in life for these two virtues:

> He gave to Mis'ry all he had, a tear,
> He gained from Heaven, 'twas all he wish'd, a Friend.

[2] Recent criticism has varied the interpretation, but this was the one widely held in
Blake's time, and to which Blake apparently subscribed.

We are asked to seek no further after his "merits" or "frailties," for they now repose in "The bosom of his Father and his God."

So the "Elegy" is a poem about "the poet"—Gray himself and the poetic role in general—and about his vision of death. It is by genre a song of mourning. And Blake, who had so often drawn heavily on Gray's figurative language for his illustrations, here confines himself almost entirely to illustrating this poem's abstract statements. Even when Gray employs vivid personifications, as in "Chill Penury repress'd their noble rage," Blake passes over the chance to visualize that cold oppressor of poets and artists—one he himself knew bitterly well—and shows instead two poor peasants working in the field. Moreover, these are all "landscape" designs, and for the first time the natural setting, colored in beautiful greens, seems as prominent a figure as its human occupants. Nothing is quite what we expect, then, especially when we consider these illustrations in relation to those Blake has done for Gray's other poems.

Let us quickly review the sequence of designs. The first—"The author writing" —has already been described. The second design is again not drawn directly from the text of the poem, but is called "Contemplation among Tombs" (a reference to Gray's "by lonely Contemplation led," but even more to "the contemplative poet" in general, as in "Ode on the Spring"); the title to this design might almost stand as a subtitle to the poem, and the design similarly unites the three chief characters of the "Elegy" sequence: man, grave, and natural setting. A large tree stands at the left of the design, its rich yellow-green leaves arching thickly over the top of the page. Next to its trunk stands Contemplation, a blue-robed young man with hands piously crossed at his chest and an open book in one hand; he stands almost rigidly straight, with his left foot forward, and looks up toward or through the branches. Behind and to the right is a large tomb, a sort of plain sarcophagus bearing a recumbent effigy; it is a simpler version of the many royal tombs Blake had seen in Westminster Abbey. Tomb, statue, and a nearby half-toppled headstone are all a cold blue-white.

The strangest element in the drawing is an object in the immediate foreground, in front of the tomb and next to Contemplation: a green, log-shaped form wrapped crisscross with a thorny vine. It is apparently a shrouded body ready for burial, though there is no sign of an open grave, and the green of the wrapping looks more like moss or grass than cloth. A similar "wrapped" form appears in design 9, below.

The third design illustrates the third and fourth lines of the poem, as Blake's title indicates:

> The plowman homeward plods his weary way,
> And leaves the world to darkness, and to me.

A yellow road winds to the distant church, and standing on the road, looking upward at the approaching darkness, is the poet. For almost the only time in this set of illustrations (the other instance is "Contemplation"), Blake picks up an implied personification—indeed, the hint is slight, for "darkness" is not even capitalized—and gives it a life it does not have in the text: for darkness is shown as a large figure who hovers gently in gray robes, filling the top of the page and leaving gray sky above and behind her. She is modeled on the figure of "benevolent" Adversity, though she has a gentler and more peaceful face. Beneath her in the distance bent, weary plowmen and their horses plod homeward at the end of the day's labor.

Design 4 shows a burial scene: the open grave occupies the center foreground, and grouped around it are a parent and three children with bowed heads, all draped in black gowns that hide every human feature except the downcast faces of two of the children; behind the grave and largely hidden by the text is the gravedigger, who throws earth into the open grave; to the right stands a bishop in his surplice, looking upward with what appears to be staged piety, one hand over his heart, the other holding the book from which he may be supposed to have been reading (his mouth is still open). To the far right, lining the side of the page, is the trunk of a tree that bursts above into blue-green leaves, spreading luxuriously over the top of the page. The church spire has been faintly sketched in the distance, but then abandoned.

The next design is a vivid and energetic one, in strong contrast to those that precede. The top half of the page shows blue sky with soft white clouds, the bottom half a yellow wheatfield; in the foreground a large peasant bends forward vigorously, grasping a bundle of wheat with huge left hand and preparing to cut it with a great sickle held in his right. The design is remarkable in that his body and left arm form a curve precisely mirroring that of the sickle blade, though larger; and his left leg, extended behind him, forms equally precisely the handle. It is a stunning visual play, for Blake makes the figure obviously a sickle and yet powerfully human, so human that it comes as a shock to see the

meaning of his form. He is a human visualization of the productive strength celebrated in the brief, unengraved Notebook lyric:

> The sword sung on the barren heath,
> The sickle in the fruitful field:
> The sword he sung a song of death,
> But could not make the sickle yield. (178)

Behind him stands a diffident young lady, at most half his size; she wears a large
sunbonnet and her summer dress has slipped half off her shoulder. To judge
from her size she is the peasant's daughter, and she brings him lunch or something to drink in a small barrel that she holds like a pocketbook at her side. The
clothes of this pair are the brightest of the "Elegy" illustrations: the man wears
an apricot shirt and blue pants, the girl a green hat, apricot dress, and bright
blue stockings.

An important analogy to this design is *Night Thoughts* no. 71 (Night VII),
which illustrates the lines,

> That tyrant, Hope! mark, how she domineers;
> She bids us quit Realities, for Dreams.

Blake shows us the same peasant in the same field, but he has dropped his sickle
and is looking up from his bent posture in response to a winged female "Hope,"
who leaps into the air, touching his forehead with her hand. This connection,
already interesting for what it tells us about Blake's view of one kind of "Realities," becomes more so when one observes that the composition of both of these
drawings has its origin in Richard Bentley's headpiece design for the "Elegy."
There one sees the same bent reapers in the middle distance, most tellingly
related to those of the Blake designs by virtue of the way the wheat is pictured
in relation to the workers, forming a sort of living wall before them. Here is
striking evidence that by the time Blake was at work on the designs to Young's
Night VII he had already studied Bentley's designs closely enough to borrow from
them. And certainly if Blake had been looking at Bentley's illustrations, he had
been thinking about Gray.

Design 6 has already been described: it is the one showing the digger whose
counterpart in the Young designs disturbed his ancestors and found "Thomas
Day." The seventh shows another of the peasant flowers "born to blush unseen":

> Some village-Hampden, that with dauntless breast,
> The little tyrant of his fields withstood.

The Hampden referred to is John Hampden, who was famous for his resistance to the obsolete tax of ship-money (finally declared illegal in 1641) and who later raised a regiment for the Parliamentary army during the first civil war, in which he was killed. Blake pictures a peasant who holds a shovel in one hand and with the other points to the sky above his head, a gesture offered in answer to a mean-faced bailiff or landlord who walks off to the left, holding out a red-sealed official paper to the peasant's view and pointing in the direction he is himself headed, as if to indicate that the peasant should accompany him. The pointed fingers of the two men clearly represent appeals to two different authorities—the bailiff to the local secular power, the peasant to God.[3] Behind the men, partially hidden by the text box, two trees entwine, and in the distance may be seen the peasant's picturesquely modest cottage; smoke curls up from its pleasant chimney, reminding one of the life inside.[4]

Design 8, described earlier, shows Blake's own tombstone. Nine illustrates the encounter of "kindred spirit" and "hoary-headed swain." The kindred spirit, dressed as a traveller, stands in the company not of the swain but rather of "lonely Contemplation," who has led him here: it is the same Contemplation we met in design 2, holding the same book in the same hand. The sarcophagus before which they stand is also similar to that in design 2, though without the recumbent effigy; and in front of it lies another wrapped body bound with thorny vines. It is to this the kindred spirit points inquiringly. Although we do not see the swain, Blake does show as background the landscape of the story he tells—the "upland lawn" to which the now-dead poet used to climb, the "nodding beech" beneath which he stretched, and the babbling brook he used to "pore upon."

The tenth design illustrates the end of the swain's story, his description of how

---

[3] The bailiff further wears a purple knit hat, possibly in acknowledgment of his position as the representative of royal power; the peasant has a red collar on his brown shirt, possibly in corroboration of his revolutionary tendencies.

Interestingly, illustrators of this scene have often depicted Gray's "Hampden" and "little tyrant" as children (see, e.g., A. W. Callcott, R.A., *Elegy* [London, 1834]), reducing the political significance on which Blake capitalizes.

[4] The cottage is similar to that in Bentley's design showing the reapers in the wheatfield, though the idiom is common enough that Blake need not have gone there to find it.

one morning the young man was missed on his "custom'd hill," only to be found the next day on his way to the grave: "Slow thro' the church-yard path we saw him borne." This last line Blake quotes for his title, and in the distance we do see a file of mourners carrying a coffin along the path toward the church, whose spire is faintly visible in the distance. But Blake is most vividly concerned with the living group under the tree, a group of three young women surrounded by playing children: one child nurses at its mother's breast, another sits on the lap of the woman in the center and hands a ball to the woman on the right, and two more stand at the knees of the grouped women. The woman at left points back toward the funeral procession. The women are carefully drawn and brightly colored, as is the tree beneath which they sit. Their expressions are nostalgic or contemplative, but the visual effect is nonetheless one of life and vitality, especially when the foreground scene is compared to the distant view of the mourners and coffin, sketchily drawn and all in blacks and grays.

Blake's eleventh illustration shows "A Shepherd reading the Epitaph": he stands in profile on one end of another plain sarcophagus, leaning pensively on his staff. Balancing this figure is a tree posed in roughly symmetrical position at the other end of the tomb and thrusting up from behind it. Again there is an interesting connection with a drawing for *Night Thoughts*. In no. 44 Blake shows Lorenzo at the grave of Philander; this grave is flush with the ground, and the positions of shepherd and trees are reversed. But more important, in the drawing for *Night Thoughts* Lorenzo is a far more vigorous figure, bareheaded, the contours of his body showing clearly through his light clothing, and on his face a light smile. And the tree at the other end bends its thin branches entirely over the grave, sprouting into greenery in the air over Lorenzo's head and shoulders. Around its slender trunk, which stands at the head of the grave, curls one of Blake's small, barren little tendrils, usually an ominous sign. The line illustrated is *"Life*, take thy chance," and here life seems firmly centered in and about the young shepherd. In the Gray design, however, shepherd and leafy tree seem to be in opposition rather than accord, and of the two the tree seems more alive. The shepherd's concealing gown and hat, limp stance, and soulful expression all combine to give him an air of life enclosed or denied rather than life triumphant—or even life chosen over death.

The final illustration for this poem, and the closing design for the entire series of 116 illustrations to Gray, is fittingly pertinent to its position in both contexts. It shows "A Spirit conducted to Paradise," and for the first time in the "Elegy" designs (excepting the figure of hovering "darkness") we see spiritual figures floating in the air as they so often have done in the designs to other poems. Here one spirit points upward, encouraging the other, whose hands are raised in rather timid awe.

There remains the question of what Blake is doing in Gray's graveyard, and beneath a stone inscribed "Dust Thou Art." It has been noted that the designs almost always illustrate Gray's statements and descriptions rather than his figurative language, and this in itself raises questions. When Blake seized on Gray's "vultures of the mind" or his "Hyperion's march . . . and glitt'ring shafts of war" and exploded them into brilliantly visualized shapes, he did so because he felt them to be the visionary truth implicit in the poems' stated meanings—sometimes in conflict with them, as in the case of the "Ode to Adversity," where the view of the goddess "in gorgon terrors clad" was to Gray an "impious" view but to Blake a truly visionary one; and sometimes consonant with them but allowing still broader implication, as in the case of "Hyperion's march." But always the visionary truth was there in the poem, available in the language to anyone who possessed the imaginative clarity of mind to see it. Similarly, when Blake presented bold and fresh compositions illustrating the subjects and statements of Gray's translations, he obviously felt that he was responding directly to the visionary capacity of ancient bards, and that their vision was its own most important meaning: the sight of the fatal sisters weaving death on a human loom, or of Owen vastly terrible in war, is truth itself. Are we to assume that the case is similar here—that Blake is confirming Gray's view of the poet and of death? But if so, why the hunched-over and self-enclosed figure of "The author writing" in the opening design? And why the uniformly tame, "unimaginative" composition of the designs, and the sense of limpness one gets, for example, in the eleventh design, "A Shepherd reading the Epitaph," where the contrasting emphasis of the comparable Young design shows that even the composition and subject matter cannot in themselves be held to account for the picture's final tone?

The problem remains and, indeed, seems to grow more intricate when viewed in relation to other aspects of the series. But we may find the beginnings of an answer by returning to the peculiar wrapped form that appears in designs 2 and 9. Although I have consulted scholars in art history and the history of church customs,[5] I have been unable to find any tradition for such a representation. It

[5] R. Wittkower of Columbia University and Canon West of the (Episcopalian) Cathedral of St. John the Divine in New York City were especially generous with their time.

may well have been simply Blake's own invention: certainly its meaning for Blake is clear.[6] We already have hints from Spring 3 and Adversity 2 of the way in which roots in Blake's work tend to suggest confinement or a death-like sleep, or more generally the restrictions of natural life and death. In the words of "The Voice of the Ancient Bard" from the *Songs of Innocence*:

> Folly is an endless maze,
> Tangled roots perplex her ways.
> How many have fallen there!
> They stumble all night over bones of the dead.   (126)

Visualizations of entangling roots occur throughout Blake's art: two convenient ones for our purposes are those of the Preludium to *America*. In the first plate, where the central figures enact the chaining of Orc, one sees among the roots of the tree next to which he is chained a crouched and miserable figure clutching its knees to its chin; in the second plate a young man rises out of the earth like a free-springing plant, pushing himself out and away from the tangling roots that we can still see in the earth beneath him.

There are, moreover, numerous other related examples to be found in works done within a few years of the Gray designs. "The Human Abstract" pictures an old man struggling with a rootlike cord that binds him down—a version of the "Net of Urizen" vividly shown in the final plate of *The First Book of Urizen*. And elsewhere we frequently see men and women bound by coiling serpents: again, a striking example occurs in *Urizen*, where three falling serpent-entwined figures accompany the verses "But Urizen laid in a stony sleep/ Unorganiz'd, rent from Eternity" and "The Eternals said: What is this? Death./ Urizen is a clod of clay" (226). A more familiar use of the same general motif occurs in "The Garden of Love":

> And I saw it was filled with graves,
> And tomb-stones where flowers should be;
> And Priests in black gowns were walking their rounds,
> And binding with briars my joys & desires.   (215)

[6] The one other example I have seen is in an illustration to the "Elegy" by R. Redgrave, A.R.A., one of a series of illustrations to the poem done by various members of "The Etching Club" (*Elegy Written in a Country Churchyard* [London, 1847]). I have been unable to discover whether Redgrave borrowed from Blake or joined him in a conventional representation; but being a friend of Flaxman, he did have access to Blake's designs.

138

In the design to this poem a kneeling priest gestures toward an open grave, and in the margin beneath we see loops of thorny vines like those binding the corpse in the illustration to Gray's "Elegy."

The network of ideas behind the motif is, then, already a central one in Blake's work, both poetry and design.[7] But to connect it specifically with the bound corpse of the Gray designs, we must turn again to the *Night Thoughts* illustrations. Design no. 34 illustrates Young's lines about the poet's effort to break free of "Grief's sharpest Thorn" by singing with the "Rage divine" of great earlier poets; Blake pictures him lying on the ground absorbed in a book, well wrapped and closely held down by thorny vines, and chained by the left foot.[8] In design no. 109 an old man representing "Death" unchains the left foot of a young man who reaches upward to follow an already soaring figure. The lines illustrated are these:

> Death wounds, to cure: We fall, we rise; we reign!
> Spring from our fetters; fasten in the skies;
> Where blooming *Eden* withers in our sight;
> Death gives us more than was in Eden lost.
> This King of Terrors is the Prince of Peace.

Death's "cure," in Blake's eyes as in Young's, is to cut the fetters binding us to earth.

Four more designs from Young complete the connection. In Night VII Young wonders why man must remain "in this thorny Wilderness so long": Blake shows (no. 311) a hunched, grieving man wandering across tangles of huge thorns, one of which winds up around the tree at his left. In Night VIII (no. 350) Young

---

[7] For examples of the continuing significance of these binding briars in Blake's pictorial art, see the rejected design for Blair's *The Grave* (1808), showing, in Flaxman's words, "A widow embracing the turf which covers her husband's grave" (reproduced by Bentley in *Blake Records*, plate XVIII; Flaxman's description is quoted on pp. 166-167) and the Rosenwald version (1809?) of *A Vision of the Last Judgment* (reproduced in Damon, *Dictionary*, plate I and in Raine, *Blake and Tradition*, II, 205). At the bottom and center of the Rosenwald *Last Judgment* a skeleton wrapped in thorny vines—he is surely the deadest of the dead—"begins to animate, starting into life at the Trumpet's sound" (609), to quote Blake's own description of the scene. The grave scene from Blair is similar in several respects to the Gray "Elegy" designs, but most notably in the thorny vines binding the "turf."

[8] As a demonstration of the difficulties in assigning right-left symbolism, one should observe that the same young man is bound in no. 34 by his left foot and in no. 35 by his right. Both designs were engraved, and the shift occurs there also.

compares "This World" to a "thorny pillow" and Blake shows a scene similar to that just described, though this time the man sleeps pillowed on the thorns. In the same Night VIII, illustrating Young's lines about how even "Virtue" has her relapses and "Foes, that n'er fail to make her feel their Hate," Blake draws (no. 366) a dead angel, rigidly outstretched on the ground, bound round and round by a coiling serpent like those of plate 7 of *Urizen* (Blake Trust facsimile). Roots, serpents, chains, or thorns: the line of connection is clear, for all are earth-binding reminders of man's natural ties to his origin in dust.

Finally, illustrating lines in which Young argues that we should learn from the example of friends' deaths the meaning and necessity of our own, Blake shows (no. 96) a form bound in briars exactly like those in his Gray designs, though with a few leaves sprouting from the thorny vine. At the foot of this form sits a mourning figure, touched from above by the soaring spirit of the departed friend for whom he mourns. Whatever that object bound by briars is, it now belongs to the earth, not to the "departed" friend, for he is a spirit in the air. We have here, if you like, a translation into visionary design of Blake's lines to Hayley about how the "ruins of Time" build "mansions in Eternity." As he argued in that letter, "I know that our deceased friends are more really with us than when they were apparent to our mortal part" (797). But in the two designs to Gray's "Elegy" in which these bound forms appear there is a notable lack of any sign of the living spirit: to the eyes of Gray's Contemplation there is none, and Blake has drawn none in his pictures.

What Blake *has* drawn, again and again, are scenes of human mourning in the midst of a green and pleasant land.[9] One is struck by contrasts throughout the designs. The burial scene of design 4 pictures the bright life of nature as opposed to the sorrowful event and the hooded, enclosed mourners; their dark and modest gowns remind us of the downcast "author writing," of "darkness" in design 3, and, by way of her, of "benevolent" Adversity and her hooded, sulky charge—all share the common shape of the life-despiser, who cloaks and regrets the body, who eyes the ground or looks straight ahead, and who responds with little expression other than sternness or sorrow. In the burial scene little humanity is to be seen, although there are six humans: the mourners seem more closely allied to death than to life, the bishop seems rather inhuman in another sense, and the gravedigger is entirely hidden except for feet and shovel, making him

---

[9] Color reproduction is essential if one is to realize the full force of Blake's technique here.

more an occupation than a man. And we have observed that the shepherd of design 11 seems less alive than the tree that faces him.

In the other pictures even the peasants—though far more vigorous than Contemplation, the mourners, the poet, unlettered muse, traveler, or shepherd—are still bowed far toward the earth: the plowman is bent almost double, the digger and the moping boy behind him both intently regard the earth, and even the reaper, splendid as he is, is a humanization of the sickle, blurring the "line" between man and tool. The one figure who looks up is the village-Hampden, and even he is anchored to the earth by his shovel and wears a face drawn with weariness. Clearly Blake respects the strong bodies and capacities of his digger, reaper, and village-Hampden; these three designs come exactly at the center of the sequence and have an earthy vigor that starkly emphasizes by contrast the marked lack of it in the other designs. For Blake the human body, even apart from its role as the receptacle of creative intellect, is beautiful; he insisted that "The Beauty proper for sublime art is lineaments, or forms and features that are capable of being the receptables of intellect" (579), but the body was not simply a "housing"—rather, its lovely form is "The Naked Human form divine" (755). Blake's whole philosophy of dress rests on one assumption, that the best is that which reveals the naked body beneath it: "Art can never exist without Naked Beauty displayed" (776); "Drapery is formed alone by the Shape of the Naked" (462). But even these splendid peasant bodies whose naked shapes are visible through their clothing (unlike those of the other figures) seem securely attached to the earth. They are alive with the life of trees and grass rather than the life of spiritual existence.

Nonetheless, the life of trees and grass is surely important to the meaning of the "Elegy" designs. We noticed earlier the living group of women and children under the tree in design 10, reminiscent of the group of adults on "The Ecchoing Green" in the *Songs of Innocence*.[10] They, too, sit beneath a tree, surrounded by children—some at their knees, as in the Gray design, others playing games out in the open. But there one of the figures is a man—the "Old John" of the poem—whereas here all three are mothers. "The Ecchoing Green" is a poem about life and vitality:

> The Sun does arise,
> And make happy the skies;

[10] I am grateful to John E. Grant for pointing out this similarity to me.

141

> The merry bells ring
> To welcome the Spring. (116)

As the youngsters sport on the green, the "old folk" recall their own youth and join in the spirit of play. In the third stanza the day ends—"The sun does descend,/ And our sports have an end"—and the children gather "Like birds in their nest" "Round the laps of their mothers." Most critics agree that the poem reflects the cycle of life in the cycle of a day and that the playing children represent the vitality of innocent joy. As E. D. Hirsch observes, "in the full cycle of life the setting of this sun" brings "'a new and greater sunrise.'" Old John's "sympathetic recollections of early childhood are prophetic intimations of eternity. . . . The pastoral landscape is at once an occasion for and the content of prophetic vision.'"[11] If this be accepted, then one may see more clearly the point in this analogous design for Gray's "Elegy." The pastoral bounty of the scene in the foreground—mothers and children, and particularly the nursing infant, in a setting of lush greenery—provides a contrast with the drab order of the distant funeral march at the same time that it reminds us that the end of life is not the grave but eternal rebirth, that "new and greater sunrise."[12]

The writing "author" of the title page, then, may be bent down and closed off from the sunlight outside (and all it implies), but the designs remind us again and again that he need not be.[13] The poet pictures himself at the opening of the poem as standing in a graveyard at "parting day," the time at which Blake's

[11] *Innocence and Experience: An Introduction to Blake* (New Haven and London, 1964), pp. 40-41.

[12] Further support for this reading is offered by another strikingly similar design, that of "Christ Blessing the Little Children," done for Thomas Butts in 1799 and now in the Tate Gallery. There Christ sits alone beneath the tree, folding children to him; adults who have brought the children stand and kneel at the sides and foreground. For Blake—as for more traditional Christian theologians—it is through Christ that eternal rebirth is achieved.

[13] Similarly, Blake's emphasis on the striking purple cloth draping the pulpit in Elegy 1—an otherwise almost hueless design—underscores in still another way what Blake felt Gray should have known about corporeal death. In the progression of liturgical colors of the Church of England, the Lenten purple marks a period of suffering and penitence; but that period is of course only a prelude to the exuberant joy and renewal of life implicit in Easter. The church in which the author writes displays the funereal colors of Lent, but the world outside springs to green life, anticipating that rebirth of which the self-enclosing mourners seem unaware, though it is manifest in the new grass and young children of design 12.

own "Ecchoing Green" ends. But what Gray then sees is no "new and greater sunrise": rather, he sees—in that one striking personification of Blake's—descending "darkness," and all about him mouldering graves whose occupants will never again be aroused by "Morn." It is now clear why Blake chose to draw out and vivify this particular example of Gray's half-obscured figurative language: it is Gray's mistaken vision that Blake advertises, rather than the half-hidden true vision so often brought to life in other poems. The "spirit" of this poem, Blake says by illustration, is not the human spirit, but Darkness personified.

"Every Mortal loss is an Immortal Gain" because to Blake death is in truth no loss at all, properly understood. In offering comfort to Hayley over the loss of his son, Blake begged him to "Forgive me for Expressing to you my Enthusiasm which I wish all to partake of Since it is to me a Source of Immortal Joy" (797). It is not surprising, then, that he should wish to express this same enthusiasm to the viewers of his designs to Gray's "Elegy." Thus the two very low-key designs to the "Epitaph on Mrs. Clarke" may be seen as an introduction to the more ambitious and more positively stated designs of this final series. Those designs argued by implication that tombbuilders are themselves already half-dead; but the designs to the "Elegy" remind one that eternal life awaits those who will have it.

What Gray, the self-enclosed "author," has forgotten in this poem about death is the world of "Imagination," which Blake believed to be eternal and open to all men. "This world of Imagination is the world of Eternity; it is the divine bosom into which we shall all go after the death of the Vegetated body" (605). It is the world in which Blake, reaping his "daily Bread" in the fields of art, disturbed his ancestor and uncovered "Thomas Day"—still alive and still stimulating. But in this "Elegy" Gray put himself in his own graveyard and wrote his own epitaph, in his closing lines placing not himself but rather his "merits" and "frailties" in "The bosom of his Father and his God." But Blake always insisted that "merits" and "frailties" are qualities, not persons or things, and reside neither in the bosom of God nor anywhere else. "Moral Virtues do not Exist" (614), nor was this a personification Blake was likely to allow to pass. What does exist—what must exist for the man ever to be alive, in vegetated body or out of it—is the divine imagination, poetic genius, creative artistic power. Viewed negatively, this is what makes, for example, the artist Correggio, though physically long dead, still greatly dangerous: "he infuses a love of soft and even tints without boundaries" (583). Similarly, "Rubens is a most outrageous demon, and by infusing the remembrances of his Pictures and style of execution, hinders all power of individual thought" (582-583). "The Eternal Body of Man is the Imagination" (776), and that Gray's imagination is very much alive, in both its positive and its negative capacities, all Blake's designs stand as proof.

Gray's "Elegy" is rich in Miltonic echoes, and in view of this the poet's own entrance into the poem at the end is particularly reminiscent of Milton's in his great elegy "Lycidas." There Milton's concern was in part with poetic continuity: at the death of one elegiac poet another will step into his place. Gray hints, though less specifically, at the same continuity in the phrase "Another came" and in the hoped-for "kindred spirit." But for Blake the continuity consists in the absoluteness of each man's art: as artist, each is eternal. Indeed, Milton, dead for more than a hundred years, is soon to return to earth as the power behind Blake's next major prophecy, which will bring about Milton's further development and bear as its title his name.

As Milton and Gray are still alive, so also was Blake's beloved brother Robert, who died in 1787. Blake wrote Hayley: "Thirteen years ago I lost a brother & with his spirit I converse daily & hourly in the Spirit & See him in my remembrance in the regions of my Imagination" (797). In his epitaph Gray asserts that his "bounty" had been large, for he had "gain'd from Heav'n, 'twas all he wished, a Friend."[14] But this is the epitaph of a poet, and in Blake's view the poet, of all people, should know that heaven has given him a bounty far greater than the one he mentions—indeed, the one bounty that makes real friendship possible. Blake's dark dictum that "Corporeal friends are spiritual enemies" may be taken to refer to those friends who are *only* corporeal friends, who are incapable of the spiritual converse that renders death meaningless and friendship rich. Thus it was that in the Young design showing Lorenzo at Philander's grave, Lorenzo could afford to choose life, and regard the grave with a gentle smile.

And in these terms, too, the meaning of the briar-wrapped shapes becomes clear. The loglike corpse is the vegetated body, and in a sense it matters little whether that body be physically alive or dead: it is bound in restricting briars in either case. The important thing is to realize that there *is* a soaring spirit above it, as we see in the Young design where the wrapped shape appears. There the

[14] Presumably Richard West is meant here, insofar as the lines are autobiographical; West had died in 1742, the year in which Gray's early editor Mason believed the poem to have been begun. Most scholars now date the composition between 1745 and 1750; certainly it was composed over a period of several years ending in 1750. (See *Complete Poems of Gray*, ed. Starr and Hendrickson, p. 222.)

spirit is touching his mourning friend, and causing tiny leaves to sprout from the thorny vines themselves. But Gray's Contemplation sees no soaring spirit, for he does not know that "in your own Bosom you bear your Heaven/ And Earth & all you behold; tho' it appears Without, it is Within" (709). So the thorns there bear no leaves, and, more important, the human mourners have little vitality; where the "author writing" is oppressed, the figures of his poem must also be oppressed. So Blake follows Gray's dictates and pictures a race of half-dead men and women deeply rooted in the earth, unable to find the "human" in the "Mould," and presented in compositions of a tameness unmatched anywhere else in the 116 designs. A sensitive viewer can hardly escape the overwhelming sense of a stifled humanity.

It is, finally, in these terms that we must appreciate the full seriousness of Blake's whimsy in inscribing "HERE LIETH Wm Blake" upon a tomb in Gray's churchyard. First of all, there is the resonance of a kind of wit that draws on the history of both painting and literature. Just as painters like Dürer—who was much admired by Blake—would find not only a place for their patrons but also a (lesser) place for themselves in their religious visions on canvas, so also Blake irreverently preempts a tomb in the country churchyard. And just as Milton, the "uncouth swain," and Gray, the "Youth" mourned by some "swain," manage to glance at themselves in the course of writing an elegy, so also Blake the painter reveals himself among his own illustrations. Second, and more significant, the joke, with Blake's millennial predictions for himself, has a moral dimension, an "eternal" meaning. What Blake has fastened on throughout the designs to this elegy is Gray's view of death as merely a petering out of life, the return to dust of a creature fundamentally earthbound even during "life." All paths "lead but to the grave"; and the inability of "storied urn" or "Honour's voice" to reenliven the "silent dust" is based for Gray not on their own inadequacy as bringers of life but rather on the absolute deadness of the dust. And the comfort offered the genius squelched by penury is that if he was never able to be great, at least he was never able to be greatly evil: better "sober wishes" and "noiseless tenour" than a life of frightening creative potential. Finally, "the poet" is characterized in Gray's elegy as a youth who stretches "his listless length" to "pore upon the brook," mutters "wayward fancies," and vascillates between the extremes of "drooping, woeful wan" and being "craz'd with care, or cross'd in hopeless love."

Blake must have found this sulky melancholic a far cry from the powerful bard. And when Gray clothes himself in the poetic role and asserts with the force of the whole of a vastly popular poem that "Dust Thou Art," Blake can only respond with a tombstone bearing his own name: the part of me that is dust, it says by implication, I willingly consign to your graveyard, for it is as dead now as it ever will be. But the part of me that lives will outlive the millennium, for it is eternal.

In the last of the 116 designs Blake shows the soaring spirits so tellingly absent in the rest of the "Elegy" designs: indeed the spirit there "conducted to Paradise" is in an important sense Gray himself, guided by his visionary illustrator.

CONCLUSION

BLAKE saw in Gray a serious and ambitious poet constantly and sensitively examining his poetic stance, one whose poetic genius, though flickering and erratic, deserved the exhaustive inspection of visionary criticism. Blake's was a time, moreover, when (despite Fuseli's experience with his Milton Gallery) poetical painting was, if not a genre, at least a recognized idiom. Flaxman illustrated not only Homer, Aeschylus, and Dante, but also Cowper's translations of Milton's Latin poems, *Pilgrim's Progress*, and (privately, for his wife) two works of his own. Stothard had illustrated not only Chaucer, but also "L'Allegro" and "Il Penseroso." Hogarth had illustrated Milton several times; Barry did so even more extensively. Boydell's Shakespeare Gallery catered to a public that liked to see its great literature translated into sumptuous paintings, and the list of contributing artists reads like a *Who's Who* of informed contemporary taste. Thus it would be surprising if an ambitious young artist did not try his hand at literary illustration. That Blake should turn to Gray reflected not only his own interests but those of his contemporaries.

Moreover, the preference for line drawing that Blake demonstrated so aggressively in all his remarks on the subject— ("Painting is drawing on Canvas" [594]; "the more distinct, sharp, and wirey the bounding line, the more perfect the work of art" [585]) and illustrated in the technique of the present series of designs was shared by a large contingent of late-eighteenth-century artists, who found their own ideals exemplified in the "simplicity" of classical art. The opposition that students of English literature are used to finding between the ideals of neoclassicism and romanticism will not hold in the visual arts, where a late-eighteenth-century rediscovery of and admiration for classical examples served to bolster several important tenets of their growing romanticism: among them, that which repudiated as decadent the showy and overwrought style then popular in favor of one more "chaste" and idealized. In *Pandora's Box* Dora and Irwin Panofsky speak of "that Romantic Classicism which dominated the taste of [the] period" and observe that one of its most characteristic aspects is that "it produced, in addition to a new interpretation of forms and subjects, a new technique

147

of visual presentation: engravings consisting of outlines without either color or modeling."[1]

In his early years Blake praised classical art and stressed its affinity with his own techniques, writing Dr. Trusler in 1799 that "the purpose for which alone I live" is "in conjunction with such men as my friend Cumberland [author of *Thoughts on Outline*] to renew the lost Art of the Greeks" (792). To Cumberland himself he wrote: "Go on, if not for your own sake, yet for ours, who love & admire your works; but, above all, For the Sake of the Arts. Do not throw aside for any long time the honour intended you by Nature to revive the Greek workmanship. I study your outlines as usual, just as if they were antiques" (795). And in 1800, "the immense flood of Grecian light & glory which is coming on Europe will more than realize our warmest wishes" (797).

The reasons for such a preference, and the unstated assumptions of Blake's own aesthetic, are finely synopsized by the Panofskys, and it is most telling that despite point for point parallels with Blake's own views, the Panofskys do not have Blake in mind at all.[2] They are explaining some of the reasons for the widespread popularity of outline drawing in the mainstream of late-eighteenth-century art, commenting on its beginnings as a technique for illustrating technical treatises, and briefly tracing its eventual broad influence. Students of Blake are familiar with his position concerning the relationship of color to line: "all depends on Form or Outline, on where that is put; where that is wrong, the Colouring never can be right" (563-564); "the disposition of forms always directs colouring" (580-581); "What kind of Intellects must he have who sees only the Colours of things & not the Forms of Things" (597). The Panofskys offer a context—indeed, even patristic support—for such dicta. Line engravings, they say, "may originally have been produced by didactic, in part even economic considerations. . . . But it was soon realized that these chaste contour prints lent tangible expression not only to the ontological superiority accorded to the line in the theory of cognition (had not Thomas Aquinas asserted that the relation between image and prototype rests on *figura* rather than *color* because 'if the color of anything is depicted on a wall, this is not called an image unless the figure is also depicted'?) [*Summa theologiae*, I, qu. 35, art. 1, c.], but also to the aesthetic superiority accorded to

---

[1] (New York, 1962), pp. 89, 90.

[2] They do discuss both Barry and Flaxman, since these artists illustrated versions of the Pandora story. (Flaxman's six outline drawings were engraved by Blake in 1816 and published early the following year.)

it by every type of Platonism. Simple line drawings, Frans Hemsterhuys wrote in 1769, retain more of the 'godlike fire of the first-conceived idea than paintings.' "[3] Hemsterhuys' view is Blake's, some forty years later: the best drawings, Blake maintained, are those done "with a firm & decided hand at once" (595); "Let a Man who has made a drawing go on & on & he will produce a Picture or Painting, but if he chooses to leave it before he has spoil'd it, he will do a Better Thing" (603).[4] Part of the reason is that painting should not be concerned with surface realism, with working up accuracy of representation: "shall Painting be confined to the sordid drudgery of fac-simile representations of merely mortal and perishing substances?" (576). This argument is by no means Blake's alone. Robert Rosenblum observes that "Beginning in the mid-eighteenth century and culminating around 1800, one can trace in certain currents of European art a gradually increasing emphasis upon outline and two-dimensionality as well as upon the rejection of art's function to render illusionistically the data of the seen world."[5] The "organic eye," as Blake called it, sees texture, shadow, mass—all perishing substances; but the eye of the imagination is concerned with quite a different level of reality. "Mental Things are alone Real; what is call'd Corporeal, Nobody Knows of its Dwelling Place. . . . I question not my Corporeal or Vegetative Eye any more than I would Question a Window concerning a Sight. I look thro' it & not with it" (617). It is just such attitudes, according to the Panofskys, that account for one of the main lines in the genealogy of modern art. "Reduced to pure contours, the visible world in general, and the precious relics of antiquity in particular, seemed to assume an unearthly, ethereal character, detached from the 'material' qualities of color, weight, and surface texture; and we can easily conceive that the line engravings found in the archaeological publications of the late

[3] *Pandora's Box*, p. 91.

[4] These terms had wide currency. Fuseli's godfather could be mistaken for either Hemsterhuys or Blake when he praises thoughts "conceiv'd in the first warmth" that are "never so well express'd as by the strokes that are drawn at that instant" ("Letter to M. Fuslin [sic] on Landscape Painting," trans. into English in 1776 by W. Hooper in *New Idylles By Gessner*; quoted by Geoffrey Grigson in "English Painting From Blake to Byron," *From Blake to Byron*, ed. Boris Ford [Aylesbury and Slough, 1957]).

[5] "The International Style of 1800: A Study in Linear Abstraction" (unpublished dissertation, New York University, 1956), pp. 3-4. Blake's place in the neoclassical movement, and particularly his curious parallels with Carstens, are stimulatingly discussed in this dissertation. Unfortunately some of the material offered there is not available in Mr. Rosenblum's recent *Transformations in Late Eighteenth Century Art* (Princeton, 1967), although *Transformations* is the best published study of the period that I have found.

eighteenth century . . . inspired creative artists from Philipp Otto Runge, Asmus Carstens, and Peter Cornelius through Ingres down to Matisse and Picasso."[6] The strong lines and restrained coloring of Blake's designs to "The Bard" and the translations—their sketchy or "unfinished" look—give evidence of his awareness that the appropriate execution for such daring and ancient pieces would necessarily be the inspired drawing that is done "with a firm & decided hand at once." His borrowings from Flaxman's own "chaste outlines" underscore the point. Thus not only the choice of literary illustration, but also the technique of line drawing and subordinated coloring—the linear rather than the painterly style—place Blake firmly in a context with many other late-eighteenth-century artists, their shared convictions not altered or perverted by Blake, but rather represented in his work with full self-awareness.

Students of Blake should realize that the issue on which he broke with his fellow artists was not one of idiom or technique, but rather a matter of what I will for the moment call moral attitude. Within a few years of finishing his Gray designs Blake had sharply shifted his ideological ground on one point at least: whereas in 1800 he had written to Cumberland of his enthusiasm for "the immense flood of Grecian light & glory," in his Preface to *Milton* he decries classical influence as "infection from the silly Greek & Latin slaves of the Sword," adding, "We do not want either Greek or Roman Models if we are but just & true to our own Imaginations" (480). Joseph Burke's argument that "style was for Blake an essential and absolute test of spiritual truth" (see above, pp. 7-9) is surely right in the negative sense that the painterly style always indicated for Blake the blurred vision that saw only nature and made no outlines, obeying material rather than mental muses, memory rather than inspiration. But in the art of the Greeks and Romans he was confronted with a perceptual approach utterly to his liking, in the service of a philosophy he came increasingly to consider the way of death—literally "the Antichrist" (786) because it revered "Glorious War" and opposed the philosophy of forgiveness.[7] Blake's views on this issue

---

[6] *Pandora's Box*, pp. 91-92.

[7] Blake makes the connection explicit in *The Everlasting Gospel*:

> The Roman Virtues, Warlike Fame,
> Take Jesus' & Jehovah's Name;
> For what is Antichrist but those
> Who against Sinners Heaven close. (758)

But this is also one of the themes of the Notebook version of "The Grey Monk," which

are familiar: "The Classics! it is the Classics, & not Goths nor Monks, that Desolate Europe with Wars" (778). Thus he was forced to insist that the writings of the classical authors were "Stolen and Perverted" from the work of "more ancient & consciously & professedly Inspired Men" (480). "Let it be here Noted that the Greek Fables originated in Spiritual Mystery & Real Visions, which are lost & clouded in Fable & Allegory" (605). "No man can believe that either Homer's Mythology, or Ovid's, were the production of Greece or of Latinum; neither will any one believe, that the Greek statues, as they are called, were the invention of Greek Artists"; with few exceptions the works are "copies, though fine ones, from greater works of the Asiatic Patriarchs." Cause and proof are one: "The Greek Muses are daughters of Mnemosyne, or Memory, and not of Inspiration or Imagination, therefore not authors of such sublime conceptions" (565-566).

Although Blake was still praising classical influence in 1800, I think we may see in these designs to Gray the beginnings of his rejection of classical ideology, particularly in the designs to the "war group" of "The Bard," "The Fatal Sisters," and "The Descent of Owen," and especially through their connection with Flaxman's Homer designs. Blake's dictum that "Imitation is Criticism" (453) had here a special application, if I am right in guessing that Blake, knowing his Gray designs were destined for the Flaxmans' library, copied from Flaxman's outlines—whose pristine beauty masks the actual carnage and brutality of the Trojan war under the appearances of dancelike postures and heroic forms—and placed these copies in contexts of grim explicitness. "These are the true shapes of war," he says through the medium of his illustrations. Surely Flaxman is among those "Sculptors! Architects!" on whom he calls in the Preface to *Milton*, urging them to "set your foreheads against" those "who would, if they could, forever depress Mental & prolong Corporeal War" (480). The mild Flaxman was hardly one to prolong corporeal war intentionally, but it may be that he saw the lines of what Blake called "spiritual agency" (579) less clearly than Blake believed he himself did. For some reason—this or another—Blake was soon to feel that Flaxman had disappointed him and was not a true friend, and even to accuse Flaxman (in the Notebook "Public Address") of having copied certain of the Homer designs from his work: "How much of his Homer & Dante he will allow to be mine I

Erdman dates 1803 (*Prophet Against Empire*, p. 458 [rev. edn., p. 497]). There Blake contends that "The Roman pride is a sword of steel" and opposes to it "The Tear of Love & forgiveness sweet" which "shall melt the sword of steel,/And every wound it has made shall heal" (420).

do not know, as he went far enough off to Publish them, even to Italy, but the Public will know & Posterity will know" (592).[8] In fact posterity still does not know; we might suppose that the copies Blake made from Flaxman were earlier copies by Flaxman from Blake, but this seems unlikely on the face of it. More likely Blake had in mind a broader influence, exercised in the early period of their friendship, before Flaxman went to Italy (1787-1794), when they were both relatively unknown artists. In view of Flaxman's subsequent great success—he had, for example, just been elected an associate to the Royal Academy (in 1797)— Blake must have found the continuing general disregard for his own work embitteringly unjustified.

I have already noted Blake's awareness that in order to communicate "spiritual ideas" or "vision" one had somehow to expand ordinary language. Such an expansion was consistently his objective—to build, like Los, "the stubborn structure of the language" of art out of "English, the rough basement" (668). This Blake sought to do for Gray in a variety of ways, adjusting his technique to the job at hand. In the Eton ode, for example, we saw "incapacity" first suggested in the limpness of the youngsters, then demonstrated as they flee the "vultures" and shuffle toward death. In the "Elegy" a similar vague lifelessness is displayed; but Blake's intention is less clear, raising the question of whether his idiosyncratic technique does not limit more than it expands, in that it requires of the viewer a special way of seeing that makes of Blake's art something approaching cryptogram. Certainly we can sense a stifling of human vigor just by looking at the "Elegy" designs and aligning them with Gray's argument, but we would hardly be able to know what that sense of stifling means, or how to overcome it, if we did not have recourse to other of Blake's works which remind us, for example, that "Active Evil is better than Passive Good" (77).

That "special way of seeing"—in part because it *is* so unfamiliar—Blake considered absolutely the central concern of art. I have said earlier that he broke with his fellow artists on the issue of "moral attitude," by which I meant to distinguish his continuing respect for the linear style of classical art from his growing re-

[8] The break does not seem to have affected his friendly feelings toward Nancy Flaxman, however, viz. the Notebook couplet:

To Nancy F.
How can I help thy Husband's copying Me?
Should that make difference 'twixt me & Thee?

pugnance for what he felt to be the moral or philosophical assumptions of classical civilization. But Blake would have referred the break to a difference in "way of seeing" (vision) and would have objected to such a use of the word "moral," insomuch as it might imply that the artist's business was to reason things into order along the axioms of one or another ethical system. It was precisely in such service to a system—to an inherited code of behavior or value—that art was most likely to founder, the artist's vision to darken and grow clouded. Such a faulty allegiance had been one of the difficulties besetting the poet Milton, who understood the "history" of the fall but assigned to the actors moral qualities that made him misinterpret his own vision. In the same way Blake often found Gray right in his vision yet wrong in his interpretation of it; right in his particulars, wrong in his abstractions. Gray could, as in the "Ode to Adversity," delineate accurately a state of mind; as poet, that was his job. But he is moral philosopher—and mistaken—when he imputes to that state of mind any creative power: a moral philosopher in a "puritan" tradition, mistaken because he refuses to recognize the overall shape of his vision, the lines of connection and distinction. Gray's vision is right in associating adversity with virtue and moral rectitude; Blake's "corrective" was to demonstrate, pictorially, that these are all allied with death and opposed to that energetic delight that claims "every thing that lives is Holy" (160). Blake's is not a moral judgment in that it imputes sin or virtue (although he occasionally speaks in these terms);[9] rather, as illustrator he sought to expose what he considered the true similarities among certain important spiritual states displayed in the poem. All bear the "outline" of the enclosed or limited. Despite Gray's stated approval of hardship and denial, his poetic genius (Blake would call it) hints at an awareness of the truth contained in such allusions as that to Adversity's "rigid lore" or Melancholy's "leaden eye that loves the ground." And so Blake isolates and magnifies that awareness by showing us bodies crouched, bent, rigidified—dead as the child of Grief among the roots of trees.

In a spectacular passage, central to his whole aesthetic as poet-artist, Blake tries to press the "rough basement" of expository language, through metaphor, into spiritual vision, and at the same time to show what he means by the proper way of seeing. If we say *There* I draw the line," we are indicating that at a given

[9] Blake's usual view on the subject is that expressed in his annotations to Boyd's Dante: "Poetry is to excuse Vice & shew its reason & necessary purgation" (412). The key word is "excuse": Blake uses it (perhaps with a glance at its etymology) in the sense of "explain" or "give the cause," *ex*cuse as opposed to *ac*cuse.

point we believe one thing becomes another: acceptable behavior becomes unacceptable, "plenty" becomes "too much." Blake suggests that this metaphorical "line"—available even in everyday speech—is the same as that which shapes prophetic vision and guides the artist, the line on whose clarity all accurate vision depends, and consequently all truly creative human activity. For line-drawing is the operation of intellect, it is what organizes all experience in life, all forms in art:

> The great and golden rule of art, as well as of life, is this: That the more distinct, sharp, and wiry the bounding line, the more perfect the work of art; and the less keen and sharp, the greater is the evidence of weak imitation, plagiarism, and bungling. Great inventors, in all ages, knew this: Protogenes and Apelles knew each other by this line. Rafael and Michael Angelo and Albert Dürer are known by this and this alone. The want of this determinate and bounding form evidences the want of idea in the artist's mind, and the pretence of the plagiary in all its branches. How do we distinguish the oak from the beech, the horse from the ox, but by the bounding outline? How do we distinguish one face or countenance from another, but by the bounding line and its infinite inflexions and movements? What is it that builds a house and plants a garden, but the definite and determinate? What is it that distinguishes honesty from knavery, but the hard and wiry line of rectitude and certainty in the actions and intentions? Leave out this line, and you leave out life itself; all is chaos again, and the line of the almighty must be drawn out upon it before man or beast can exist. (585)

The true prophet is he who sees these lines clearly and recognizes the similarities of shape and meaning. Among Chaucer's pilgrims (and recall that "Chaucer's characters live age after age" [570]) the good parson is "a real Messenger of Heaven, sent in every age for its light and its warmth." "Search, O ye rich and powerful, for these men and obey their counsel, then shall the golden age return: But alas! you will not easily distinguish him from the Friar or the Pardoner; they, also, are 'full solemn men,' and their counsel you will continue to follow" (570). To differentiate parson from pardoner is at once to recognize the "Visionary Form" of each and to "draw the line" between them. The bounding outline that circumscribes in the negative sense of restricting or perverting is quite another thing—the product of that fallen intellect which, having eaten of the tree of knowledge of good and evil, has become concerned not with accuracy of

154

vision but with accusation, repression, and coercion, with forcing lines of vision to take the shapes of moral evaluation. The result is destructive of life and art, and Blake identifies these areas of destruction—"identifies" in the special sense in which he so often used the word, that is, as meaning that at the level of vision both areas have the same form, the same "identity."

In *A Vision of the Last Judgment*, from the Notebook writings of about 1810, Blake anticipates the apocalypse that closes *Jerusalem*: he envisions the inhabitants of paradise "walking up & down in Conversations concerning Mental Delights." The point is that "they are no longer talking of what is Good & Evil, or of what is Right or Wrong, & puzzling themselves in Satan's Labyrinth, But are Conversing with Eternal Realities as they Exist in the Human Imagination." And Blake's next lines point to the crux of the matter for art, defined through the opposition of linear to painterly: "We are in a World of Generation & death, & this world we must cast off if we would be Painters such as Rafael, Mich. Angelo & the Ancient Sculptors; if we do not cast off this world we shall be only Venetian Painters, who will be cast off & Lost from Art" (613). The artist whose work does not reveal where the human form leaves off and its shadow begins is in trouble all the way to eternity, and the reason is that he does not care about the "true forms" of things but only about appearances. The artist who does not respect the true forms of things in perishing nature can never expect to see the eternal form of anything. He is a man who does not respect lines, who does not make distinctions: he is a blurrer.

Such language of line applies to poetic as well as pictorial art, as Blake shows in his *Public Address*; arguing that no "Original Invention" can exist without "Execution, Organized & minutely delineated & Articulated, Either by God or Man," he draws parallel examples from art and poetry. "I do not mean smooth'd up & Niggled & Poco-Pen'd, and all the beauties pick'd out & blurr'd & blotted, but Drawn with a firm & decided hand at once, like Fuseli & Michel Angelo, Shakespeare & Milton" (595). The creative act is always the same, whether considered the act of God or of man, painter or poet.[10] Later Blake assimilated to these terms the language of Christianity as well, arguing in *The Laocoön* that

---

[10] I do not know whether it has ever been pointed out that Blake's verb "organize"—a key word in his vocabulary—concerns this creative act. One reason Blake's uses of the verb sometimes seem odd is that for him the word still carries in it the implications of the noun "organ," as when he speaks of historians who "being weakly organized themselves, cannot see either miracle or prodigy" (578). "The clearer the organ the more dis-

A Poet, a Painter, a Musician, an Architect: the Man or Woman who is not one of these is not a Christian.

You must leave Fathers & Mothers & Houses & Lands if they stand in the way of Art.

Prayer is the Study of Art.

Praise is the Practice of Art.

Fasting &c., all relate to Art.

The outward Ceremony is Antichrist.

The Eternal Body of Man is the Imagination . . .

It manifests itself in his Works of Art (In Eternity All is Vision). (776)

And, to repeat, "Vision" is the capacity to see clearly, to recognize lines and to draw them accurately.

There can be no doubt that Blake's illustrations testify to the mixed regard in which he held Gray, but the poet's weaknesses seem to have been not so much in a blurring of vision as in a rational uncertainty as to what his vision meant. For Blake the "Poetic Genius" was life itself, the "true Man," as he asserted in his early manifesto *All Religions are One* (98), and (to repeat) to the poetic genius death in the physical sense is wholly irrelevant. Blake's brother Robert was not dead in Blake's view; Milton was not dead; indeed, Gray himself was alive and vigorous. Yet Blake found Gray continually misled by his "Contemplation" into the grievously mistaken belief that "the race of man" comes finally "in dust to rest." We have seen that such is the argument of Gray's first and his last poem in this illustrated series, and as an unstated assumption it lies behind most of the remaining poems. But Blake appears to have sensed a counterargument struggling toward the surface of Gray's thought, never entirely reaching it and yet again and again making itself felt in the language of the early poems and the content of some of the later ones. Gray, Blake was sure, was in these poems more "of the Devil's party" than he knew. And as with Milton, Blake found that

---

tinct the object" (576), Blake maintained, so that "If Perceptive Organs vary, / Objects of Perception seem to vary" (661). This is of course why "The unorganized Blots and Blurs of Rubens and Titian are not Art" (596) and why Blake concluded emphatically, if rather cryptically by standards of normal word usage, *"Unorganiz'd Innocence: An Impossibility"*—adding, as if in explanation, "Innocence dwells with Wisdom, but never with Ignorance" (380). "Wisdom" presupposes the visionary capacity to see clearly, a necessary prerequisite for drawing accurately and indeed for excellence in any art.

his job here was to uncover and display that true and admirable allegiance in its prophetic splendor.

With "The Progress of Poesy," however, Blake seemed to feel that Gray had assumed the dishonorable role of Virgil to a corrupt Augustus, so that while, as before, certain of Gray's poetic insights emerge as true and richly suggestive, the argument of the poem taken as a whole is degrading to the poet and destructive of his muse-seeing "infant eyes." That those eyes were not permanently blurred or destroyed "The Bard" stands as powerful evidence, for there poetic prophecy addresses itself fearlessly to kingship. Yet the "Ode for Music" and, for other reasons, the "Epitaph on Mrs. Clarke" and the "Elegy Written in a Country Churchyard" betrayed (to Blake) how fallible Gray could be in his role as poet of vision.

In his illustrations to "The Bard" Blake allowed certain of his own developing mythological elements to entangle themselves with Gray's, drawing together sometimes contradictory lines of association: chief of these are the glimpses of the dead bards as ancient Britons (later described by Blake as "naked civilized men, learned, studious . . . wiser than after-ages" [577]) and at the same time as a trio of vindictive and punishing furies.

There are, to be sure, suggestions of both prophecy and vengeance in Gray's portrayal of the bards, and in another mood Blake might have found it important to separate the two in the name of eternal salvation. But I suspect that Blake's mood was influenced in part by the conditions of the time, and that he was willing to let such contradictions pass—and indeed to build on them in his designs—in his greater eagerness to display the necessity and potential power of bardic denunciation of a government founded on war and the persecution of poets. It has always been true, he maintained, that "Art Degraded, Imagination Denied, War Governed the Nations" (775), and while Gray doubtless intended no radicalism, still his poem does present a vision of poetic power in the face of bloody suppression, of the final victory of art and imagination over a government that degraded and denied them, and ruled by war.

When Blake illustrated Gray's poems England was engaged in a war that weighed heavily on Blake's conscience; and bardic insurgencies were being suppressed by a conservatism that provided a painful analogy to Edward I's suppression of the Welsh bards. The treason trials of 1794 were past, but political dissension was by no means to be permitted, as Blake well knew and rediscovered to his horror when he found himself accused of seditious speech and brought to trial in 1803.[11] If the bard's prophetic account of the evils to ensue from Edward's example and lineage is seen at times as exultantly vindictive, still it is the denunciation itself that mattered to Blake. Such prophecy as the bard's is the business of any artist—indeed, of any honest man—for a nation survives by its seers: "Every honest man is a Prophet; he utters his opinion both of private & public matters. Thus: If you go on So, the result is So. He never says, such a thing shall happen let you do what you will. A Prophet is a Seer, not an Arbitrary Dictator" (392). In Blake's view, any honest man could have predicted the evil that was to result from Edward's persecution of the Welsh poets, because such persecution always results in evil; Gray's bard, having the advantage of the author's hindsight, only offers greater accuracy of historical detail, and (perhaps because of his increased knowledge) a greater virulence of denunciation.

In this context, too, we can understand more clearly what Blake saw in the two translations of ancient poems about war, "The Fatal Sisters" and "The Triumphs of Owen," and much of the point of his illustrations. Any man who sees war clearly, whose vision is not blurred, or perverted by false notions of glory or heroism, must see that "The god of war is drunk with blood" (13) and that "war is the Tyrant's gain" (420). But should we miss the point he still provides us with the silent comment of Owen 6, in which the Liberal Man invites the traveller into his house and so repudiates a society grounded in terror and death.

Blake's visionary reading of these poems, then, is largely available to any attentive and sensitive viewer; but would such a viewer, even under ideal circumstances, be able to understand Blake's quite specific critical reading of the "Elegy Written in a Country Churchyard," that most famous of all Gray's poems and one of the most loved of its century? I cannot doubt that Blake considered the proper reading of this poem to be of the highest importance: he set the poem apart from all the rest, with its own introductory portrait of "The author writing"; he placed his own signature in the graveyard; and finally, as "Lycidas" had been Milton's vision of the poet as individual and yet as one in a continuing line of poets, so this was Gray's. The designs are Blake's answer, and at the same time a statement of his own visionary credo.

Blake's defense of the obscurity of his own art is well known; in 1799 he wrote Dr. Trusler, "What is Grand is necessarily obscure to Weak men. That which can

[11] Blake's turmoil during this entire period and its record in the developing *Vala* are discussed in detail by Erdman in *Prophet Against Empire*, Part V.

be made Explicit to the Idiot is not worth my care. The wisest of the Ancients consider'd what is not too Explicit as the fittest for Instruction, because it rouzes the faculties to act" (793). But he is dedicated to educating those faculties, as no one can doubt who has read his *Descriptive Catalogue* and *Public Address.* And I think the progress of these designs may be seen as at least partly educative. We recall that Spring 3 refers in its title to the "roots of nature," and we are shown these roots in the design itself; we are, moreover, shown their relationship to the whole life of the picture, for in springing into that life, the young Year pushes up and away from the roots. His grotesque posture calls further attention to this wrenching from the "natural" life of rooty growth to that life Blake says the ancient poets saw when they "animated all sensible objects with Gods or Geniuses," perceiving with "their enlarged & numerous senses" (153). In the designs to "Ode on the Spring" Blake tried to show the necessity of using human capacities fully, in "Ode on a Distant Prospect of Eton College" the spiritual terror and death that results from the unused capacity, in "Ode to Adversity" the connections between grief, hardship, and related natural evils that starve the spirit and blunt the mind. The two lighter poems, the "Ode on the Death of a Favourite Cat" and "A Long Story," served among other things to remind us in the first instance of the relationships of allegory to vision and in both instances of the visionary potential of a wit not used to destroy or to confine the mind. We are, then, already somewhat educated in Blake's vocabulary of vision by the time we reach the varied commentaries of the later poems and perceive the loss of Gray's "infant eyes" at the close of "The Progress of Poesy," the power of prophecy in "The Bard," the terrors of war and its mechanized goddesses, and the living death to which tombbuilders commit themselves.

Thus when we finally reach the "Elegy," after this Blakean tour de force of 104 varied and bold compositions, we should know at the very least that something is missing in this final, earthbound sequence; and the bright coloring of nature alone shows us that it is not a failure of the natural capacities of life. Surely we know by now where to look. On the other hand, the specific terms supplied by the connections with the Young designs are not available unless one does look there, or (for slightly less precise analogies) at other of Blake's pictures. To this extent the vocabulary of Blake's language must be explicated from his other works, even though the grammatical frame is fully displayed within this sequence. We cannot ask much more of an artist, if we interpret his task to be one of showing us the object anew without our failing to recognize it. Blake really wished to share his visionary capacity: "If the Spectator could Enter into these Images in his Imagination, . . . or could make a Friend & Companion of one of these Images of wonder, which always intreats him to leave mortal things (as he must know), then would he arise from his Grave, then would he meet the Lord in the Air & then he would be happy" (611). That he was able to share only fitfully, and with so few, was one of the recurring disappointments of his career as an artist.

The importance of these designs lies first of all in their commanding effects as an artistic series, but of course they are significant as well insofar as they may be considered documents in the history of Blake's own artistic development. This period of Blake's life, the late 1790's, has left us very few records of other kinds. The portion of *Vala* written during this period was at least partly destroyed in the process of its evolution into *The Four Zoas*, and it is hard to distinguish with any exactness the various layers of its history and to date them with certainty.[12] A bare half dozen of Blake's letters survive from the entire period before 1800, and after 1795 he had stopped writing short prophecies. In brief, the designs to Young and Gray, and a set of tempera paintings done for his then-new patron Thomas Butts around 1799-1800, are practically the only evidence that remains of a tumultuous and important period in Blake's life.

They show us a Blake returning from the disillusionment of the early 1790's to a renewed optimism based on a fresh belief in the power of man to create in the fallen world a spiritual home—the "Paradise within thee, happier far" that Michael promised to Adam and Eve. The views of adversity and war do argue a continuing capacity for dark vision, and Blake was to face one more period of deep melancholy (according to his letter of July 2, 1800 to Cumberland) before the momentous removal to Felpham. For the Blake of the "Elegy" designs it is entirely true that

> Whate'er is Born of Mortal Birth
> Must be consumed with the Earth
> To rise from Generation free.

Yet the question raised by the next line—"Then what have I to do with thee?"— Blake here answers in a gentler and more flexible voice than that heard in the poem of bitter repudiation from which these lines are taken, "To Tirzah" (220). For it is the beauty of the natural world that teaches us what is missing in the

---

[12] The facsimile edited by G. E. Bentley, Jr. (Oxford, 1963), should open the way to much fuller scholarship in that area.

"Elegy" designs. And as we learned from the Young design which showed the corpse's burial briars sprouting leaves, the felt life and beauty of thorny nature does not disappear when one reaches a visionary understanding of its limitations and transience, but rather fully emerges only with that understanding.

> . . . in your own Bosom you bear your Heaven
> And Earth & all you behold; tho' it appears Without, it is Within,
> In your Imagination, of which this World of Mortality is but a
> Shadow. (709)

Yet a shadow retains the shape of that which casts it; and the man who can recognize and feel the life within him will recognize and feel it outside as well.

I think Blake's poem dedicating his work "To Mrs. Ann Flaxman" may be read on one level as explaining to her the value of what he has done for Gray's vision. Gray had spoken in his "Elegy" of the potentially great, the geniuses that never reach the light: "Full many a flower is born to blush unseen/ And waste its sweetness on the desert air." Blake picks up the figure, connecting it to Gray through his self-description as one "to Fame unknown," and translates it into his own view of what visionary enlargement could do for the poetry of the partial poet, the genius who only fitfully reached the light.

> A little Flower grew in a lonely Vale
> Its form was lovely but its colours pale
> One standing in the Porches of the Sun
> When his Meridian Glories were begun
> Leapd from the steps of fire & on the grass
> Alighted where this little flower was
> With hands divine he movd the gentle Sod
> And took the Flower up in its native Clod
> Then planting it upon a Mountains brow
> 'Tis your own fault if you dont flourish now

If Gray does not flourish now, Blake implies, if his vision is not clarified and his true bardic power revealed, it must be his own fault, for Blake feels that he has done for him all that was needed. Keeping the poetry intact—in its "native Clod" —he had nonetheless exposed its prophetic meanings and repudiated its errors. Its fate now lay with its viewers. And so it still lies almost 175 years later, as Blake continues to converse with Gray—and with us—in "Visionary forms dramatic."

LIST OF WORKS CITED

Anon. "Blake's Designs for Gray. Light on their History." *The Times* (London), November 5, 1919, p. 15.

Antal, Frederick. *Fuseli Studies*. London, 1956.

Baker, C. H. Collins. *Catalogue of William Blake's Drawings and Paintings in the Huntington Library*. San Marino, California, 1957.

Bentley, G. E., Jr., and Martin K. Nurmi. *A Blake Bibliography*. Minneapolis, 1964.

Bentley, G. E., Jr., ed. *Vala or The Four Zoas*. Oxford, 1963.

———. *Blake Records*. Oxford, 1969.

Bentley, Richard. *Designs by Richard Bentley, for Six Poems by Mr. Thomas Gray*. London, 1753.

Blake, William. *Poems by Mr. Gray: Drawings by William Blake* (the unique copy).

———. *The Complete Writings of William Blake*. Sir Geoffrey Keynes, ed. London and New York, 1957.

———. *William Blake's "Heads of the Poets."* Ed. with an Introduction and notes by G. L. Conran and William Wells. Manchester, England, n.d. [1969?].

———. *William Blake's Illustrations to the Bible*. A Catalogue compiled by Geoffrey Keynes. London, 1957.

Blunt, Anthony. *The Art of William Blake*. New York, 1959.

Bronowski, J. *A Man Without A Mask: William Blake 1757-1827*. London, 1947.

Bronson, Bertrand H. "Personification Reconsidered," *ELH*, XIV (1947), 163-77.

Burke, Joseph. "The Eidetic and the Borrowed Image: an Interpretation of Blake's Theory and Practice of Art," *In Honour of Daryl Lindsay*. Melbourne, 1964.

Chapin, Chester F. *Personification in Eighteenth-Century English Poetry*. New York, 1955.

Coleridge, Samuel Taylor. *Complete Works*, ed. W.G.T. Shedd. 7 vols. New York, 1871-76.

Damon, S. Foster, *A Blake Dictionary*. Providence, Rhode Island, 1965.

———. *Blake's Grave, A Prophetic Book*. Providence, Rhode Island, 1963.

———. *William Blake: His Philosophy and Symbols*. Boston and New York, 1924.

Eglington, Guy. "Blake Illustrates Gray," *International Studio*, LXXIX (1924), 39-47.

Erdman, David V. *Blake: Prophet Against Empire*. Revised Ed. Princeton, 1969.

———. *The Poetry and Prose of William Blake*. New York, 1965.

——— and John E. Grant, eds. *Blake's Visionary Forms Dramatic*. Princeton, 1970.

Evans, B. Ifor. *Tradition and Romanticism.* London, 1940.

Farington, Joseph. *The Farington Diary,* ed. James Grieg. 8 vols. London, 1922-28.

Frye, Northrop. *Fearful Symmetry.* Princeton, 1947.

Fuseli, Henry, illustrator in part. *The Poems of Gray,* anon. ed. London, 1800.

Gilchrist, Alexander. *Life of William Blake, "Pictor Ignotus."* 2 vols. London and Cambridge, 1863.

Gosse, Edmund. *More Books on the Table.* London, 1923.

Grant, John E. "Interpreting Blake's 'The Fly,'" *BNYPL,* LXVII (1963), 593-615.

Gray, Thomas. *The Poems of Gray,* anon. ed. London, 1800.

Grierson, H.J.C. "Blake's Designs for Gray. Discovery in Hamilton Palace." *The Times* (London), November 4, 1919, p. 15.

————, ed. *William Blake's Designs for Gray's Poems: Reproduced Full-size in Monochrome or Colour.* London, 1922.

Hagstrum, Jean H. *The Sister Arts.* Chicago, 1958.

————. *William Blake: Poet and Painter.* Chicago and London, 1964.

Hirsch, E. D., Jr. *Innocence and Experience: An Introduction to Blake.* New Haven and London, 1964.

Irwin, David. *English Neoclassical Art.* London, 1966.

Johnson, Samuel. *The Works of Samuel Johnson LL.D. in Nine Volumes.* Oxford, 1825.

Johnston, Arthur. "The Purple Year in Pope and Gray," *RES,* XVI (1963), 389-93.

Keynes, Sir Geoffrey. *Blake Studies: Notes on his Life and Works in Seventeen Chapters.* London, 1949.

————, ed. *The Complete Writings of William Blake.* London and New York, 1957.

————. *Pencil Drawings by William Blake.* Second Series. Holland, 1956.

Lowery, Ruth. "Blake and the Flaxmans," *The Age of Johnson,* ed. F. W. Hilles, New Haven and London, 1949.

Mason, Eudo C. *The Mind of Henry Fuseli.* London, 1951.

Milton, John. *Poems in English with Illustrations by William Blake.* 2 vols. London, 1926.

Miner, Paul. "William Blake: Two Notes on Sources," *BNYPL,* LXII (1958), 203-7.

Monk, Samuel. *The Sublime.* Ann Arbor, 1960.

Panofsky, Dora and Erwin. *Pandora's Box.* New York, 1962.

Plowman, Max. "A Note on William Blake's 'Marriage of Heaven and Hell,'" *The Marriage of Heaven and Hell* (color facsimile). London and Toronto, 1927.

Pointon, Marcia R. *Milton & English Art.* Manchester, 1970.

Preston, Kerrison. *The Blake Collection of W. Graham Robertson.* London, 1952.

Raine, Kathleen. *Blake and Tradition.* 2 vols. Princeton, 1968.

LIST OF WORKS CITED

Rosenblum, Robert. *The International Style of 1800: A Study in Linear Abstraction.* Unpublished doctoral dissertation. New York University, 1956.

————. *Transformations in Late Eighteenth Century Art.* Princeton, 1967.

Schiff, Gert. *Johann Heinrich Füsslis Milton Galerie.* Zurich and Stuttgart, 1963.

Schorer, Mark. *William Blake: The Politics of Vision.* New York, 1959.

Sherburn, George. "The Restoration and Eighteenth Century," *A Literary History of England,* ed. Albert C. Baugh. New York, 1948.

Spacks, Patricia Meyer. *The Poetry of Vision: Five Eighteenth-Century Poets.* Cambridge, Massachusetts, 1967.

Starr, H. W. and J. R. Hendrickson, eds. *The Complete Poems of Thomas Gray.* Oxford, 1966.

Wicksteed, Joseph. *Blake's Vision of the Book of Job.* London and New York, 1910.

INDEX

"Ancients" (followers of Blake), 6, 7
Antal, Frederick, 15
Apelles, as referred to by Blake, 154
Aquinas, St. Thomas, 148

Bacon, Francis, mentioned by Blake, 124
Baker, C. H. Collins, 87
Barry, James, 148; illustrator of Milton, 147
Basire, James, 14, 46
Baugh, A. C., 83
Beckford, William, 4
Bentley, G. E., Jr., *Blake Records*, 3, 139; ed. *Vala*, 10, 12, 16, 17, 160; with Martin K. Nurmi, *A Blake Bibliography*, 4, 102
Bentley, Richard, illustrator of Gray, 24, 28; designs for Gray's Cat Ode, 59-61, 62, 70; Elegy, 134, 135; Eton Ode, 28-31, 36, 42, 43, 45, 97; Long Story, 71, 74, 75, 122; Ode on the Spring, 49
Bible, as Vision, 9, 60; referred to by Blake, 17; *see also* Blake, illustrations to Job; *and* Blake, Separate Pictures
Bicknell, John, 130
Blair, Robert, *see* Blake, as illustrator of Blair's *The Grave*
Blake, Catherine, 12
Blake, Robert, 144, 156
Blake, William, pencil sketch by Flaxman, 20; as illustrator of Blair's *The Grave*, 6, 7, 15, 107, 139; Bunyan's *Pilgrim's Progress*, 7, 33; Dante, 3, 7, 33; Job, 3, 6, 33; Milton, 3, 7, 33, 51, 66-67, 69, 70, 87, 97; Shakespeare, 7; Young's *Night Thoughts* (general mention), 3-20 *passim*, 33, 129, 131, 137, 144, 159, 160, 161 (references to specific designs), 78-79, 92, 99, 107, 111, 124, 130, 134, 136, 139, 140
    Separate Pictures, "Ancient Britons," 107-108; "The Bard, from Gray" (tempera), 14, 30 (watercolor), 14; "Christ Blessing the Little Children," 142; "Death of Abel," 13; "Edward **and** Elanor," 102; "Ghost of the Flea," 29; "Heads of the Poets," 104; "Joseph of Arimathea," 88; "The Poet Gray," 46; "The Virgin and Child in Egypt," 122; "Vision of the Last Judgement," 139; "Whore of Babylon," 119

Blunt, Sir Anthony, 5, 87, 102
Boccaccio, 122
Boydell's Shakespeare Gallery, 18, 147
British Museum, 10, 11, 13
Bronowski, J., 4-5, 12
Bronson, Bertrand H., 28, 42, 44
Bunyan, John, 9; *see also* Blake, as illustrator, and Flaxman, as illustrator
Burke, Joseph, 7-9, 150
Butts, Thomas, 17, 18, 97, 142, 160
Byron, Lord, 105

Calcott, A. W., 135
Carstens, Asmus, 150
Chapin, Chester, 42, 43
Chatterton, Thomas, 55
Chaucer, Geoffrey, 8, 9, 43, 72, 122, 124, 154
Christie's, 3, 4
Clarke, William, 4
Cornelius, Peter, 150
Correggio, 143
Cowper, William, 18
Cumberland, George, 16, 17, 19, 80, 148, 150, 160

Damon, S. Foster, 5, 76-77, 107, 109, 139
Dante, 8; *see also* Blake, and Flaxman, as illustrators
Day, Thomas, 130, 131, 135, 143
Drake, Nathan, 23
Dryden, John, 60, 82, 90, 91, 92, 93
Dürer, Albrecht, 145, 154

Edward I, 94-110 *passim*, 157, 158
Edward III, 99, 100, 125

PLATES

William Blake

Drawn by John Flaxman

Ode on the Spring

Design.

1 The Pindaric Genius receiving his Lyre

2 Gray writing his Poems

3 The Purple Year awaking from the Roots of
Nature & the Hours suckling their
Flowery Infants

4 "With me the Muse shall sit & think
At ease reclind in rustic State"

5 "Brush'd by the hand of rough Mischance
Or chill'd by Age"

6 Summer Flies reproaching the Poet

Around the Springs of Gray my wild root weaves
Traveller repose & Dream among my leaves.
Will. Blake

O D E

ON THE

S P R I N G.

L O! where the rofy-bofom'd hours,
  Fair VENUS' train, appear,
Difclofe the long-expected flowers,
  And wake the purple year!
The Attic warbler pours her throat,
Refponfive to the cuckow's note,
The untaught harmony of fpring:
While, whifp'ring pleafure as they fly,
Cool Zephyrs thro' the clear blue fky
  Their gather'd fragrance fling.

D   Where-

Where-e'er the oak's thick branches stretch
A broader browner shade;
Where-e'er the rude and moss-grown beech
O'er-canopies the glade;
Beside some water's rushy brink
With me the Muse shall sit, and think,
(At ease reclin'd in rustic state),
How vain the ardour of the crowd,
How low, how little are the proud,
How indigent the great!

Still is the toiling hand of Care;
The panting herds repose:
Yet hark, how thro' the peopled air
The busy murmur glows!
The insect youth are on the wing,
Eager to taste the honied spring,

And

ODE ON THE SPRING.   45

And float amid the liquid noon:
Some lightly o'er the current skim,
Some shew their gaily-gilded trim
Quick-glancing to the sun.

To Contemplation's sober eye
Such is the race of man:
And they that creep, and they that fly,
Shall end where they began.
Alike the busy and the gay
But flutter thro' life's little day,
In Fortune's varying colours drest:
Brush'd by the hand of rough Mischance,
Or chill'd by Age, their airy dance
They leave in dust to rest.

Methinks I hear, in accents low,
The sportive kind reply;
Poor Moralist! and what art thou?
A solitary fly!

D 2   Thy

ODE ON THE SPRING.

Thy joys no glitt'ring female meets,
No hive haft thou of hoarded sweets,
No painted plumage to display:
On hasty wings thy youth is flown;
Thy sun is set, thy spring is gone—
We frolic while 'tis May.

ODE

ON THE DEATH OF A

FAVOURITE CAT.

Drowned in a Tub of Gold Fishes.

D 3

2

O D E

ON THE DEATH OF A

FAVOURITE CAT.

Drowned in a Tub of Gold Fishes,

'TWAS on a lofty vase's side,
 Where China's gayest art had dy'd
  The azure flowers, that blow;
Demurest of the tabby kind,
 The pensive Selima reclin'd,
  Gaz'd on the lake below.

Her conscious tail her joy declar'd;
The fair round face, the snowy beard,
 The velvet of her paws;
    D 4   Her

50 ODE ON THE DEATH

Her coat, that with the tortoise vies,
Her ears of jet, and emerald eyes,
 She faw; and purr'd applaufe.

Still had fhe gaz'd; but 'midft the tide
Two angel forms were feen to glide,
 The Genii of the ftream:
Their fcaly armour's Tyrian hue,
Thro' richeft purple to the view
 Betray'd a golden gleam.

The haplefs nymph with wonder faw:
A whifker firft, and then a claw,
 With many an ardent wifh,
She ftretch'd, in vain, to reach the prize.
What female heart can gold defpife?
 What cat's averfe to fifh?

         Prefump-

OF A FAVOURITE CAT.   5t

Presumptuous maid! with looks intent
Again she stretch'd, again she bent,
    Nor knew the gulph between:
(Malignant Fate sat by, and smil'd)
The slipp'ry verge her feet beguil'd,
She tumbled headlong in.

Eight times emerging from the flood
She mew'd to ev'ry wat'ry God,
    Some speedy aid to send.
No Dolphin came, no Nereid stirr'd,
Nor cruel Tom, nor Susan heard,
    A fav'rite has no friend!

From hence, ye beauties, undeceiv'd,
Know, one false step is ne'er retriev'd,
    And be with caution bold.

                                    Not

52   O D E,   &c.

Nor all that tempts your wand'ring eyes,
And heedless hearts, is lawful prize ;
  Nor all that glisters, gold.

                              O D E

O D E

ON A

DISTANT PROSPECT

OF

ETON COLLEGE.

Ἄνθρωπος ἱκανὴ πρόφασις εἰς τὸ δυστυχεῖν.
MENANDER.

ODE

ON A DISTANT PROSPECT OF

ETON COLLEGE.

YE diſtant ſpires, ye antique towers,
  That crown the wat'ry glade,
Where grateful Science ſtill adores
+ Her HENRY's holy ſhade;
And ye, that from the ſtately brow
Of WINDSOR's heights th' expanſe below
Of grove, of lawn, of mead ſurvey,
Whoſe turf, whoſe ſhade, whoſe flowers among
Wanders the hoary Thames along
His ſilver-winding way.

                                    Ah

4

56 ODE ON A DISTANT PROSPECT

Ah happy hills! ah pleasing shade!
Ah fields belov'd in va n!
Where once my careless childhood stray'd,
A stranger yet to pain!
I feel, the gales that from ye blow,
A momentary bliss bestow,
As waving fresh their gladsome wing,
My weary soul they seem to sooth,
And, redolent of joy and youth,
To breathe a second spring.

Say, Father THAMES, for thou hast seen
Full many a sprightly race
Disporting on thy margent green
The paths of pleasure trace;
Who foremost now delight to cleave,
With pliant arms, thy glassy wave?

The

OF ETON COLLEGE.   57

The captive linnet, which enthral?
What idle progeny succeed
To chase the rolling circle's speed,
Or urge the flying ball?

While some on earnest business bent
Their murm'ring labours ply
'Gainst graver hours, that bring constraint
To sweeten liberty :
Some bold adventurers disdain
The limits of their little reign,
And unknown regions dare descry :
Still as they run they look behind,
They hear a voice in every wind,
And snatch a fearful joy.

Gay hope is theirs by fancy fed,
Less pleasing when possest ;
The tear forgot as soon as shed,
The sunshine of the breast :
                                    Theirs

6

58 ODE ON A DISTANT PROSPECT

Theirs buxom Health, of rosy hue,
Wild wit, Invention ever-new,
And lively Cheer of Vigour born;
The thoughtless day, the easy night,
The spirits pure, the slumbers light,
That fly th' approach of morn.

Alas! regardless of their doom,
The little victims play!
No sense have they of ills to come,
Nor care beyond to-day:
Yet see, how all around 'em wait
The ministers of human fate,
And black Misfortune's baleful train!
Ah, show them where in ambush stand,
To seize their prey, the murderous band!
Ah, tell them they are men!

These shall the fury passions tear,
The vultures of the mind,
                                    Disdainful

Disdainful Anger, palid Fear,
And Shame that skulks behind;
Or pining Love shall waste their youth,
Or Jealousy, with rankling tooth,
That inly gnaws the secret heart:
And Envy wan, and faded Care,
Grim-visag'd comfortless Despair,
And Sorrow's piercing dart.

Ambition this shall tempt to rise,
Then whirl the wretch from high,
To bitter scorn a sacrifice,
And grinning Infamy.
The stings of Falsehood those shall try,
And hard Unkindness alter'd eye,
That mocks the tear it forc'd to flow;
And keen Remorse with blood defil'd,
And moody Madness laughing wild
Amid severest woe.

E   Lo,

60 ODE ON A DISTANT PROSPECT

Lo, in the Vale of Years beneath,
A grisly troop are seen,
The painful family of Death,
More hideous than their queen:
This racks the joints, this fires the veins,
That every labouring sinew strains,
Those in the deeper vitals rage:
Lo, Poverty, to fill the band,
That numbs the soul with icy hand,
And slow-consuming Age.

To each his suff'rings: all are men,
Condemn'd alike to groan;
The tender for another's pain;
Th' unfeeling for his own.
Yet, ah! why should they know their fate!
Since sorrow never comes too late,

    And

OF ETON COLLEGE.   61

And happineſs too ſwiftly flies.
Thought would deſtroy their paradiſe.
No more—where ignorance is bliſs,
'Tis folly to be wiſe.

E 2   A LONG

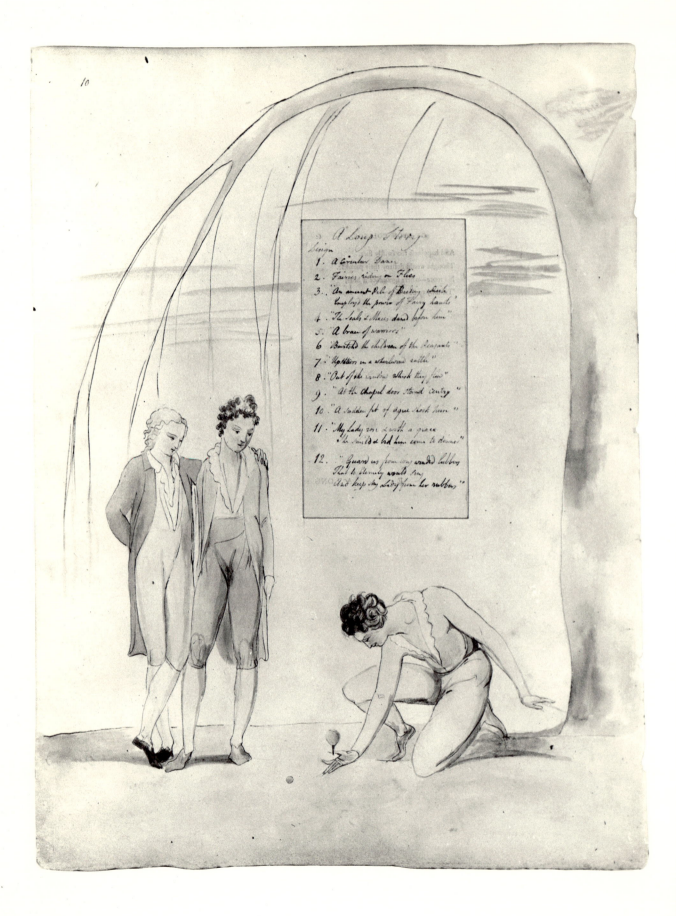

MR. GRAY'S Elegy in the Country Church-Yard, before it appeared in print, was handed about in manuscript; and amongst other eminent personages who saw and admired it, was the Lady Cobham, who resided at the Mansion-house at Stoke-Pogeis. The performance induced her to wish for the author's acquaintance; and Lady Schaub and Miss Speed, then at her house, undertook to effect it. These two ladies waited upon the author at his aunt's solitary mansion, where he at that time resided; and not finding him at home, they left their names. Mr. Gray, surprised at such a compliment, returned the visit. And as the beginning of this acquaintance wore a little of the face of romance, he soon after gave a fanciful and pleasant account of it in the following copy of verses, which he entitled A LONG STORY.

ALTHOUGH this performance certainly possesses great humour, yet it is not immediately perceived; and has not been *universally* relished. The author perceived this himself, and owned it candidly.— " The verses," he writes to Dr. Wharton, " you " so kindly try to keep in countenance, were writ- " ten merely to divert Lady Cobham and her fa- " mily, and succeeded accordingly; but being " shewed about in town, are not liked at all." This last consideration induced Mr. Gray to reject them in the Collection which he himself made of his poems.

MR. GRAY'S Executor having thought fit to restore them, they are retained here.

A

LONG STORY.

IN Britain's isle, no matter where,
    An ancient pile of building stands:
The Huntingdons and Hattons there
    Employed the power of Fairy hands

To raise the ceiling's fretted height,
    Each pannel in atchievements clothing,
Rich windows that exclude the light,
    And passages, that lead to nothing.

E 4   Full

66   A LONG STORY.

Full oft within the ſpacious walls,
When he had fifty winters o'er him,
My grave Lord-Keeper led the Brawls:
The Seals and Maces danc'd before him.

His buſhy beard, and ſhoe-ſtrings green,
His high-crown'd hat, and ſatin doublet,
Mov'd the ſtout heart of England's Queen,
Tho' Pope and Spaniard could not trouble it.

What, in the very firſt beginning!
Shame of the verſifying tribe!
Your Hiſt'ry whither are you ſpinning?
Can you do nothing but deſcribe?

A Houſe there is, (and that's enough)
From whence one fatal morning iſſues
A brace of warriors, not in buff,
But ruſtling in their ſilks and tiſſues.

                                    The

The first came cap-a-pee from France
Her conqu'ring destiny fulfilling,
Whom meaner beauties eye askance,
And vainly ape her art of killing.

The other Amazon kind heaven
Had arm'd with spirit, wit, and satire:
But Cobham had the polish given,
And tipp'd her arrows with good-nature.

To celebrate her eyes, her hair—
Coarse panegyrics would but teaze her,
Melissa is her *Nom de Guerre*.
Alas, who would not wish to please her!

With bonnet blue and capuchin,
And aprons long they hid their armour,
And veil'd their weapons bright and keen
In pity to the country-farmer.

Fame

68   A LONG STORY.

Fame in the shape of Mr. P—tt
(By this time all the parish know it)
Had told, that thereabouts there lurk'd
A wicked Imp they call a Poet;

Who prowl'd the country far and near,
Bewitch'd the children of the peasants,
Dried up the cows, and lam'd the deer,
And suck'd the eggs, and kill'd the pheasants.

My Lady heard their joint petition,
Swore by her coronet and ermine,
She'd issue out her high commission
To rid the manor of such vermin.

The Heroines undertook the task,
Thro' lanes unknown, o'er stiles they ventur'd,
Rapp'd at the door, nor stay'd to ask,
But bounce into the parlour enter'd.
                                    The

A LONG STORY.   69

The trembling family they daunt,
They flirt, they fing, they laugh, they tattle.
Rummage his Mother, pinch his Aunt,
And up ftairs in a whirlwind rattle.

Each hole and cupboard they explore,
Each creek and cranny of his chamber,
Run hurry-fkurry round the floor,
And o'er the bed and tefter clamber;

Into the Drawers and China pry,
Papers and books, a huge Imbroglio!
Under a tea cup he might lie,
Or creafed like dog-ears, in a folio.

On the firft marching of the troops
The Mufes, hopelefs of his pardon,
Convey'd him underneath their hoops,
To a fmall clofet in the garden.

                                                 So

So Rumour says: (Who will, believe.)
But that they left the door a-jar,
Where, safe and laughing in his sleeve,
He heard the distant din of war.

Short was his joy.   He little knew
The power of magic was no fable ;
Out of the window, whisk, they flew,
But left a spell upon the table.

The words too eager to unriddle
The poet felt a strange disorder :
Transparent birdlime form'd the middle,
And chains invisible the border,

So cunning was the Apparatus,
The powerful pothooks did so move him,
That, will he, nill he, to the Great-house
He went, as if the devil drove him.

Yet

Yet on his way (no sign of grace,
  For folks in fear are apt to pray)
To Phœbus he preserr'd his case,
  And begg'd his aid that dreadful day.

The Godhead would have back'd his quarrel,
  But with a blush on recollection
Own'd that his quiver and his laurel
  'Gainst four such eyes were no protection.

The Court was sat, the Culprit there,
  Forth from their gloomy mansions creeping
The Lady *Janes* and *Joans* repair,
  And from the gallery stand peeping:

Such as in silence of the night
  Come (sweep) along some winding entry
(*Styack* has often seen the sight)
  Or at the chapel-door stand sentry;

                        In

A LONG STORY.

In peaked hoods and mantles tarnifh'd,
Sour vifages, enough to fcare-ye,
High Dames of honour once, that garnifh'd
The drawing-room of fierce Queen Mary!

The Peerefs comes. The Audience ftare,
And doff their hats with due fubmiffion:
She curtfies, as fhe takes her chair,
To all the People of condition.

The Bard with many an artful fib,
Had in imagination fenc'd him,
Difprov'd the arguments of *Squib*,
And all that *Groom* could urge againft him:

But foon his rhetoric forfook him,
When he the folemn hall had feen;
A fudden fit of ague fhook him,
He ftood as mute as poor *Macleane*.

Yet

Yet fomething he was heard to mutter,
' How in the Park beneath an old tree,
' (Without defign to hurt the butter,
' Or any malice to the poultry,)

' He once or twice had penn'd a fonnet ;
' Yet hop'd that he might fave his bacon :
' Numbers would give their oaths upon it,
' He ne'er was for a conj'rer taken.'

The ghoftly prudes with hagged face
Already had condemn'd the finner,
My Lady rofe, and with a grace—
She fmil'd, and bid him come to dinner.

' Jefu-Maria ! Madam Bridget,
' Why what can the Vifcountefs mean ?'
(Cried the fquare Hoods in woeful fidget)
' The times are alter'd quite and clean !

                                ' Decorum's

74   A LONG STORY.

'Decorum's turned to mere civility;
'Her air and all her Manners shew it.
'Commend me to her affability!
'Speak to a Commoner and Poet!'

[Here 500 Stanzas are lost.]

And so God save our noble King,
And guard us from long-winded Lubbers,
That to eternity would sing,
And keep my Lady from her Rubbers.

ODE

2
Ode to Adversity
Design
1. A Widower & children
2. Grief among the roots of trees
3. "Purple tyrants vainly groan"
4. "Stern rugged Nurse"
Virtue Nursd in the Lap of Adversity
5. "In thy Gorgon terrors clad
Screaming Horrors funeral cry
Despair & Fell Disease & ghastly Poverty"
6. "Oh gently on thy Suppliants head
Dread Goddess lay thy chastening hand

ODE

TO

ADVERSITY.

———

DAUGHTER of Jove, relentless power,
   Thou tamer of the human breast,
Whose iron scourge, and tort'ring hour,
The bad affright, afflict the best!
Bound in thy adamantine chain,
The proud are taught to taste of pain,
And purple tyrants vainly groan
With pangs unfelt before, unpitied and alone.

F 2   When

38   ODE TO ADVERSITY.

When first thy Sire to send on earth
Virtue, his darling child, defign'd,
To thee he gave the heavenly birth,
And bade to form her infant mind.
Stern rugged nurfe! thy rigid lore
With patience many a year fhe bore:
What forrow was, thou bad'ft her know,
And from her own fhe learn'd to melt at others
            woe.

Scar'd at thy frown terrific, fly
Self-pleafing Folly's idle brood,
Wild Laughter, Noife, and thoughtlefs Joy,
And leave us leifure to be good,
Light they difperfe; and with them go
The fummer-friend, the flatt'ring foe;
By vain Profperity receiv'd,
To her they vow their truth, and are again
            believ'd.

                            Wifdom

Wisdom in sable garb array'd,
Immers'd in rapt'rous thought profound,
And Melancholy, silent maid
With leaden eye, that loves the ground,
Still, on thy solemn steps attend:
Warm Charity, the general friend,
With Justice to herself severe,
And Pity, dropping soft the sadly-pleasing tear.

Oh, gently on thy suppliant's head,
Dread Goddess, lay thy chast'ning hand!
Not in thy Gorgon terrors clad,
Nor circled with the vengeful band
(As by the impious thou art seen)
With thund'ring voice, and threat'ning mien,
With screaming Horror's funeral cry,
Despair, and fell Disease, and ghastly Poverty.

F 3   Thy

ODE TO ADVERSITY.

Thy form benign, oh Goddess, wear,
Thy milder influence impart,
Thy philosophic train be there
To soften, not to wound my heart.
The gen'rous spark extinct revive,
Teach me to love, and to forgive,
Exact my own defects to scan,
What others are to feel; and know myself a
    man.

THE

PROGRESS of POESY.

ADVERTISEMENT.

PINDARIC ODE.

Φωνᾶντα συνετοῖσι· ἐς
Δὲ τὸ πᾶν ἑρμηνέων
Χατίζει. ——
PINDAR, Olymph. II.

F 4

PROGRESS of POESY.

A PINDARIC ODE.

I. 1.

AWAKE, Æolian lyre, awake,
And give to rapture all thy trembling
        strings.
From Helicon's harmonious springs
A thousand rills their mazy progress take:
The laughing flowers, that round them blow,
Drink life and fragrance as they flow.
Now the rich stream of music winds along,
Deep, majestic, smooth, and strong,

                                      Thro'

Thro' verdant vales, and Ceres' golden reign:
Now rolling down the steep amain,
Headlong, impetuous, see it pour:
The rocks and nodding groves rebellow to the
        roar.

II. 2.

Oh! Sovereign of the willing soul,
Parent of sweet and solemn-breathing airs,
Enchanting shell! the sullen Cares,
And frantic Passions, hear thy soft controul.
On Thracia's hills the Lord of War
Has curb'd the fury of his car,
And drop'd his thirsty lance at thy command.
Perching on the sceptred hand
Of Jove, thy magic lulls the feather'd king
With ruffled plumes, and flagging wing:
Quench'd in dark clouds of slumber lie
The terror of his beak, and light'nings of his eye.

                                    I. 3.

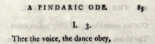

A PINDARIC ODE. 85

I. 3.

 Thee the voice, the dance obey,
Temper'd to thy warbled lay.
O'er Idalia's velvet-green
The rosy- crowned loves are seen
On Cytherea's day
With antic Sports, and blue-ey'd Pleasures,
Frisking light in frolic measures;
Now pursuing, now retreating,
Now in circling troops they meet:
To brisk notes in cadence beating,
Glance their many-twinkling feet.
Slow melting strains their Queen's approach
   declare:
Where-e'er she turns the Graces homage pay.
With arms sublime, that float upon the air,
In gilding state she wins her easy way:

         O'er

85   THE PROGRESS OF POESY.

O'er her warm cheek, and rising bosom, move
The bloom of young desire, and purple light
        of Love.

                II. 1.

    Man's feeble race what ills await!
Labour, and Penury, the racks of Pain,
Disease, and Sorrow's weeping train,
And Death, sad refuge from the storms of Fate!
The fond complaint, my song, disprove,
And justify the laws of Jove.
Say, has he given in vain the heav'nly Muse?
Night, and all her sickly dews,
Her spectres wan, and birds of boding cry,
He gives to range the dreary sky:
Till down the eastern cliffs afar
Hyperion's march they spy, and glitt'ring
        shafts of war.

                II. 2.

A PINDARIC ODE. 87

II. 2.

Or where

In climes beyond the folar road,
Where fhaggy forms o'er ice-built mountains
         roam,
The Mufe has broke the twilight gloom,
To cheer the fhiv'ring native's dull abode.
And oft beneath the od'rous fhade
Of Chili's boundlefs forefts laid,
She deigns to hear the favage youth repeat
In loofe numbers wildly fweet
Their feather-cinctur'd chiefs, and dufky loves.
Her track, where-e'er the Goddefs roves,
Glory purfue, and gen'rous Shame,
Th' unconquerable mind, and Freedom's holy
         flame.

II. 3.

Woods that wave o'er Delphi's fteep,
Ifles, that crown th' Egean deep,

                              Fields,

Fields, that cool Ilissus laves,
Or where Mæander's amber waves
In lingering lab'rinths creep,
How do your tuneful echoes languish,
Mute, but to the voice of Anguish?
Where each old poetic mountain
Inspiration breath'd around;
Ev'ry shade and hallow'd fountain
Murmur'd deep a solemn sound:
Till the sad Nine, in Greece's evil hour,
Left their Parnassus for the Latian plains.
Alike they scorn the pomp of tyrant Power,
And coward Vice, that revels in her chains.
When Latium had her lofty spirit lost,
They sought, oh Albion! next thy sea-en-
    circled coast.

III. 1.

A PINDARIC ODE. 29

III. 1.

Far from the sun and summer gale,
In thy green lap has Nature's darling laid,
What time, where lucid Avon stray'd,
To him the mighty mother did unveil
Her awful face: the dauntless child
Stretch'd forth his little arms, and smil'd.
This pencil take (she said) whose colours clear
Richly paint the vernal year:
Thine too these golden keys, immortal boy!
This can unlock the gates of Joy;
Of Horror that, and thrilling Fears,
Or ope the sacred source of sympathetic Tears.

III. 2.

Nor second he, that rode sublime
Upon the seraph-wings of Ecstasy,
The secrets of th' abyss to spy.
He pass'd the flaming bounds of Place and Time:

The

90 THE PROGRESS OF POESY.

The living throne, the fapphire blaze,
Where angels tremble, while they gaze,
He faw; but, blafted with excefs of light,
Clos'd his eyes in endlefs night.
Behold, where Dryden's lefs prefumptuous car,
Wide o'er the fields of glory bear
Two courfers of ethereal race,
With necks in thunder cloth'd, and long-
 refounding pace.

III. 3.

Hark, his hands the lyre explore!
Bright-eyed Fancy, hov'ring o'er,
Scatters from her pictur'd urn
Thoughts that breathe, and words that burn.
But ah ! 'tis heard no more—
Oh! Lyre divine, what daring fpirit
Wakes thee now ? tho' he inherit

                                    Nor

A PINDARIC ODE.   91

Nor the pride, nor ample pinion,
That the Theban Eagle bear,
Sailing with ſupreme dominion
Thro' the azure deep of air:
Yet oft before his infant eyes would run
Such forms as glitter in the Muſe's ray,
With orient hues, unborrow'd of the ſun:
Yet shall he mount, and keep his diſtant way
Beyond the limits of a vulgar fate,
Beneath the Good how far—but far above the
     Great.

G   THE

The Bard.

1. A Welch Bard.
2. The Slaughterd Bards. taken from this line "The famish'd Eagle screams & passes by" Aug.98.
3. The Bard weaving Edwards fate
4. Edward & his Queen & Nobles astonish'd at the Bard's Song
5. "Hark how each Giant Oak & Desart Cave Sigh to the Torrents awful voice beneath"
6. "On yonder Cliffs. "I see them sit"
7. "Ver thy country hangs The scourge of heaven"
8. The Whirlwind "Hush'd in grim repose"
9. "Fill thirst & Famine Scowl A baleful smile upon their baffled guest"
10. The death of Edwards Queen Eleanor from this line "Half of thy heart we consecrate"
11. Elizabeth "Girt with many a Baron bold"
12. Spenser creating his Fairies.
13. "Leading from the Mountains height Deep in the roaring tide he plung'd to endless night"
14. A poor Goatherd in Wales.

THE

B A R D.

A

PINDARIC ODE.

G 2

ADVERTISEMENT.

The following Ode is founded on a Tradition current in Wales, that Edward the First, when he completed the conquest of that country, ordered all the Bards that fell into his hands to be put to death.

T H E

B A R D.

A PINDARIC ODE.

I. 1.

' RUIN seize thee, ruthless King.
　' Confusion on thy banners wait ;
' Tho' fann'd by Conquest's crimson wing,
' They mock the air with idle state !
' Helm, nor Hauberk's twisted mail,
' Nor even thy virtues, Tyrant, shall avail

G 3　　　　　' To

96   THE BARD.

' To save thy secret soul from nightly fears,
' From Cambria's curse, from Cambria's tears!'
Such were the sounds that o'er the crested pride
Of the first Edward scatter'd wild dismay,
As down the steep of Snowdon's shaggy side
He wound with toilsome march his long array.
Stout Glo'ster stood aghast in speechless trance!
To arms! cried Mortimer, and couch'd his
       quiv'ring lance.

I. 2.

On a rock, whose haughty brow
Frowns o'er old Conway's foaming flood,
Robed in the sable garb of woe,
With haggard eyes the Poet stood ;
(Loose his beard, and hoary hair
Stream'd, like a meteor, to the troubled air ;)
And with a master's hand, and prophet's fire,
Struck the deep sorrows of his lyre.

               ' Hark,

'Hark, how each giant-oak, and defert-cave,
'Sigh to the torrent's awful voice beneath!
'O'er thee, oh King! their hundred arms
  'they wave,
'Revenge on thee in hoarfer murmurs breathe;
'Vocal no more, since Cambria's fatal day,
'To high-born Hoel's harp, or soft Llewel-
  'lyn's lay.

I. 3.

'Cold is Cadwallo's tongue,
'That hush'd the stormy main:
'Brave Urien sleeps upon his craggy bed:
'Mountains, ye mourn in vain
'Modred, whose magic song
'Made huge Plinlimmon bow his cloud-top'd
  'head.

G 4   'On

92   THE BARD.

'On dreary Arvon's shore they lie,
'Smear'd with gore, and ghastly pale:
'Far, far aloof th' affrighted ravens sail;
'The famish'd eagle screams, and passes by.
'Dear lost companions of my tuneful art,
'Dear, as the light that visits these sad eyes,
'Dear, as the ruddy drops that warm my heart,
'Ye died amidst your dying country's cries—
'No more I weep. They do not sleep.
'On yonder cliffs, a griesly band,
'I see them sit, they linger yet,
'Avengers of their native land:
'With me in dreadful harmony they join,
'And weave with bloody hands the tissue of
'thy line.'

II. 1.

"Weave the warp, and weave the woof,
"The winding-sheet of Edward's race.
"Give

A PINDARIC ODE.   99

" Give ample room, and verge enough
" The characters of hell to trace.
" Mark the year, and mark the night,
" When Severn shall re-echo with affright
" The shrieks of death, thro' Berkley's roofs
        " that ring,
" Shrieks of an agonizing King!
" She-wolf of France, with unrelenting fangs,
" That tear'st the bowels of thy mangled mate,
" From thee be born, who o'er thy country
        " hangs
" The scourge of Heav'n.   What terrors
        " round him wait!
" Amazement in his van, with flight combin'd,
" And Sorrow's faded form, and Solitude
        " behind.

II. 2.

" Mighty Victor, mighty Lord,
" Low on his funeral couch he lies!
                            " No

THE BARD.

"No pitying heart, no eye, afford

"A tear to grace his obsequies.

"Is the sable warrior fled?

"Thy son is gone. He rests among the dead.

"The swarm that in thy noon-tide beam were

born?

"Gone to salute the rising Morn.   [blows,

"Fair laughs the Morn, and soft the zephyr

"While proudly riding o'er the azure realm

"In gallant trim the gilded vessel goes;

"Youth on the prow, and pleasure at the helm;

"Regardless of the sweeping Whirlwind's sway,

"That, hush'd in grim repose, expects his

"evening-prey.

II. 3.

"Fill high the sparkling bowl,

"The rich repast prepare,

"Reft of a crown, he yet may share the feast;

"Close by the regal chair

A PINDARIC ODE. 101

" Fell thirst and famine scowl
" A baleful smile upon their baffled guest.
" Heard ye the din of battle bray,
" Lance to lance, and horse to horse?
" Long years of havoc urge their destin'd course,
" And thro' the kindred squadrons mow their
        " way.
" Ye tow'rs of Julius, London's lasting shame,
" With many a foul and midnight murder fed,
" Revere his consort's faith, his father's fame,
" And spare the meek usurper's holy head.
" Above, below, the rose of snow,
" Twin'd with her blushing foe we spread!
" The bristled boar in infant gore
" Wallows beneath the thorny shade.
" Now, Brothers, bending o'er th' accursed
        " loom
" Stamp we our vengeance deep, and ratify
        " his doom.

III.

THE BARD.

III. 1.

" Edward, lo! to sudden fate
" (Weave we the woof. The thread is spun,)
" Half of thy heart we consecrate.
" (The web is wove. The work is done.)"
' Stay, oh stay! nor thus forlorn,
' Leave me unbless'd, unpity'd, here to mourn :
' In yon bright track, that fires the western skies,
' They melt, they vanish from my eyes.
' But oh! what solemn scenes on Snowdon's
        ' height
' Descending slow their glitt'ring skirts unroll?
' Visions of glory! spare my aching sight,
' Ye unborn ages, crowd not on my soul!
' No more our long-lost Arthur we bewail.
' All-hail, ye genuine Kings, Britannia's issue,
        ' hail!

III.

A PINDARIC ODE. 103

III. 2.

‘ Girt with many a Baron bold
‘ Sublime their ſtarry fronts they rear;
‘ And gorgeous Dames, and Stateſmen old
‘ In bearded majeſty, appear.
‘ In the midſt a form divine!
‘ Her eye proclaims her of the Briton-line;
‘ Her lion-port, her awe-commanding face,
‘ Attempered ſweet to virgin-grace.
‘ What ſtrings ſymphonious tremble in the air!
‘ What ſtrains of vocal tranſport round her play!
‘ Hear from the grave, great Talieſſin, hear;
‘ They breathe a ſoul to animate thy clay.
‘ Bright Rapture calls, and ſoaring, as ſhe ſings,
‘ Waves in the eye of Heaven her many-co-
      ‘ lour'd wings.

III.

104   THE BARD.

III. 3.

' The verse adorn again
' Fierce War, and faithful Love,
' And Truth severe, by fairy Fiction dreſt.
' In buſkin'd meaſures move
' Pale Grief, and pleaſing pain,
' With Horror, tyrant of the throbbing breaſt.
' A voice, as of the cherub-choir,
' Gales from blooming Eden bear;
' And diſtant warblings leſſen on my ear,
' That loſt in long futurity expire.
' Fond impious man, thinkſt thou yon ſan-
      ' guine cloud,
' Rais'd by thy breath, has quench'd the orb
      ' of day?
' To-morrow he repairs the golden flood,
    And warms the nations with redoubled ray.

                        ' Enough

A PINDARIC ODE.   105

' Enough for me: with joy I see

' The different doom our fates affign.

' Be thine Defpair, and fcepter'd Care;

' To triumph, and to die, are mine.'

He fpoke, and headlong, from the mountain's
    height,

Deep in the roaring tíde he plung'd to endlefs
    night.

THE

THE

FATAL SISTERS.

AN ODE.

(From the NORSE TONGUE.)

To be found in the ORCADES of THERMODUS
TORFÆUS; HAFNIÆ, 1697, Folio; and
also in BARTHOLINUS.

VITT ER ORPIT FYRIR VALFALLI, &c.

H

ADVERTISEMENT.

The author once had thoughts (in concert with a friend) of giving *A History of English Poetry:* In the Introduction to it he meant to have produced some specimens of the style that reigned in ancient times among the neighbouring nations, or those who had subdued the greater part of this island, and were our progenitors: the following three imitations made a part of them. He afterwards dropped his design; especially after he had heard, that it was already in the hands of a person well qualified to do it justice, both by his taste, and his researches into antiquity.

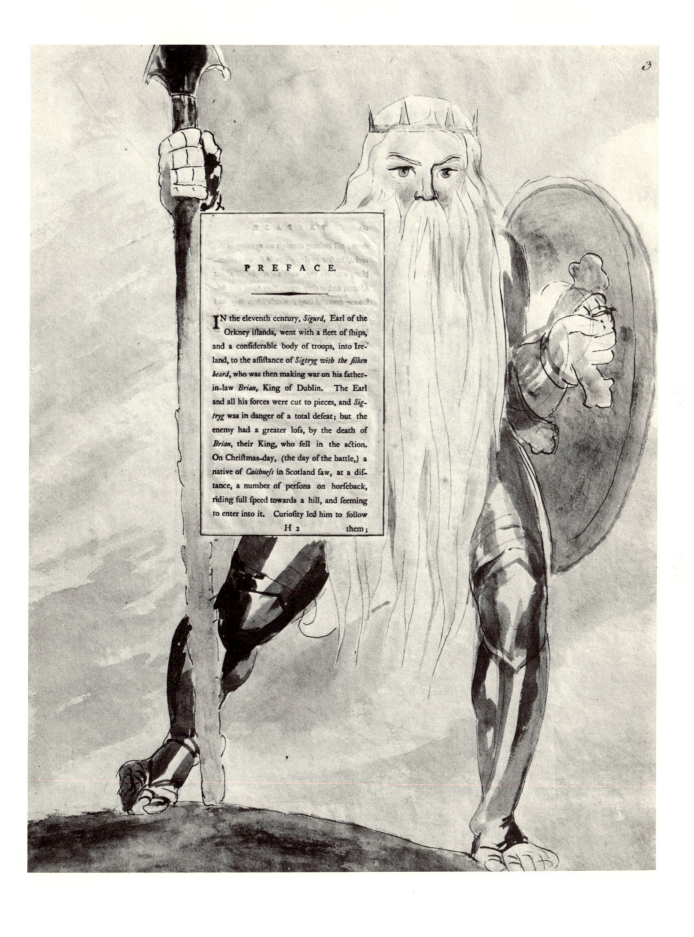

PREFACE.

IN the eleventh century, *Sigurd*, Earl of the
Orkney islands, went with a fleet of ships,
and a confiderable body of troops, into Ireland, to the affiftance of *Sigtryg with the filken
beard*, who was then making war on his father-
in-law *Brian*, King of Dublin. The Earl
and all his forces were cut to pieces, and *Sigtryg* was in danger of a total defeat; but the
enemy had a greater lofs, by the death of
Brian, their King, who fell in the action.
On Chriftmas-day, (the day of the battle,) a
native of *Caithnefs* in Scotland faw, at a dif-
tance, a number of perfons on horfeback,
riding full fpeed towards a hill, and feeming
to enter into it. Curiofity led him to follow

H 2   them;

4

them; till looking through an opening in the
rocks, he saw twelve gigantic figures resembling women: they were all employed about
a loom, and as they wove, they sung the following dreadful song; which when they had
finished, they tore the web into twelve pieces,
and, each taking her portion, galloped six to
the north, and as many to the south.

THE

FATAL SISTERS.

AN ODE.

———

NOW the storm begins to lour,
    (Haste, the loom of hell prepare,)
Iron fleet of arrowy shower
Hurtles in the darkened air.

Glitt'ring lances are the loom,
Where the dusky warp we strain,
Weaving many a soldier's doom,
Orkney's woe, and Randver's bane.

            H 3   See

112   THE FATAL SISTERS.

See the grisly texture grow!
('Tis of human entrails made,)
And the weights that play below,
Each a gasping warrior's head.

Shafts for shuttles, dipt in gore,
Shoot the trembling cords along.
Sword, that once a monarch bore,
Keep the tissue close and strong.

Mista, black terrific maid,
Sangrida, and *Hilda*, see!
Join the wayward work to aid:
'Tis the woof of victory.

Ere the ruddy sun be set,
Pikes must shiver, javelins sing,
Blade with clatt'ring buckler meet,
Hauberk crash, and helmet ring.

                (Weave

AN ODE.   113

(Weave the crimfon web of war,)
Let us go, and let us fly,
Where our friends the conflict fhare,
Where they triumph, where they die.

As the paths of fate we tread,
Wading thro' th' enfanguin'd field,
Gondula, and *Geira*, fpread
O'er the youthful King your fhield.

We the reins to flaughter give,
Ours to kill, and ours to fpare :
Spite of danger he fhall live.
(Weave the crimfon web of war.)

They, whom once the defert-beach
Pent within its bleak domain,
Soon their ample fway fhall ftretch
O'er the plenty of the plain.

H 4   Low

114　THE FATAL SISTERS.

Low the dauntlefs Earl is laid,
Gor'd with many a gaping wound:
Fate demands a nobler head:
Soon a King fhall bite the ground.

Long his lofs fhall Eirin weep,
Ne'er again his likenefs fee;
Long her ftrains in forrow fteep:
Strains of immortality!

Horror covers all the heath,
Clouds of carnage blot the fun.
Sifters, weave the web of death.
Sifters, ceafe: The work is done.

Hail the tafk, and hail the hands!
Songs of joy and triumph fing;
Joy to the victorious bands;
Triumph to the younger King.

Mortal,

Mortal, thou that hear'st the tale,
Learn the tenour of our song.
Scotland, thro' each winding vale,
Far and wide the notes prolong.

Sisters, hence, with spurs of speed!
Each her thundering faulchion wield;
Each bestride her sable steed.
Hurry, hurry, to the field!

THE

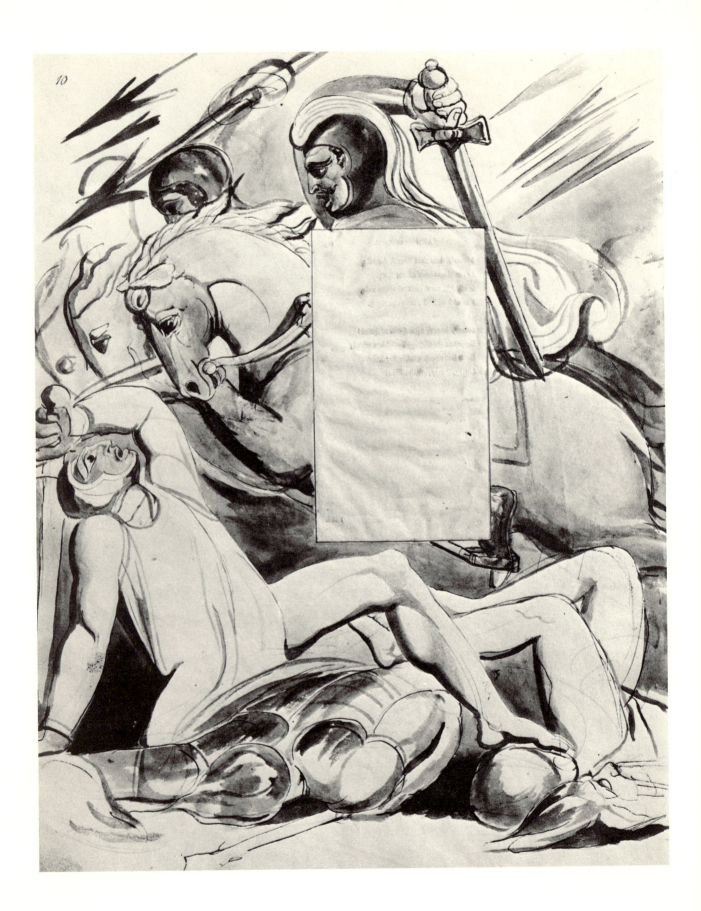

THE

DESCENT of ODIN.

AN ODE.

(From the Norse Tongue.)

To be found in Bartholinus, de caufus contemnendæ mortis; Hafniæ, 1689, Quarto.

Upreis Odinn Allda gautr, &c.

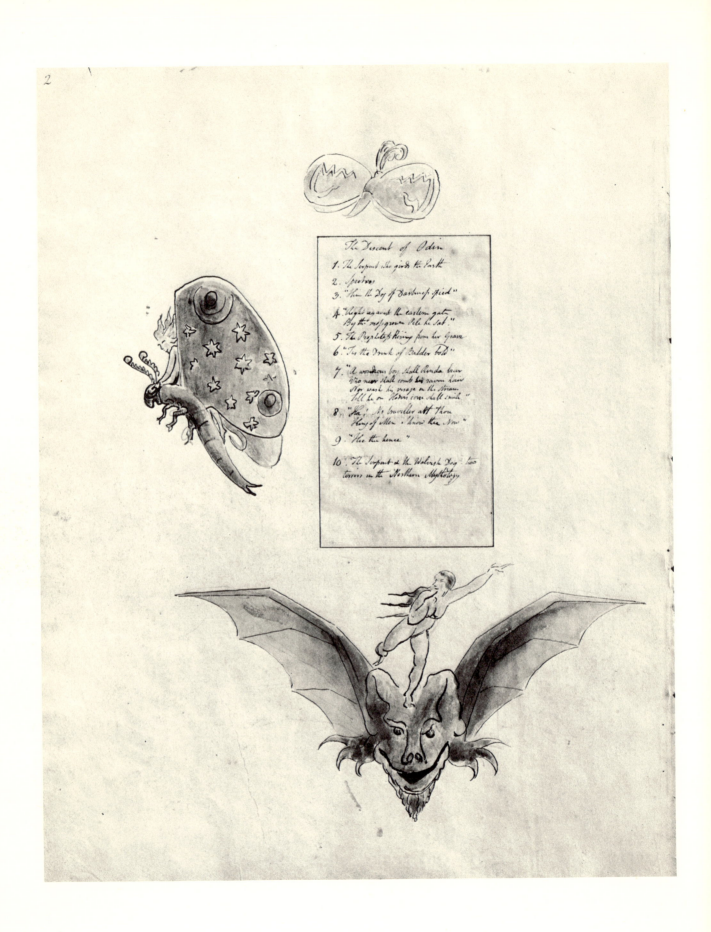

The Descent of Odin

1. The Serpent who girds the Earth

2. Spectres

3. "When the Day of Darkness speed"

4. "Right against the eastern gate
By the moss-grown Pile he Sat."

5. The Prophetess Rising from her Grave

6. "Tis the Drink of Balder bold"

7. "A wondrous boy shall Rinda bear
Who ne'er shall comb his raven hair
Nor wash his visage in the Stream
Till he on Hoders corse shall smile"

8. "Ha! No Traveller art Thou
King of Men I know thee Now"

9. "Hie thee hence"

10. The Serpent & the Wolvish Dog: two
terrors in the Northern Mythology

THE

DESCENT of ODIN.

AN ODE.

————

UPROSE the King of men with speed,
        And saddled strait his coal-black steed;
Down the yawning steep he rode,
That leads to HELA's drear abode.
Him the dog of darkness spied;
His shaggy throat he opened wide,
While from his jaws, with carnage fill'd,
Foam and human gore distill'd.
Hoarse he brays with hideous din,
Eyes that glow, and fangs that grin;

                                                And

And long pursues, with fruitless yell,
The father of the powerful spell.
Onward still his way he takes,
(The groaning earth beneath him shakes,)
Till full before his fearless eyes
The portals nine of hell arise.

    Right against the eastern gate,
By the moss-grown pile he sat,
Where long of yore to sleep was laid
The dust of the prophetic Maid.
Facing to the northern clime,
Thrice he trac'd the Runic rhyme;
Thrice pronounc'd, in accents dread,
The thrilling verse that wakes the dead;
Till from out the hollow ground
Slowly breath'd a sullen sound.

PRO-

AN ODE.   121

PROPHETESS.

What call unknown, what charms, presume
To break the quiet of the tomb?
Who thus afflicts my troubled sprite,
And drags me from the realms of night?
Long on these mould'ring bones have beat
The winter's snow, the summer's heat,
The drenching dews, and driving rain!
Let me, let me sleep again.
Who is he, with voice unblest,
That calls me from the bed of rest?

ODIN.

A Traveller to thee unknown,
Is he that calls, a warrior's son.
Thou the deeds of light shalt know;
Tell me what is done below,
For whom yon glitt'ring board is spread,
Drest for whom yon golden bed.

PRO-

6

::: THE DESCENT OF ODIN.

PROPHETESS.

Mantling in the goblet see
The pure bev'rage of the bee;
O'er it hangs the shield of gold:
'Tis the drink of *Balder* bold.
Balder's head to death is giv'n.
Pain can reach the Sons of Heav'n!
Unwilling I my lips unclose:
Leave me, leave me to repose.

ODIN.

Once again my call obey.
Prophetess, arise, and say,
What dangers *Odin*'s child await,
Who the author of his fate.

PROPHETESS.

In *Hoder*'s hand the hero's doom;
His brother sends him to the tomb.

Now

AN ODE.   123

Now my weary lips I close:
Leave me, leave me to repose.

ODIN.

Prophetess, my spell obey:
Once again arise, and say,
Who th' avenger of his guilt,
By whom shall *Hoder*'s blood be spilt.

PROPHETESS.

In the caverns of the west,
By *Odin*'s fierce embrace comprest,
A wond'rous boy shall *Rinda* bear,
Who ne'er shall comb his raven hair,
Nor wash his visage in the stream,
Nor see the sun's departing beam,
Till he on *Hoder*'s corse shall smile
Flaming on the funeral pile.
Now my weary lips I close:
Leave me, leave me to repose.

I   ODIN.

124 THE DESCENT OF ODIN.

ODIN.

Yet awhile my call obey;
Prophetefs, awake, and fay,
What Virgins thefe, in fpeechlefs woe,
That bend to earth their folemn brow,
That their flaxen treffes tear,
And fnowy veils, that float in air.
Tell me whence their forrows rofe:
Then I leave thee to repofe.

PROPHETESS.

Ha! no Traveller art thou,
King of Men, I know thee now;
Mightieft of a mighty line——

ODIN.

No boding Maid of fkill divine
Art thou, nor Prophetefs of good,
But mother of the giant-brood!

PRO-

AN ODE.   125

PROPHETESS.

Hie thee hence, and boaſt at home,
That never ſhall enquirer come
To break my iron-ſleep again;
Till *Lok* has burſt his tenfold chain.
Never, till ſubſtantial Night
Has reaſſum'd her ancient right;
Till wrapt in flames, in ruin hurl'd,
Sinks the fabric of the world.

I 2   THE

The Triumphs of Owen

1. A Standard bearer fainting in the routed battle

2. A Festal board

3. The Bard singing Owens praise

4. "Dauntless on his native sands
   The Dragon son of Mona stands"

5. "Fear to stop & shame to fly"

6. The Liberal Man inviting the traveller into his house

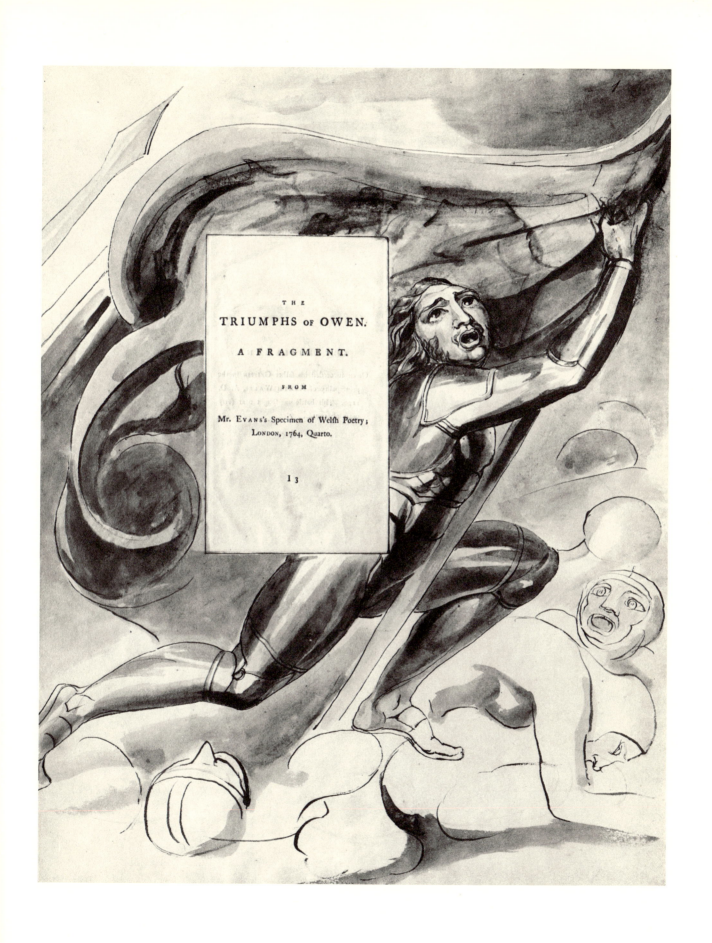

THE
TRIUMPHS OF OWEN.

A FRAGMENT.

FROM

Mr. EVANS's Specimen of Welsh Poetry;
LONDON, 1764, Quarto.

I 3

ADVERTISEMENT.

Owen succeeded his father Griffin in the
principality of North Wales, A. D.
1120. This battle was fought near forty
years afterwards.

THE

TRIUMPHS of OWEN.

A FRAGMENT.

OWEN's praise demands my song,
Owen swift, and Owen strong;
Faireſt flower of Roderic's ſtem,
Gwyneth's ſhield, and Britain's gem.
He nor heaps his brooded ſtores,
Nor on all profuſely pours;
Lord of every regal art,
Liberal hand, and open heart.

I 4   Big

130 TRIUMPHS OF OWEN.

Big with hosts of mighty name,
Squadrons three against him came;
This the force of Eirin hiding;
Side by side as proudly riding,
On her shadow long and gay
Lochlin plows the wat'ry way:
There the Norman sails afar
Catch the winds, and join the war:
Black and huge along they sweep,
Burthens of the angry deep.

Dauntless on his native sands
The dragon-son of Mona stands:
In glittering arms and glory dress,
High he rears his ruby crest.
There the thund'ring strokes begin,
There the press, and there the din;
Talymalfra's rocky shore
Echoing to the battle's roar.

Where

A FRAGMENT.   131

Where his glowing eye-balls turn,
Thousand banners round him burn:
Where he points his purple spear,
Hasty, hasty Rout is there;
Marking with indignant eye
Fear to stop, and shame to fly.
There Confusion, Terror's child;
Conflict fierce, and Ruin wild;
Agony, that pants for breath;
Despair, and honourable Death.

* * * * * * * *

ODE

ODE FOR MUSIC.

PERFORMED IN THE

SENATE-HOUSE

AT

CAMBRIDGE, July 1, 1769,

At the INSTALLATION of his Grace
AUGUSTUS-HENRY FITZROY, Duke of
GRAFTON, CHANCELLOR of the University.

Ode for Music.

1. Fame.

2. A bird singing

3. A Genius drawing away "Comus & his
   midnight crew"

4. Milton struck the sorided Bell
   Newtons selt bends from his State Sublime

5. "I wood the gleam of Cynthia silver bright
   Where willowsy Camus lingers with delight"

6. "Great Edward with the lillies on his brow
   To hail the fatal morning come"

7. "Leaning from her golden cloud
   The venerable Margaret"

8. "The Laureate wreath"

9. "Nor fear the rocks nor seak the shore"

10. Fame.

ODE FOR MUSIC.

IRREGULAR.

I.

"HENCE, avaunt, ('tis holy ground)
    "Comus, and his midnight-crew,
"And Ignorance with looks profound,
"And dreaming Sloth of palid hue,
"Mad Sedition's cry profane,
"Servitude that hugs her chain,
"Nor in these consecrated bowers
"Let painted Flatt'ry hide her serpent-train
        "in flowers.
                        "Nor

136   ODE FOR MUSIC.

" Nor Envy bafe, nor creeping Gain
" Dare the Mufe's walk to ftain,
" While bright-eyed Science watches round:
" Hence, away, 'tis holy ground!"

II.

From yonder realms of empyrean day
Burfts on my ear th' indignant lay:
There fit the fainted Sage, the Bard divine,
The Few, whom Genius gave to fhine
Thro' every unborn age, and undifcover'd
          clime.
Rapt in celeftial tranfport they,
Yet hither oft a glance from high
They fend of tender fympathy
To blefs the place, where on their opening foul
Firft the genuine ardor ftole.
'Twas Milton ftruck the deep-ton'd fhell,
And, as the choral warblings round him fwell,
                                    Meek

Meek Newton's self bends from his state sublime,
And nods his hoary head, and listens to the
        rhyme.

III.

" Ye brown o'er-arching Groves,
" That Contemplation loves,
" Where willowy Camus lingers with delight!
" Oft at the blush of dawn
" I trod your level lawn,
" Oft woo'd the gleam of Cynthia silver-bright
" In cloisters dim, far from the haunts of Folly,
" With Freedom by my side, and soft-ey'd
        " Melancholy."

IV.

But hark! the portals sound, and pacing forth
With solemn steps and flow,
High Potentates, and Dames of royal birth,
And mitred fathers in long order go:

                                    Great

138   ODE FOR MUSIC.

Great Edward, with the lilies on his brow
From haughty Gallia torn,
And sad Chatillon, on her bridal morn
That wept her bleeding Love, and princely
        Clare,
And Anjou's Heroine, and the paler Rose,
The rival of her crown and of her woes,
And either Henry there,
The murder'd Saint, and the majestic Lord,
That broke the bonds of Rome.
(Their tears, their little triumphs o'er,
Their human passions now no more,
Save Charity, that glows beyond the tomb)
All that on Granta's fruitful plain
Rich streams of regal bounty pour'd,
And bad these awful fanes and turrets rise,
To hail their Fitzroy's festal morning come;
And thus they speak in soft accord
The liquid language of the skies.
                                        V.

V.

" What is grandeur, what is Power?

" Heavier toil, superior pain.

" What the bright reward we gain?

" The grateful memory of the Good.

" Sweet is the breath of vernal shower,

" The bee's collected treasures sweet,

" Sweet music's melting fall, but sweeter yet

" The still small voice of Gratitude."

VI.

Foremost and leaning from her golden cloud

The venerable Marg'ret see!

" Welcome, my noble Son, (she cries aloud)

" To this, thy kindred train, and me:

" Pleas'd in thy lineaments we trace

" A Tudor's fire, a Beaufort's grace.

" Thy liberal heart, thy judging eye,

" The flower unheeded shall descry,

K   " And

140   ODE FOR MUSIC.

" And bid it round heav'ns altars shed

" The fragrance of its blushing head:

" Shall raise from earth the latent gem

" To glitter on the diadem.

VII.

" Lo, Granta waits to lead her blooming band,

" Not obvious, not obtrusive, She

" No vulgar praise, no venal incense flings:

" Nor dares with courtly tongue refin'd

" Profane thy inborn royalty of mind:

" She reveres herself and thee.

" With modest pride to grace thy youthful

  " brow

" The laureate wreath, that Cecil wore, she

  " brings,

" And to thy just, thy gentle hand

" Submits the Fasces of her sway,

     " While

ODE FOR MUSIC. 141

" While Spirits bleſt above and Men below

" Join with glad voice the loud ſymphonious

" lay.

VIII.

" Thro' the wild waves as they roar

" With watchful eye and dauntleſs mien

" Thy ſteady courſe of honour keep,

" Nor fear the rocks, nor ſeek the ſhore:

" The ſtar of Brunſwick ſmiles ſerene,

" And gilds the horrors of the deep."

K 2 EPI-

EPITAPH

ON

MRS. CLARKE.

L O! where this silent marble weeps,
   A Friend, a Wife, a Mother sleeps;
A Heart, within whose sacred cell
The peaceful Virtues lov'd to dwell.
Affection warm, and Faith sincere,
And soft Humanity were there.
In agony, in death resign'd,
She felt the wound she left behind;

K 4   Her

146   EPITAPH, &c.

Her infant image, here below,
Sits smiling on a father's woe:
Whom what awaits, while yet he strays
Along the lonely vale of days?
A pang to secret sorrow dear;
A sigh; an unavailing tear;
Till time shall ev'ry grief remove,
With Life, with Memory, and with Love.

ELEGY

WRITTEN IN A

COUNTRY CHURCH-YARD.

———

THE Curfew tolls the knell of parting day,
   The lowing herd wind slowly o'er the lea,
The plowman homeward plods his weary way,
   And leaves the world to darkness, and to me.
Now fades the glimmering landscape on the sight,
   And all the air a solemn stillness holds,
Save where the beetle wheels his droning flight,
   And drowsy tinklings lull the distant folds;
                       Save

4

ELEGY WRITTEN IN A

Save that from yonder ivy-mantled tower,
The moping owl does to the moon complain
Of such, as wand'ring near her secret bower,
Molest her ancient solitary reign.

Beneath those rugged elms, that yew-tree's shade,
Where heaves the turf in many a mouldring heap,
Each in his narrow cell for ever laid,
The rude Forefathers of the hamlet sleep.

The breezy call of incense breathing Morn,
The swallow twitt'ring from the straw-built shed,
The cock's shrill clarion, or the echoing horn,
No more shall rouse them from their lowly bed.

For them no more the blazing hearth shall burn,
Or busy housewife ply her evening-care;
No children run to lisp their sire's return,
Or climb his knees the envied kiss to share.

Oft

Oft did the harvest to their sickle yield,
Their furrow oft the stubborn glebe has broke:
How jocund did they drive their team afield!
How bow'd the woods beneath their sturdy stroke!

Let not Ambition mock their useful toil,
Their homely joys, and destiny obscure;
Nor grandeur hear with a disdainful smile,
The short and simple annals of the poor.

The boast of heraldry, the pomp of power,
And all that beauty, all that wealth e'er gave,
Await alike th' inevitable hour.
The paths of glory lead but to the grave.

Nor you, ye proud, impute to these the fault,
If Memory o'er their tomb no trophies raise,
Where thro' the long-drawn aisle and fretted vault,
The pealing anthem swells the note of praise.

Can

152 ELEGY WRITTEN IN A

Can storied urn or animated buft,
Back to its manfion call the fleeting breath?
Can Honour's voice provoke the filent duft,
Or flattery footh the dull cold ear of Death?

Perhaps in this neglected fpot is laid
Some heart once pregnant with celeftial fire;
Hands that the rod of empire might have fway'd,
Or wak'd to ecftafy the living lyre.

But Knowledge to their eyes her ample page
Rich with the fpoils of Time did ne'er unroll;
Chill Penury reprefs'd their noble rage,
And froze the genial current of the foul.

Full many a gem of pureft ray ferene,
The dark unfathom'd caves of Ocean bear:
Full many a flower is born to blufh unfeen,
And wafte its fweetnefs on the defert air.

Some

COUNTRY CHURCH-YARD. 153

Some village-Hampden, that with dauntless breast,
The little tyrant of his fields withstood,
Some mute inglorious Milton here may rest,
Some Cromwell guiltless of his country's blood.

Th' applause of list'ning senates to command,
The threats of pain and ruin to despise,
To scatter plenty o'er a smiling land,
And read their hist'ry in a nation's eyes,

Their lot forbade: nor circumscrib'd alone
Their growing virtues, but their crimes confin'd;
Forbade to wade thro' slaughter to a throne,
And shut the gates of mercy to mankind.

The struggling pangs of conscious Truth to hide,
To quench the blushes of ingenuous Shame,
Or heap the shrine of Luxury and Pride
With incense kindled at the Muses flame.

Far

154. ELEGY WRITTEN IN A

Far from the madding crowd's ignoble ſtrife,
Their ſober wiſhes never learn'd to ſtray;
Along the cool ſequeſter'd vale of life
They kept the noiſeleſs tenour of their way.

Yet ev'n theſe bones from inſult to protect
Some frail memorial ſtill erected nigh,
With uncouth rhymes and ſhapeleſs ſculpture
Implores the paſſing tribute of a ſigh.   [deck'd,

Their name, their years, ſpelt by th' unletter'd
The place of fame and elegy ſupply;   [Muſe,
And many a holy text around ſhe ſtrews,
That teach the ruſtic moraliſt to die.

For who, to dumb Forgetfulneſs a prey,
This pleaſing anxious being e'er reſign'd,
Left the warm precincts of the chearful day,
Nor caſt one longing ling'ring look behind?

                                        On

On some fond breast the parting soul relies,
Some pious drops the closing eye requires;
Ev'n from the tomb the voice of Nature cries,
Ev'n in our ashes live their wonted fires.

For thee, who mindful of th' unhonour'd Dead,
Dost in these lines their artless tale relate;
If chance, by lonely Contemplation led,
Some kindred spirit shall inquire thy fate,

Haply some hoary-headed swain may say,
' Oft have we seen him at the peep of dawn,
' Brushing with hasty steps the dews away,
' To meet the sun upon the upland lawn.

' There at the foot of yonder nodding beech,
' That wreathes its old fantastic roots so high,
' His listless length at noon-tide would he stretch,
' And pore upon the brook that babbles by.

L   ' Hard

156   ELEGY WRITTEN IN A

'Hard by yon wood, now smiling as in scorn,
'Mutt'ring his wayward fancies he would rove;
'Now drooping, woeful wan, like one forlorn,
'Or craz'd with care, or crofs'd in hopelefs love.

'One morn I mifs'd him on the custom'd hill,
'Along the heath and near his favourite tree;
'Another came; nor yet beside the rill,
'Nor up the lawn, nor at the wood was he;

'The next with dirges due in fad array
'Slow thro' the church-way path we faw him
        'borne,
'Approach and read (for thou canst read) the lay
'Grav'd on the ftone beneath yon aged thorn.'

                              THE

COUNTRY CHURCH-YARD. 157

The EPITAPH.

HERE rests his head upon the lap of Earth
A Youth, to Fortune and to Fame unknown:
Fair Science frown'd not on his humble birth,
And Melancholy mark'd him for her own.

Large was his bounty, and his soul sincere,
Heav'n did a recompence as largely send:
He gave to Mis'ry all he had, a tear,
He gain'd from Heav'n, 'twas all he wish'd, a
   Friend.

No farther seek his merits to disclose,
Or draw his frailties from their dread abode,
(There they alike in trembling hope repose,)
The bosom of his Father and his God.

L 2   N O T E S.

12.
To Mrs Ann Flaxman
A little Flower grew in a lonely Vale
Its form was lovely but its colours pale
One standing in the Porches of the Sun
When his Meridian Glories were begun
Leapd from the steps of fire & on the grass
Alighted where this little Flower was
With hands divine he movd the gentle Sod
And took the Flower up in its native Clod
Then planting it upon a Mountains brow
'Tis your own fault if you dont flourish now
William Blake